بسم الله الرحمن الرحيم

"The house of al-Arqam is the house of Islām"

Al-Ḥākim (d. 405/1014) in *al-Mustadrak ʿala al-Ṣaḥiḥayn* (6185)

دليل الطالب لنيل المطالب

A Ḥanbalī Epitome

THE STUDENT'S GUIDE

for accomplishing the pursued objectives pertaining to worship

Marʿī b. Yūsuf al-Karmī al-Ḥanbalī (d. 1033/1623)

Translated with an Introduction & Notes by Dr Jewel Jalil
Forewords by Professor Robert Gleave and Dr Fāris b. Fāliḥ al-Khazrajī

DAR AL-ARQAM

ISBN: 978-1-068309601

British Library Cataloguing in Publishing Data
A catalogue record for this book is available from the British Library

First edition, 2020
Second edition, 2025

Prepared and published by Dar al-Arqam Publishing
Birmingham, United Kingdom

www.daral-arqam.co.uk
Email: daralarqam@hotmail.co.uk

Translated by Dr Jewel Jalil

Printed in Türkiye by Mega | export@mega.com.tr

A Ḥanbalī Epitome

THE STUDENT'S GUIDE

for accomplishing the pursued objectives pertaining to worship

Marʿī b. Yūsuf al-Karmī al-Ḥanbalī (d. 1033/1623)

Translated with an Introduction & Notes by Dr Jewel Jalil

Forewords by Professor Robert Gleave and Dr Fāris b. Fāliḥ al-Khazrajī

DAR AL-ARQAM

Contents

Acknowledgements

It was in the summer of 2005 I first attended some of the study sessions of *Manār al-sabīl fī sharḥ al-dalīl* in London with the encouragement of my friend, Alomgir Ali. I did not know adequate Arabic but fortunate for me the lessons were being taught in English. The following year on a trip to Saudi Arabia I purchased a copy of *Dalīl al-ṭālib* and its commentary *Manār al-sabīl*. I acquired the manuals to primarily encourage myself to study Arabic and fit in with the study group – most of the attendees had their personal copies of *Dalīl al-ṭālib* or *Manār al-sabīl*. The study of *Manār al-sabīl* commenced around 2001 and was stopped in the summer of 2006, reaching the Chapter of the Congregation Prayer. The few sessions I managed to attend helped me to be better informed about *Dalīl al-ṭālib* and its associated works. I am very indebted to the teacher who delivered these lessons; he was dynamic, passionate, and distinctive in the way he simplified and presented the articles of Islamic law.

After the publication of *An Epitome of Ḥanbalī Substantive Law* of Yūsuf b. ʿAbd al-Hādī al-Ḥanbalī (d. 909/1503) with Dar al-Arqam in 2018, I started translating *Dalīl al-ṭālib*. Owing to the manual's straightforward nature, it seemed like a logical choice of progression after Yūsuf b. ʿAbd al-Hādī's primer. It is hoped that the current translation compliments and expounds on the legal articles of the former translation. The present translation has been kept simple and straightforward; it is hoped that the readers will be able to fathom the legal articles without much toil. I used simple words and expressions for it to make sense to the reader; to convey the spirit and manner of the original; to have a natural and easy form; and to produce a similar response. Despite all efforts made to keep the translation accurate, a work of this nature is bound to have errors in it; some will be questions of interpretation, others will be mistakes. I am alone responsible for these.

The road to rendering the manual has been long and slow in the midst of my PhD, full time work, and family life; I thank Allāh for enabling me to complete the translation. I would like to thank Professor Robert Gleave and Dr Fāris b. Fāliḥ al-Khazrajī for kindly writing the forewords; I feel very honoured to have such exceptional personalities involved in this humble project. I also extend my deepest gratitude to Alomgir Ali, Saqib Qureshi and Refi Shafi, for reviewing and commenting on draft material and helping to improve the accuracy of the translation. I would also like to thank my family and friends for their love and support. The greatest gratitude, however, I owe to my wife, Shireen, and my children, Siyaam, Safiyya, Zakariya, and little Abdullah. Their sacrifice has been enormous and the time I spent away from them can never be made up for. I just hope they will understand and that their sacrifice was worthwhile. I am forever indebted to my father, Abdul Jalil, and my late mother, Kulsum Jalil, to whom I dedicate this work. Finally, I am very grateful to the editorial team at Dar al-Arqam Publications, especially Adnan Karim for tirelessly working on the script.

Foreword I

Professor Robert Gleave

What sort of book do you have in your hands, and how should you use it? To answer these questions, it might be worth pondering what al-Karmī was doing when he wrote *Dalīl al-Ṭālib* in the first place.

The work so ably translated here by Jewel Jalil is a brief epitome (*mukhtaṣar*) of Ḥanbalī law, and by writing such a work al-Karmī is participating in a long, illustrious tradition of *mukhtaṣar* writing by Muslim jurists across the centuries. Many hundreds, perhaps thousands, of *mukhtaṣar* works like *Dalīl al-Ṭālib* have been written by Muslim jurists – both well- and little-known – before and since al-Karmī composed the *Dalīl al-Ṭālib*. Some have been more popular than others, and each school (*madhhab*) has its own favourites. The format of a text like this, though, is one of the most enduring of all the types of literature written by the jurists of Islam.

Mukhtaṣar works like the one you are reading have defining features. In *mukhtaṣar* works, the rules and regulations for the community of Muslim believers are laid out clearly and briefly, but rarely does one find any justification or explanation for the rules. For example, al-Karmī says that consuming camel meat is one of the "nullifiers" of the minor state of ritual impurity (*wuḍū'*). Where does this rule come from? One would never know from al-Karmī's text – one simply has to accept that a believer who eats camel meat must renew his or her state of purity before praying. Al-Karmī in this text just gives the rule – there is no justification for it – no attempt to persuade the reader of its suitability. A scholar, though, who reads this rule will most likely know that it is justified by reference to Prophetic reports – reports like the one from Jābir b. Samura. A man asked the Prophet "Should one do minor ritual purification on account of camel meat?" (*a-tawaḍḍa'u min luḥūm al-ibl?*) to which the Prophet replies "Yes" (Muslim, *Ṣaḥīḥ*, Kitāb al-Ḥayḍ, Chapter 25, Ḥadīth 123). This report, and others like it, are not cited in al-Karmī's *mukhtaṣar*, even though they are essential for an understanding of *why* the Ḥanbalīs believe one should perform *wuḍū'* after eating camel meat. And it is not as if this rule is universally accepted amongst the various schools. Other schools are much less demanding on the issue of *wuḍū'* after camel's meat: for them, reports like this one only show it is recommended (*mustaḥabb*) to perform *wuḍū'*, not obligatory (as al-Karmī and the Ḥanbalīs more generally stipulate).

Why should anyone follow the rules al-Karmī lays in this text? If he produces no evidence, then, surely, there is no reason to adopt his rules. Any reason to follow al-Karmī's rules cannot come from arguments within the text of *Dalīl al-Ṭālib* because there are very few arguments. Al-Karmī is clearly not trying to *convince* the reader that one must do something (in this case *wuḍū'* after eating camel meat): he is simply informing the reader of what he must do. The whole book of *Dalīl al-Ṭālib* could be seen as a plea to the reader to *follow* the rules, but not an explanation as to *why* he or she should do so.

And yet, Ḥanbalī Muslims for many centuries have turned to this text, and others like it, for study, and ultimately to inform their religious practice. The authority of a text like *Dalīl al-Ṭālib* does not come from its internal arguments. Instead, its authority comes from the respect the book has been given within a tradition of Ḥanbalī scholarship. This respect stems from a number of factors: the standing of al-Karmī, as a religious authority; his reputation as a teacher and an author, within the Ḥanbalī school; his scholarly skills, demonstrated in his abbreviation in a clear and concise manner in a condensed but readable text all the rules of the Ḥanbalī school and also in other works. Perhaps most importantly, the popularity of *Dalīl al-Ṭālib* comes from al-Karmī's ability to write a book which subsequent teachers want to teach, and on which illustrious commentators will wish to comment.

It is this last feature which invariably dictates a *mukhtaṣar's* popularity: is the work written in such a way that inspires future generations of commentators? Subsequent scholars do not even have to agree with all of the regulations in *Dalīl al-Ṭālib* – that they choose to use this book as the starting point means they recognise it as authoritative. A good *mukhtaṣār* must invite commentary and discussion, and this, as often as not, explains one *mukhtaṣar's* popularity when compared with other *mukhtaṣar* attempts. That, in large part, explains *Dalīl al-Ṭālib*'s popularity. It is not necessarily the universal acceptance of the text's regulations which gives it fame; more important is its scholarly potential. Successful *mukhtaṣars* are coat-pegs on which subsequent scholars can hang an *abā'*.

All this does not mean that this translation will be used by readers in the same way as it was by the scholars of old. Perhaps today's readers are not looking for a teaching text, or a text on which to comment. Instead, today's readers may wish to know what the rules of the Ḥanbalī school are: and following on from this, they may, potentially, adopt these rules in their everyday religious life. In evaluating al-Karmī's text in this way, such readers might consider whether the rules accord with their own sense of what is right and proper, and in accordance with the Sharīʿa; and they might accept some of al-Karmī's regulations - and they may reject others. I would say that this was probably not the reading practice al-Karmī envisaged when he wrote *Dalīl al-Ṭālib*. This is not to say that these potential ways of using *mukhtaṣar* texts are "incorrect" or "deviant". It is simply to say the following: when you read texts like *Dalīl al-Ṭālib* in this way (that is, finding and adopting elements which chime with your own notions of what the Sharīʿa demands of the individual), then you are doing something new. Your reading practice represents a fresh way in which Islamic legal texts are put to use; you are participating in a re-reading of an old text in a modern context. Al-Karmī has no control over how we read and use his text today; this is not only a fact, it is also perhaps a good thing. Potential new readings are unleashed by good translations of old texts. These re-readings are, perhaps, the most exciting prospective effects of the publication of Jewel Jalil's accomplished new translation of *Dalīl al-Ṭālib*.

Professor Robert Gleave
University of Exeter
January 2020

Foreword II

Dr Fāris b. Fāliḥ al-Khazrajī

In the name of Allāh, the Gracious, the Merciful. All praise belongs to Allāh, who has made knowledge a testament for Him. I bear witness that there is no god besides Allāh and I bear witness that Muḥammad is His servant and messenger – may Allāh's abundant peace and blessings be upon him. To proceed:

Allāh the Exalted has singled out sacred knowledge and its people with honourable virtues. He likewise placed sacred knowledge and belief as a mode for elevating oneself in the world and the hereafter. Writing books without a doubt is a momentous position. Ḥājī Khalīfa (d. 1068/1657) mentioned seven reasons which called for the need to author books. A reason he perhaps missed to mention is the translation of books from one language to another. This is a fitting reason when the goal behind authoring is to translate *fiqh* manuals in order to benefit people who do not know the Arabic language.

Jewel Jalil exerted himself in this by undertaking the task of translating the *fiqh* manual, *Dalīl al-ṭālib* from the original Arabic into the English language – namely, the sections of worship. This is a great effort, especially considering the manual's status in Ḥanbalī *fiqh*. The manual stands out because *Shaykh* Mar'ī authored it based on the *mu'tamad* (reliable) opinions of the Ḥanbalī school's later-generation. The scholars dedicated much attention to the manual by authoring commentaries for it, clarifying its content, and they still continue to do so. Other qualities that distinguish the manual are its numerous sub-sections (of the chapter contents) and simplicity of the phrases therein. The Ḥanbalī scholars have commended this manual greatly – may Allāh have mercy on them all.

تقديم

الشيخ فارس بن فالح الخزرجي

بسم الله الرحمن الرحيم. الحمد لله الذي جعل العلم دليًلا عليه ، وأشهد أن لا إله إلا الله وأن محمدًا عبده ورسوله ، صلى الله عليه وسلم تسليمًا كثيرًا .

أما بعد:

فإن الله تعالى خصَّ العلم والمشتغلين به بمناقب فضيلة ، وجعل العلم والايمان صفة للرفعة في الدنيا والآخرة . ولا شك أن تأليف الكتب من أبواب العلم الجليلة القدر . وقد ذكر حاجي خليفة رحمه الله سبعة أسباب تدعو للتأليف ولعله فاته أن يذكر منها ترجمة الكتاب من لغة إلى أخرى ، وهو سبب جدير أن يكون من جملة أغراض التأليف لما لترجمة كتب الفقه من نفع لغير الناطقين باللغة العربية.

ولقد سعى الأخ الأستاذ الفاضل : جُوَيْل جليل في سلوك هذا الغرض حيث أقدم على ترجمة كتاب (دليل الطالب لنيل المطالب قسم العبادات) من اللغة العربية إلى اللغة الإنكليزية ، وهو جهد متميز لاسيما وأن للكتاب مكانة في الفقه الحنبلي حيث صنفه الشيخ مرعي وفق معتمد المذهب عند المتأخرين ولقد اعتنى به العلماء شرحًا وبيانًا ولا زالوا ، ومما تميز به الكتاب بكثرة تقاسيمه واختصار عبارته ولقد أثنى عليه علماء المذهب رحم الله الجميع .

Jewel Jalil put in much toil in publishing a portion of the manual; and before this manual, he published *Kitāb furū' al-fiqh.* We ask Allāh to grant him success and assistance. And we ask Allāh to pave the way for him to translate and render a greater number of Ḥanbalī *fiqh* manuals.

Dr Fāris b. Fāliḥ al-Khazrajī

Written just before the Maghrib prayer of Friday, 1st Jumādā al-Ūlā 1441

27th December 2019

ولقد بذل الأستاذ جُوَيْل جليل جهدًا كبيرًا ومتميزًا في اخراج جزء من هذا المصنف ولا سيما أنه قد سبق هذا الكتاب بكتاب الفروع ، فنسأل الله له التوفيق والسداد والاعانة ، وأن يهئ الله له الأسباب لترجمة أكبر عدد ممكن من كتب الفقه الحنبلي ، وان يبارك في وقته وعلمه إنه ولي ذلك والقادر عليه .

وكتب

فارس بن فالح الخزرجي

قبيل صلاة المغرب يوم الجمعة ١/ جمادي الأولى / ١٤٤١

٢٧ / ١٢ / ٢٠١٩

Translator's Introduction

Translation is a process of changing the original written text (the source text or ST) in the original verbal language (the source language or SL) into a written text (the target text or TT) in a different verbal language (the target language or TL). In short, it is rendering the meaning of a text into another language in the way the author intended the text.[1] Therefore, it is incumbent to fully comprehend the ST for the correct application of the TL syntax and lexis. Inadequate understanding of the ST brings about errors pertaining to syntax and grammar in the TL. Thus, thorough research is required to fully understand the ST and become acquainted with the subject matter. According to Nida, the 'basic requirements' of a translation must consist of four elements. Firstly, it must make sense. Secondly, it must convey the spirit and manner of the original. Thirdly, it must have a natural and easy form of expression. Fourthly, it must produce a similar response.[2]

Translators take different positions in portraying a specific text into English; some prefer 'free translations' over 'literal translations' while others prefer 'translations with commentaries'.[3] The three different styles of translations have their merits and their shortfalls. Translators have also disputed whether a legal text should be translated literally or contextually owing to its sensitive nature.[4] Those who preferred literal translation argued that legal texts are complicated as a whole and authoritative in their nature; therefore, vagueness must be avoided in the rendition and thus a literal equivalence should be opted for. Proponents of this methodology also stress on the importance

1 Paul Newmark, *A Textbook of Translation* (Hertfordshire: Prentice Hall International Ltd, 1998), 5.
2 Basil Hatim, *Discourse and the Translator* (New York: Longman, 1990), 16.
3 Hatim, *Discourse*, 36.
4 Susan Sarcevic, *New Approach to Legal Translation* (The Hague: Kluwer Law International, 1997), 23.

of fidelity in translation of law,[5] thus they argue that a literal equivalence is the preferred choice for legal translation. It is undeniable that the TT must be precise and accurate; however, owing to the nature of the Arabic ST, a literal translation focusing on lexical equivalence does not always bring about a successful outcome; translations of concise law manuals (*mukhtaṣarāt*) enters into this category.

Concise Islamic law manuals in Arabic were generally authored for people aspiring to be jurists and judges. The concise law manuals do not normally include passages of the Qur'ān or Prophetic reports as supportive material for the legal opinions therein; the genre endorses the technique of paraphrasing rulings rather than presenting the evidences for the stated legal rulings. *Mukhtaṣar fī al-fiqh* was the first abridged Ḥanbalī manual which al-Khiraqī (d. 324/935) authored towards the latter part of his life.[6] Ibn Qudāma (d. 620/1223) in the thirteenth century authored a series of law manuals, as a curriculum, to progressively develop Ḥanbalī law students. The manuals he authored differed in their levels, ranging from the beginner level to the scholarly. Some of the concise law manuals authored by Ḥanbalī scholars became more celebrated than others. Celebrated manuals among the later-generation Ḥanbalīs include: *Zād al-mustaqni'* of al-Ḥajjāwī (d. 968/1560); *Dalīl al-ṭālib* of Mar'ī b. Yūsuf (d. 1033/1623); and *Akhṣar al-mukhtaṣarāt* of Ibn Balbān (d. 1083/1672).

Methodology and issues associated with the translation

The objective of this translation of *Dalīl al-ṭālib* is to render its Arabic text into English which will be clear and concise for the English speaker. Bearing in mind the 'basic requirements' of a translation, the rendition will focus on conveying the meanings premeditated by the author while trying to maintain as much as possible the lexical, grammatical, and syntactical aspects of it in the translation. Throughout the translation, to maintain the grammatical rules of English while trying to keep the TT as close as possible to the Arabic, it was necessary to restructure parts of the text entirely or partially.

5 Rafat Alwazna, *Translating Ḥanbalī Sharī'a code from Arabic to English* (Saarbrucken: Lambert Academic Publishing, 2013), 262.

6 Bakr b. Abū Zayd, *Al-Madkhal al-mufaṣṣal* (Riyadh: Dār al-'Āsima, 1997), vol.1 p.687.

While keeping the translation accurate and precise, the language employed in the translation has been made simple and modern to make it accessible to everyone who speaks English – law student or otherwise. The present translation is an easy-read and it is hoped that the legal language used therein does not descend to an unfitting level.

In the past, the chapters pertaining to crimes and legal punishments from *Dalīl al-ṭālib* were translated by George M. Baroody in English as part of his Masters' thesis, *Crime and Punishment under Islamic Law*. The thesis was initially published by The American University in Cairo in 1961, and then Regency Press (London) published the second edition in 1979. The current translation of *Dalīl al-ṭālib* focuses on the articles of worship only. The rendition was based on its first Arabic edition, published by Dār al-Ṭayyiba in 2004, and edited by Naẓr Muḥammad al-Fāriyābī. In order to convey the premeditated meanings, the translation relied on some well-known commentaries. Two of the earliest works were given special attention to, namely: *Sharḥ dalīl al-ṭālib* of ʿAbdullāh b. Aḥmad al-Maqdisī (d. 1091/1680) and *Ḥāshiyat ibn ʿawaḍ ʿalā dalīl al-ṭālib* of Aḥmad b. ʿAwaḍ al-Mardāwī (d. 1105/1693). Other secondary works cited include: *Nayl al-maʾārib* of ʿAbd al-Qādir al-Taghlibī (d. 1135/1722); *Ḥāshiyat ʿalā dalīl al-ṭālib* of Muṣṭafā al-Dūmānī (d. 1200/1785); *Manār al-sabīl fī sharḥ al-dalīl* of Ibrāhīm b. Ḍuwayyān (d. 1353/1934); *Shifāʾ al-ʿalīl sharḥ manār al-sabīl* of ʿAbdullāh al-Jibrīn (d. 1430/2009); and *Al-Salsabīl fī sharḥ al-dalīl* of Sʿad al-Khathlān.

The translation generally follows the system of transliteration used in *The Encyclopaedia of Islam*. Arabic terminologies that did not have an English equivalent, which are few in number – have not been translated. For such terminologies, the transliteration of the terms has been written in italic, however the meanings of the terms have been explained in the annotations. Arabic words and expressions that initially appear in the translation have been written in italic between brackets, and thereafter, only the Arabic transliterations appear without its English equivalence. The transliterations do not differentiate between *alif-lām* before sun and *alif-lām* before moon letters, hence the definite article has been written as *ʿal-ʾ* throughout. The abbreviation 'b.' has been employed after the mention of a forename, whether it follows the name of the individual's actual father or otherwise. It does not distinguish between names that follow the actual father's name (e.g. Anas bin Mālik) and names that do not (e.g. Aḥmad ibn Ḥanbal).

The years have been cited firstly according to the Hijrī calendar, then according to the Gregorian calendar; e.g., (d. 505/1111), the year in which al-Ghazālī died. Glorifications and invocations after certain names have not been included in the rendition to maintain the flow of the script, but as Muslims, one ought to say the dictums where necessary. The wedging of parenthetical interpolations into the text has also been kept very minimal to prevent the reader from being side tracked. The editor's format and layout of the original Arabic text is very commendable, but I did not limit myself to the editor's format while presenting the English translation, although I tried my best to maintain its foundation.

The Chicago notes and referencing system has been used. Throughout the translation, footnotes have been employed to assist the reader to understand the text easily. The purpose of the annotations is not to present a commentary to the manual. The main purpose of this rendition is to present Marʿī b. Yūsuf's *Dalīl al-ṭālib*. The notes that appear at the bottom of the translated text have been kept short. But where I felt the text of *Dalīl al-ṭālib* required extra clarification, I supplemented it with notes from its explanations and super-commentaries, primarily summarised from *Sharḥ dalīl al-ṭālib* of ʿAbdullāh b. Aḥmad al-Maqdisī and *Ḥāshiyat* of Ibn ʿAwaḍ. The reader should note that the opinions expressed in the translated text are those of the author, Marʿī b. Yūsuf, and not necessarily of the translator.

Virtues of learning Islamic law

The knowledge of Islamic law has numerous virtues. It is also required to perform devotional acts of worship correctly and carry out social dealings properly. The scholars have compiled works which specifically deal with the merits of learning and teaching Islamic knowledge. In this section, a few Prophetic traditions along with its commentaries have been included to shed some light on the merits of learning Islamic law.

Al-Bukhārī (d. 256/870) reported: Saʿīd narrated to us, he said: Ibn Wahb narrated to us from Yūnus who narrated from Ibn Shihāb, he said: Ḥumayd b. ʿAbd al-Raḥmān said: I heard Muʿāwiya preaching and he said: I heard the Prophet saying:

> **If Allāh wants good for a person, He gives him understanding of the religion.**

Al-Nawawī (d. 676/1277) understood this narration to indicate the excellence of knowledge and the excellence of understanding religious matters. The narration encourages people to understand the religion,[7] which includes knowing the legal rulings of the religion.[8] While explaining this ḥadīth, Ibn Ḥajar (d. 856/1452) mentioned:

> It's implied from the ḥadīth: if a person does not try to understand the religion, then the person will be deprived of much good. Therefore, an individual who did not acquire any knowledge related to the foundations of Islam and its branches will be included in this category of people.[9]

---

7 Muḥī al-Dīn al-Nawawī, *Al-Minhāj* (Beirut: Dār al-Maʿrifa, 2009), vol.7 p.127.

8 Muṣṭafā al-Bughā, *Nuzhat al-muttaqīn* (Damascus: Dār al-Muṣṭafā, 2006), vol.2 p.188.

9 Aḥmad b. Ḥajar al-Asqalānī, *Fatḥ al-bārī bi-sharḥ ṣaḥīḥ al-bukhārī* (Riyadh: Dār

In his lengthy discussion, Ibn al-ʿUthaymīn explained that motives behind acquiring religious knowledge are very important; he also discussed the importance of implementing knowledge, he said:

> If Allāh knows there is some goodness in a person, He will want good for that person and consequently, He will grant him understanding of Islam, which includes His laws and regulations. Deep understanding does not mean mere accumulation of knowledge, but also its implementation.[10]

In a different narration, Ibn ʿAdī (d. 365/975) reported: Aḥmad b. Ḥafṣ narrated to us, he said: Suwaid narrated to us, he said: Al-Walīd b. Muḥammad al-Mūqirī narrated to us from Thawr b. Yazīd, who narrated from Khālid b. Maʿdān on the authority of Muʿāwiya, who said that the Prophet said:

> **If Allāh wants good for a person, He gives him understanding of the religion. Whoever does not try to understand the religion, Allāh does not care about such an individual.**[11]

Ibn Ḥajar and others considered this narration to be *ḍaīʿf* (weak) but considered the meaning of the latter part of the ḥadīth to be correct. This is because one who does not acquaint himself with the matters of Islam will not be considered as a legist or even a law student and thus, divine goodness will be deprived from such individuals.

Al-Tirmidhī (d. 279/892) reported: Muḥammad b. Ismāʿīl narrated to us, he said: Ibrāhīm b. Mūsā informed us, he said: Al-Walīd, the son of Muslim informed us, he said: Rawḥ b. Janāḥ narrated from Mujāhid: Ibn ʿAbbās said that the Prophet said:

> **A well-versed jurist is more powerful against the Satan than a thousand regular worshippers.**[12]

---

al-Ṭayyiba, 2011), vol.1 p.290.

10 Muḥammad b. al-ʿUthaymīn, *Sharḥ riyāḍ al-ṣāliḥīn* (Riyadh: Madār al-Waṭn, 2006), vol.5 p.422.

11 Abū Aḥmad b. ʿAdī al-Jurjānī, *Al-Kāmil fī ḍuʿafāʾ al-rijāl* (Beirut: Dār al-Kutub al-ʿIlmiyya, 1997), vol.8 p.351.

12 Al-Tirmidhī (2681) and others. This narration was graded as *ḥasan* (fair) by al-Tirmidhī

Al-Mubārakfūrī (d. 1353/1934) clarified why a well-versed jurist is more powerful against the Satan compared to regular worshippers:

> The person well-versed in law does not accept any of the deceptions of the Satan. Furthermore, the person well-versed in law commands people to goodness, which is the opposite of what Satan commands people to do. The saying in the ḥadīth, 'than a thousand' – numerousness is the intention for stating that particular figure. So, every time the Satan opens up a door of passion and stimulates desires in the hearts of people, the well-versed jurist clarifies the plots and traps of the Satan for them. The jurist blocks off these doors and makes Satan's plots unsuccessful. This is contrary to the regular worshipper, who may be engaged and busy in worship while in the snares of Satan without even being aware.[13]

What we learn from the Prophetic narrations is that when a person tries to understand Islam, including its laws, it shows that Allāh wants well for such an individual. The one who attains religious knowledge, understands it, and implements it, is considered to be a successful person in the sight of Allāh. The accomplishment of Islamic knowledge is achieved through divine assistance as well as hard work. The classical scholars considered it essential to have righteous intentions to study Islamic law. A well-versed jurist is believed to be more austere against the Satan than a normal worshipper. Therefore, an educated person will naturally be more honorable in the sight of Allāh than an ignorant person.

13 Muḥammad al-Mubārakfūrī, *Tuḥfat al-aḥwadhī* (Beirut: Dār al-Kutub al-'Ilmiyya, 2010), vol.7 p.450.

Chronology of the Ḥanbalī school

Gregorian	
780	Birth of Aḥmad b. Ḥanbal in Baghdad, the epicenter of the Ḥanbalī school.
833	The inquisition of Aḥmad regarding the Qurʾān being created.
855	Death of Aḥmad b. Ḥanbal. His law school crystallised after the law schools of Abū Ḥanīfa (d. 150/767), Mālik (d. 179/795), and al-Shāfiʿī (d. 204/820).
855 – 1012	Era of the early-generation Ḥanbalī scholars.
888	Death of al-Marrūdhī, a close student of Aḥmad.
	Around this time, al-Khallāl, a disciple of al-Marrūdhī near-completed his voluminous compendium, *al-Jāmiʿ*. The compendium included Aḥmad's legal verdicts and the raw material for the Ḥanbalī school. It existed in twenty volumes which al-Khallāl amassed in twenty-five years, after being encouraged by his teacher, al-Marrūdhī.
935	Death of al-Khiraqī, first to compose a concise Ḥanbalī law manual.
1012	Death of Ibn Ḥāmid, first to write a manual on Ḥanbalī legal theory.
1012 – 1479	Era of the mid-generation Ḥanbalī scholars. During the later phase of this era, a number of Ḥanbalī scholars were appointed as formal judges for the first time in Mecca, Medina,

	Aleppo, Hama, Damascus, Jerusalem, Ramla, Gaza, and in other cities.
1480	Era of the later-generation Ḥanbalī scholars; it began with the death of 'Alā' al-Dīn al-Mardāwī, the verifier of the Ḥanbalī school.
1480 –	During this era, around five hundred law manuals were authored. Ibn Qudāma's manual, *al-Muqni'*, became the foundation material for the law manuals of the later-generation Ḥanbalī scholars. Reliable manuals of this era include: *al-Iqnā'; Zād al-mustaqni'; Muntahā al-irādāt; Ghāyat al-muntahā; Dalīl al-ṭālib; 'Umdat al-ṭālib; Kāfī al-mubtadī; and Akhṣar al-mukhtaṣarāt.*
1485	Birth of Mūsā al-Ḥajjāwī, author of *Zād al-mustaqni'*. He became a reference point owing to his diligence in critically revising (*taṣḥīḥ*) Aḥmad's law school.
1564	Death of Ibn al-Najjār, author of *Muntahā al-irādāt.*
1591	Birth of al-Buhūtī, he was known to be *Shaykh al-Ḥanābila* of Egypt and was considered to be the last of its prominent Ḥanbalī scholars.
1610	Mar'ī al-Karmī finishes authoring the epitome, *Dalīl al-ṭālib.*
1740	The Ḥanbalī school starts to spread from Najd to the other regions of Saudi Arabia under Muḥammad b. 'Abd al-Wahhāb's propagation.
1871 – 1874	Ibn Ḥumayd authors' *al-Ṣuḥub al-wābila,* a biographical dictionary. The works of Ibn Abī Ya'lā, Ibn Rajab, and Ibn Ḥumayd in this genre documents Aḥmad's legacy, covering over 1200 years.

1897	Walter Patton produces the first Western work on Aḥmad b. Ḥanbal as a PhD thesis entitled, *Ahmed ibn Hanbal and the Mihna* (Leiden University)
1927	King ʿAbd al-ʿAzīz issues a proclamation stating that the Ḥanbalī doctrine should be uniformly applied in Saudi Courts.
1961	George M. Baroody produces a part-translation of *Manār al-sabīl fī sharḥ al-dalīl* as a Masters thesis entitled, *Crime and Punishment under Islamic Law* (The American University in Cairo)
2010	Death of ʿAbdullāh b. ʿAqīl, he was considered to be *Shaykh al-Ḥanābila* of the modern era.

Principles of Aḥmad b. Ḥanbal's law

The Ḥanbalī scholars have written at length about the sources Aḥmad b. Ḥanbal used to infer his legal verdicts (*fatāwā*). Aḥmad b. Ḥanbal himself did not author any documented work on legal theory (*uṣūl al-fiqh*), that is, the science which deals with the sources of Islamic law, its order of priority, and the procedures by which substantive laws (*fiqh*) are inferred. The Ḥanbalī jurists filled this gap and wrote on the topic; one of the earliest jurists to write on the subject was Ibn Ḥāmid (d. 403/1012).[14] By studying and examining Aḥmad b. Ḥanbal's responsa collections (*masā'il*), the scholars generally agreed that he used five primary sources to issue his legal verdicts.[15] Ibn al-Qayyim (d. 751/1350) and Ibn Badrān (d. 1346/1927) listed the primary sources:[16]

1. **Text of the Qur'ān and the Prophetic traditions.**

   If textual evidence was available, Aḥmad would base the legal verdicts on the Qur'ān and the Prophetic traditions, and would not opt for anything else.

2. **Legal verdicts of the Companions, which they did not differ upon.**

   In absence of the first source, Aḥmad would resort to the legal verdicts of the Companions of the Prophet. He would not base his legal verdicts upon practices (*'amal*), opinions or upon analogy (*qiyās*) if such legal verdicts of the Companions were available.

14 Abū Zayd, *Al-Madkhal al-mufaṣṣal*, vol.1 p.604.

15 Abdul Hakim al-Matroudi, *The Hanbalī School of Law and Ibn Taymiyyah* (New York, Routledge, 2006), 32.

16 'Abd al-Qādir b. Badrān, *Al-Madkhal*, (Damascus: Mu'assasat al-Risāla, 2011), 113-119. This categorisation mentioned by Ibn Badrān is of Ibn al-Qayyim (d. 751/1350).

3. **Legal verdicts of the Companions, which they differed upon.**

   Aḥmad would select one of their opinions, which he regarded to be closest to the Qur'ān and the Prophetic traditions. If the closest opinion was unclear to him, he would transmit the various opinions of the Companions.

4. **Weakly attested Prophetic traditions and *mursal* reports.**[17]

5. **Analogy.**[18]

17 A narration attributed to the Prophet without naming the intermediating Companion. It is worth noting that during Aḥmad b. Ḥanbal's time, the Prophetic traditions were divided only into two main categories in terms of soundness: authentic (*ṣaḥīḥ*) and weak (*ḍaʿīf*). The latter category varied in its strength of soundness.
18 Ibn Badrān, *al-Madkhal*, 113-119. Ibn al-Qayyim mentioned that Aḥmad b. Ḥanbal used analogy out of necessity.

The Five Legal Rulings

The action of a person who is deemed legally responsible under Islamic law enters into one of the five legal rulings (*aḥkām*). The legal theorists went into great depths in clarifying the premeditated meanings and associated issues surrounding these five legal rulings. In this section, a summary of Ibn al-ʿUthaymīn's (d. 1421/2001) description[19] of the five legal rulings has been presented.

1. ***Wājib*** (obligatory)

   It is something the Lawgiver has commanded to do without a choice. The person, who performs the obligatory act out of obedience to Allāh, is rewarded, and the person who leaves it is liable for punishment.

2. ***Mandūb*** (recommended/commendable)

   It is something the Lawgiver has commanded to with a choice. The person, who performs the recommended act out of obedience to Allāh, is rewarded, and the person who leaves it is not liable for punishment.

3. ***Ḥarām*** (prohibited/impermissible)

   It is something the Lawgiver has forbidden from doing, which must be avoided. The person, who leaves the prohibited act out of obedience to Allāh, is rewarded, and the person who falls into it is liable for punishment.

4. ***Makrūh*** (detested/reprehensible)

   It is something the Lawgiver has forbidden from doing but left it optional. The person, who leaves the disliked act out of obedi-

19 Muḥmammad b. al-ʿUthaymīn, *Al-Uṣūl min ʿilm al-uṣūl* (Cairo: Dār ʿUmar b. Khaṭṭāb, 2006), 8-10.

ence to Allāh, is rewarded, and the person who falls into it is not liable for punishment.

5. ***Mubāḥ*** (permissible)

   It is something, which is not connected to a command or a prohibition in and of itself. As long as the action is deemed permissible, the concept of reward or punishment will not directly result from the act.

Determining the official opinions of the Ḥanbalī school

Ḥanbalī jurists such as Ibn Ḥāmid, Abū Ya'lā (d. 458/1066), Ibn Qudāma, al-Mardāwī (d. 885/1480), and others attempted to establish the 'correct' legal positions for Aḥmad. To ascertain Aḥmad's 'correct' juristic position for a particular issue, the participants must be definite about Aḥmad's closing opinion (i.e. the juristic opinion he did not change his mind about later). This can be problematic because the reports in the *Masā'il* and *Jāmi'* collections were not chronologically arranged, and perhaps for this reason al-Ṭūfī (d. 716/1316) was inclined to say:

> It is improper for us to be certain about an imam's position until we know his final position before he died. This is ascertained from his works or what has been narrated from him close to his death. Hence, it is impossible for us to know this regarding Aḥmad. As for the critical revisions of Aḥmad's legal positions, they are in fact, diligent enquiries of Aḥmad's associates, who came after him such as Ibn Ḥāmid, Abū Ya'lā and later jurists like Ibn Qudāma.[20]

Nevertheless, certain revision methods (*tarājīḥ*) were put in place to determine the 'correct or official' positions of the Ḥanbalī school. That is, if there were numerous opinions from Aḥmad for a legal issue, the Ḥanbalī scholars opted for one of these opinions following certain revision methods. The 'correct' opinions were determined by three different techniques: by analysing the reporters of Aḥmad's responsa; by selecting the preferred opinions of the Ḥanbalī masters (*shuyūkh al-madhhab*); and finally, by examining the reliable Ḥanbalī law manuals. The last method (*tarjīḥ bi-l-kutub*) is similar to the second method; it follows a type of tier system (according to each era) to determine the 'correct or official' opinion. In general, to establish the

---

20 Najm al-Dīn b. al-Ṭūfī, 2011. *Sharḥ mukhtaṣar al-rawḍah* (Damascus: Mu'assasat al-Risāla, 2011), vol.3 p.627.

official positions, some scholars opted for the following manuals from the mid-generation era:

> (1) The agreement between *al-Muḥarrar* and *al-Muqniʿ*. If the two manuals differed on a legal opinion, the official position will be what Ibn Qudāma opted for in his manual, *al-Kāfī*. (2) The opinions which Abū al-Khaṭṭāb (d. 510/1116) opted for in his manual, *Ruʾūs al-masāʾil*. (3) The opinions which Ibn Qudāma opted for in his manual, *al-Mughnī*. (4) The opinions which al-Majd (d. 652/1254) opted for in his work, *Sharḥ al-hidāya*.

From the later-generation manuals, the following law manuals were selected to determine the 'correct or official' positions:

> The opinions in *al-Iqnāʿ* and *al-Muntahā*. If the two manuals differed on a matter, the official position will be what's in the manual, *Ghāyat al-muntahā*.[21]

21 Abū Zayd, *Al-Madkhal al-mufaṣṣal*, vol.1 p.295; vol.1 p.293-320.

Methodology for studying Ḥanbalī law manuals

It is important to understand how to study Islamic law and what law manuals to select to commence one's studies. It was a regular practice of scholars from the different law schools to author a series of law manuals, as curriculums, to progressively develop their law students. The manuals authored in substantive law and legal theory varied in levels, ranging from beginner to scholarly level. In the past as well as present, scholars pointed out that adopting incorrect methodologies to study law will lead students to waste many years without progressing properly – they may not even go past the beginners' level. The scholars pointed out two main factors which lead to this: firstly, one is not naturally bright; and secondly, one is ignorant in the ways to teach.[22] Unfortunately, a lot of teachers fall into the latter category; so for example, a beginner student may come to learn a discipline but the teacher floods the student with unnecessary information. This method does not permit the student to develop and build himself.

The Ḥanbalī school's beginner level

For substantive law (*fiqh*), one of the five reliable (*mu'ṭamad*) manuals according to the later-generation[23] is selected for study. Preferably in the following order but it's not a must:

- *Akhṣar al-mukhtaṣarāt* of Ibn Balbān (d. 1083/1672)
- *'Umdat al-ṭālib* of Manṣūr al-Buhūtī (d. 1051/1641)
- *Dalīl al-ṭālib* of Mar'ī b. Yūsuf (d. 1033/1623)

22 Ibn Badrān, *Madkhal*, 485.

23 The early-generation Ḥanbalī era stretched between 241/855 and 403/1012; the mid-generation Ḥanbalī era between 404/1013 and 884/1479; and the later-generation Ḥanbalī era starts from the year 885/1480, it coincides with the death date of 'Alā' al-Dīn al-Mardāwī, founder of the later-generation Ḥanbalī school.

- *Kāfī al-mubtadī* of Ibn Balbān (d. 1083/1672)
- *Zād al-mustaqniʿ* of Mūsā al-Ḥajjāwī (d. 968/1560)

The teachers navigate the students through these manuals, explaining the content of texts without falling short or adding extra. The main objective at the beginners' level is to understand technical wordings of the author, the legal articles therein, the rulings, and to get acquainted with the evidences for these rulings along with it's points of inference (*waj al-dalāla*). The students are required to put in a lot of effort to fully comprehend each legal article before moving to the next one. The teacher helps to build the students' understanding and teaches in a manner so the students can capture and internalise the legal articles in their minds. The past and present scholars also emphasised a lot on memorising legal manuals. It was a regular custom for aspiring law students to memorise legal texts by heart, and jurists have practiced this for many centuries.[24] If a student decides to memorise a Ḥanbalī legal manual, the person selects one of the following, in the preferable order:

- *Zād al-mustaqniʿ*
- *Dalīl al-ṭālib*
- *Akhṣar al-mukhtaṣarāt*
- *ʿUmdat al-ṭālib*
- *Kāfī al-mubtadī*

Memorisation is an excellent way to retain the legal articles and recall its rulings, but it is best to combine between comprehension and memorisation of a legal manual. A student may be too occupied with memorising while falling short in his understanding of the legal articles or vice versa. In summary, a beginner student of Ḥanbalī law should memorise a law manual and study with a proficient Ḥanbalī teacher, with the aim of fully understanding the manual's content. In the long run, the student studies the remaining four manuals from the beginners' level with a teacher, if this is possible. Thereafter, he moves on to the next level. Of course, for a student to fully progress within and beyond the beginners' level, they are required to learn

24 Aḥmad b. Nāsir al-Quʿaymī, *Madārij tafaqquh al-ḥanbalī* (London, Takween: 2014), 33-34.

the Arabic language at an advanced level. The other law manual included in this level by some scholars is al-Buhūtī's *Al-Rawḍ al-murbiʿ* – a commentary of *Zād al-Mustaqniʿ*. This can actually be classed as the intermediate level. Once a student completes studying the five 'reliable' manuals or most of them, one starts *al-Rawḍ al-murbiʿ* with a proficient Ḥanbalī scholar. It is the final manual to be studied before the advanced level.[25] Certain scholars preferred that students go through a basic Ḥanbalī legal theory manual before beginning *al-Rawḍ al-murbiʿ*.[26]

Considering our lifestyle in the West, it is often difficult to complete a law manual from the beginning to the end. As I have previously experienced, at times a basic primer in law would require several years to complete in English when it really should not take more than a few months. For a number of reasons, Western teachers choose even shorter law manuals than the aforementioned to teach. I for example started by teaching *An Epitome of Ḥanbalī Substantive Law* of Yūsuf b. 'Abd al-Ḥādī al-Ḥanbalī (d. 909/1503) before moving on to *Akhṣar al-mukhtaṣarāt*, while other teachers preferred to teach *The Path of the Wayfarer* of 'Abd al-Raḥmān b. Nāṣir al-Saʿdī (d. 1376/1956) first. One of the primary reasons is the teachers' consideration of the students they are delivering to. Most of us in the West have little to no elementary knowledge of substantive law or of the Arabic language, so it's better to start with a much easier and shorter law manual. This also allows students to at least complete one law manual within a short time period. It is better for students to cover and learn all aspects of Islamic law to some degree from a shorter manual, than to cover some aspects from a longer manual.

In closing this discussion, I will end with an excellent advise from Ibn Badrān (d. 1346/1927), he explains how he studied substantive law:

> During the days of our studies, by God's grace we were guided to a method for studying substantive law (*fiqh*).
>
> We would open up a law epitome (*matn*) and select a clause from it to study. Once we selected a clause, we tried to understand the

25 Al-Quʿaymī, *Madārij*, 36.
26 Ibn Badrān, *Madkhal*, 488.

legal articles therein without citing the law epitome's commentary (*sharḥ*). We did this until we thought to have understood the clause properly. Thereafter, we read the commentary; the first reading of the commentary was read to test our understanding and comprehension. If we understood things from the clause incorrectly, it was corrected. In the next stage, we tried to understand the commentary in the same manner we did for the epitome (i.e. by selecting clauses etc.) Once we thought to have understood the commentary properly, we read its super-commentary (*ḥāshiya*), that is, if there was one. Again, the super-commentary was read to test our understanding and comprehension.

If we knew that we understood the lesson, we left the law epitome and preoccupied ourselves in capturing and internalising the legal articles in our minds. In this way, we memorised the law epitome, that is, a memorisation of comprehension and capturing, not through preserving its clauses and wordings. Thereafter, we tried our best to express these legal articles using our wordings without copying or adhering to the author's. Finally, we went to the teacher to read to him and test our comprehension while going through the lesson. We amended what was incorrect and documented anything important the teacher mentioned that was additional to the epitome and commentary.

I realised that if someone studied one book in a science in the aforementioned manner, the rest of the books in the science will be made easy for him – whether the books happen to be long or short.[27]

The Ḥanbalī school's advanced level

At the advanced level, the students study three extended reliable manuals according to the later-generation, they are as follows:

- *Muntahā al-irādāt* of Ibn al-Najjār (d. 972/1564)
- *Al-Iqnāʿ* of Mūsā al-Ḥajjāwī (d. 968/1560)
- *Ghāyat al-muntahā* of Marʿī b. Yūsuf (d. 1033/1623)

The advanced level requires a lot of patience and endurance from the stu-

27 Ibn Badrān, *Madkhal*, 489-490.

dents. The extended-manuals are studied as listed. *Muntahā al-irādāt* is studied before *al-Iqnāʿ* for a number of reasons: the later-generation regarded it to be reliable manual; they also authored a lot more works based on the former; it is better refined; and contains fewer legal articles.[28] The way to study these manuals is more complex. It generally entails citing their commentaries and super-commentaries systematically and cross-referencing them to understand and unfold the legal articles therein. The extended-manuals are usually studied more than once for a person to retain the intricate details and the legal rulings they contain.

28 Al-Quʿaymī, *Madārij*, 102.

Marʿī b. Yūsuf al-Karmī al-Ḥanbalī

He is Marʿī b. Yūsuf b. Abī Bakr b. Aḥmad b. Abī Bakr b. Yūsuf al-Karmī (then) al-Maqdisī. His agnomen was Zayn al-Dīn.[29] The ascription 'al-Karmī' refers to where he was originally from. Al-Karmī originated from Tulkarm, a small town near Nablus, Palestine.[30] The historical sources do not provide information about his birth, his childhood, nor about the elementary stages of his education. As with many notable scholars, al-Karmī probably started his quest for sacred knowledge at an early stage. After completing his studies with the resident scholars of his locality, he made his trip to Jerusalem for advanced studies. It was perhaps his initial excursion away from Tulkarm. He remained in Jerusalem for some period, hence the ascription 'al-Maqdisī' after his name. The historical sources do not inform us when al-Karmī made the journey to Jerusalem and how long he remained there to study.

After leaving Jerusalem, al-Karmī relocated to Cairo, where he studied in the famous al-Azhar Mosque. While residing in Cairo, he sought sacred knowledge from a great number of scholars. Having excelled in his studies under the instruction of many specialists, al-Karmī gained licenses to teach. Consequently, he began to teach in al-Azhar Mosque and then held the professorial role (*al-Mashyakha*) in The Mosque of Sultan Hasan.[31] His prominent teachers in Cairo include Muḥammad Ḥijāzī al-Wāʿiẓ (d. 1035/1625) and Aḥmad al-Ghunaymī (d. 1044/1634).[32] Al-Karmī's life was occupied

29 'Abdullāh bin 'Abd al-Muḥsin al-Turkī, *Al-Madhhab al-ḥanbalī* (Beirut: Mu'assasat al-Risāla, 2002), vol.2 p.501.

30 Muḥammad b. Ḥumayd, *Al-Suḥub al-wābila* (Beirut: Mu'assasat al-Risāla, 2017), vol.3 p.1118.

31 Ibn Humayd, *Suḥub*, vol.3 p.1119

32 'Abdullāh al-Ṭurīqī, *Al-Ḥanābila khilāl thalātha 'ashara qarna* (Beirut: Sharikat Fawā'id, 2012), vol.8 p.332.

with learning, teaching, issuing legal verdicts, editing works, and writing books. Regarding al-Karmī, Dr. ʿAbd al-Raḥmān al-ʿUthaymīn said:

> He was among the leading imams and verifiers of the Ḥanbalī school. Al-Karmī combined between writing books and teaching others; he was a student and a pupil of the great Ḥanbalī scholars of Egypt, al-Shām, and Najd. Students from one generation to another are always preoccupied with his writings and books.[33]

Al-Karmī was a leading figure for the later Ḥanbalī school. He authored approximately eighty works, which included books and long essays; a lot of his writings are still extant in manuscript form. Only twenty of his works have been edited but some of them are yet to be published. The works he produced, especially his *Dalīl al-ṭālib* and *Ghāyat al-muntahā* supported the Ḥanbalī school to progress and consolidate further. Al-Karmī resided in Egypt until he passed away after leading a great life of knowledge. The biographers generally agreed that Marʿī b. Yūsuf al-Karmī al-Ḥanbalī passed away in the year 1033/1623.

33 Ibn Ḥumayd, *Suḥub*, vol.3 p.1118 (see footnote no. 760).

Dalīl al-Ṭālib

Dalīl al-ṭālib has always been a popular law manual among the Ḥanbalī scholars and its law students. It was among the celebrated works and received numerous commentaries; many other manuals were authored based on the text of *Dalīl al-ṭālib*. In praising the manual, some scholars composed couplets, for instance ʿAbd al-Salām al-Shaṭṭī (d. 1295/1878) said:

O who desires to understand
the religion, in accomplishing the pursued objectives
Read Sharḥ al-muntahā,
and memorise Dalīl al-ṭālib.

Since the manual was a significant contribution of the later-generation Ḥanbalīs, a number of scholars discussed its origin and its unique qualities, for example al-Turkī stated:

> *Dalīl al-ṭālib* is a concise text similar to *Zād al-mustaqniʿ*. In his methodology, the author states only one opinion, namely the more accepted opinion (*rājiḥ*) of the Ḥanbalī school. The author mentioned in his introduction that he 'did not include anything therein except what the celebrated imams of the Ḥanbalī school corroborated and asserted to be correct – and upon which legal verdicts were authored by its prominent scholars and verifiers.' The author did not signpost if there are any links between his manual and previous law manuals (i.e. whether he cited them for his manual etc.) However, considering the way his chapters and the sub-chapters are arranged, the manual resembles *al-Iqnāʿ* and *Muntahā al-irādāt* – two preceding Ḥanbalī law manuals. In fact, a collection of scholars believed that *Dalīl al-ṭālib* is a summary of *Muntahā al-irādāt*. Scholars such as Ṣāliḥ al-Buhūtī (d. 1121/1709), Aḥmad b. ʿAwaḍ al-Mardāwī (d. 1105/1693), ʿUthmān b. Bishr (d. 1290/1794), and Ibn Māniʿ (d.

1385/1965) endorsed this view.[34]

Abū Zayd seemed to have adopted the aforementioned view too; he cited the wordings used by the author in the introduction and said:

> Marīʿ al-Karmī abridged *Muntahā al-irādāt* of Ibn al-Najjār to produce his manual and he certainly alluded to this in his introduction, he said, 'I also bear witness that Muḥammad is His servant and messenger, who clarified the laws of Islam and succeeded – in reaching its utmost desired levels – (*bi-muntahā al-irādāt*) with his Lord.'
>
> *Dalīl al-ṭālib* stands out from *Zād al-mustaqniʿ* owing to it being much easier, in terms of the language and phrases used therein, making it less complex. As a result, it became a reliable manual for the generation of that era and those after them among the scholars of *al-Shām* and *al-Qaṣīm*. Whereas *Zād al-mustaqniʿ* became more popular among the people of *al-Jazīra* owing to the great number of legal issues it encompassed.[35]

Ibn Badrān in his introductory work to the Ḥanbalī school, *Madkhal,* discussed about different law manuals, including *al-Iqnāʿ*, *Muntahā al-irādāt,* and *Dalīl al-ṭālib*. However, he did not suggest or conclude whether *Dalīl al ṭālib* is an abridgement of *Muntahā al-irādāt.*[36] It has been suggested that *Dalīl al-ṭālib* is a summary of *Ghāyat al-muntahā*, an extended-manual of the same author; but this claim seems to be incorrect.[37]

34 Al-Turkī, *Al-Madhhab al-ḥanbalī*, vol.2 p.503.
35 Abū Zayd, *Al-Madkhal al-mufaṣṣal*, vol.2 p.791.
36 Ibn Badrān, *al-Madkhal*, 439-443.
37 Khālid al-Rabbāṭ, *Al-Jāmiʿ li-ulūm al-Imām Aḥmad* (Riyadh: Dār al-Fallāḥ, 2009), vol.1 p.474.

Development & Reception

Centuries

7th/13th Ibn Qudāma (d. 620/1223) composes *al-Muqniʿ*, an intermediate epitome to progressively develop Ḥanbalī law students.

9th/15th Al-Mardāwī (d. 885/1480) edits, refines, authenticates, and adds a commentary to the legal articles of *al-Muqniʿ*. In doing so, he produced his voluminous critical-explanation, *al-Inṣāf*. Around May 1468, al-Mardāwī completed summarising *al-Inṣāf* into a single volume, commonly known as *al-Tanqīḥ*.

10th/16th Ibn al-Najjār (d. 972/1564) merges the contents of *al-Muqniʿ* and *al-Tanqīḥ* with additional materials to produce the extended-epitome, *Muntahā al-irādāt*. It becomes a reliable manual for the later-generations and legal verdicts are issued based on its content.

11th/17th Marʿī b. Yūsuf al-Karmī (d. 1033/1623) abridges *Muntahā al-irādāt* and produces the epitome, *Dalīl al-ṭālib*. Shortly after its publication, it received two commentaries: *Sharḥ dalīl al-ṭālib* by ʿAbdullāh al-Maqdisī (d. 1091/1680), a student of al-Karmī; and *Maslak al-rāghib* of Ibrāhīm b. al-ʿAuwfī (d. 1093/1681).

12th/18th A number of explanations (*shurūḥ*) and super-commentaries (*ḥawāshi*) of *Dalīl al-ṭālib* emerged. The explanations include: *Nayl al-maʾārib* of ʿAbd al-Qādir al-Taghlibī (d. 1135/1722); and *Sharḥ al-dalīl* of Muḥammad al-Saffārīnī

(d. 1188/1774). The earliest super-commentary was of Aḥmad b. ʿAwaḍ al-Mardāwī (d. 1105/1693). His son, Aḥmad compiled and edited his father's notes and then renamed the super-commentary as *Fatḥ wahhāb al-maʾārib.*

13th/19th The following explanations appeared: *Sharḥ dalīl al-ṭālib* of Ismāʿīl al-Jurāʿī (d. 1202/1788) and later, *Manār al-sabīl* of Ibrāhīm b. Ḍuwayyān (d. 1353/1934). Also, super-commentaries of earlier explanations materialised, including: *Ḥāshiyat ʿalā nayl al-maʾārib* of Muṣṭafā al-Dūmānī (d. 1200/1785) and later, *Ḥāshiyat ʿalā nayl al-maʾārib* of ʿAbd al-Ghanī b. Yāsīn al-Labadī (d. 1319/1901).

Dalīl al-ṭālib is abridged for the first time and renamed as, *Mukhtaṣar al-ghālib.* It was part-summarised by the female Ḥanbalī scholar, Fāṭima al-Faḍīliyya (d. 1247/1831). She summarised up to the chapter of the congregational prayer before passing away.

14th/20th During this century more super-commentaries were authored, namely that of Ṣāliḥ b. ʿUthmān al-Qāḍī (d. 1351/1932), ʿUthmān b. Ṣāliḥ b. ʿUthmān al-Qāḍī (d. 1366/1946), and Ibn Māniʿ. The commentary of ʿAbd al-ʿAzīz b. Bishr (d. 1359/1940) also emerged.

Based on the material of *Dalīl al-ṭālib*, two new genres of works appeared: (i) poems and (ii) 'question and answer' books. A total of seven poems of different lengths were authored. The 'question and answer' books include: *Al-Ajwiba al-jaliyya* of Mūsā b. ʿĪsā al-Qadūmī (d. 1336/1917) and *Al-Masāʾil al-fiqhiyya al-ḥanbaliyya* of ʿAbdullāh al-Khalaf al-Duḥyān (d. 1349/1930).

In 1961, George M. Baroody presented the first English part-translation of *Manār al-sabīl fī sharḥ al-dalīl.*

15th/21st Works that emerged in this era include ḥadīth excerptions (*takhrīj*), namely, *Irwāʾ al-ghalīl* of Nāṣir al-Dīn al-Albānī

(d. 1420/1999). The work attempts to trace the Prophetic narrations and reports to its original sources, which were used in *Manār al-sabīl* – a commentary of *Dalīl al-ṭālib.*

It was followed by smaller works such as *Al-Takmīl* of Ṣāliḥ b. ʿAbd ʿAzīz Āl al-Shaykh; *Al-Taḥjīl* of ʿAbd al-ʿAzīz al-Ṭarīfī; and *Mustadrak al-taʿlīl* of Aḥmad b. al-Khalīl, which all traced the Prophetic narrations and reports that were missed out in *Irwāʾ al-ghalīl.*

Contemporary commentaries of *Dalīl al-ṭālib* that materialised include: *Nayl al-maṭālib* of Muḥammad b. Sulaymān al-Jarrāḥ (d. 1417/1996); *Idrāk al-maṭālib* of ʿAbdullāh b. al-ʿAqīl (d. 1432/2011); and *Al-Salsabīl fī sharḥ al-dalīl* of Sʿad al-Khathlān.

Commentaries of *Manār al-sabīl* include: *Shifāʾ al-ʿalīl sharḥ manār al-sabīl* of ʿAbdullāh al-Jibrīn (d. 1430/2009); *Manār al-sabīl wa ḥāshiyatuh al-anwār ʿalā manār al-sabīl min irwāʾ al-ghalīl* of Zuhayr al-Shāwish (d. 1434/2013); *Fatḥ al-jalīl bayān masāʾil manār al-sabīl* of ʿAbd al-Karīm al-Namla; and *Rafʿ al-wishāḥ ʿan ḥāshiyat ibn jarrāḥ ʿan manār al-sabīl* of Muḥammad b. Sulaymān al-Jarrāḥ

Dalīl al-ṭālib went through another abridgement, a follow on from the previous incomplete abridgement. It was summarised by Fayṣal Aḥmad al-ʿAlī and entitled, *Al-Kawkab al-ghārib.*

Jewel Jalil

دليل الطالب لنيل المطالب

Author's Introduction

In the name of Allāh, the Gracious, the Merciful

All praise belongs to Allāh, the Lord of the worlds. I bear witness that there is none worthy of worship except Allāh, Master of the Day of Judgement, who has no partners. I also bear witness that Muḥammad is His servant and messenger, who clarified the laws of Islam and succeeded in reaching its utmost desired levels with his Lord. Therefore, whomsoever adheres firmly to his laws will be from among the successful. May Allāh's blessings be upon him, the prophets and messengers, his household, and his Companions.

To commence:

This is an epitome of substantive law according to the most praiseworthy law school, that is, the law school of Aḥmad. I went to great lengths in elucidating the Ḥanbalī school hoping for Allāh's forgiveness. In the epitome, I clarified the legal rulings clearly. I did not include anything therein except what the celebrated imams of the Ḥanbalī school corroborated and asserted to be correct – and upon which legal verdicts were authored by its prominent scholars and verifiers. I have named the book: *Dalīl al-ṭālib* (*The Student's Guide*). I ask Allāh to make this book beneficial for those who occupy themselves with it; I ask Allāh to have mercy upon the Muslims and me, for certainly He is the most Merciful.

[مقدمة]

بِسْمِ اللَّهِ الرَّحْمَٰنِ الرَّحِيمِ

الحمدُ للهِ ربِّ العالمينَ، وأشْهدُ أنْ لا إلهَ إلا اللهُ وحْدهُ لا شريكَ لهُ مالكُ يومِ الدينِ. وأشهدُ أنَّ محمدًا عبدهُ ورسولُهُ، المبينُ لأحكامِ شرائعِ الدينِ، الفائزُ بمنتهى الإراداتِ منْ ربهِ، فمن تمسكَ بشريعتِهِ فهو من الفائزينَ، صلى اللهُ وسلمَ عليهِ وعلى جميعِ الأنبياءِ والمرسلينَ، وعلى آلِ كلٍّ وصحبِهِ أجمعينَ.

وبعد: فهذا مختصرٌ في الفقهِ، على المذهبِ الأحمدِ، مذهبِ الإمامِ أحمدَ، بالغتُ في إيضاحِهِ رجاءَ الغفرانِ، وبينتُ فيه الأحكامَ أحسنَ بيانٍ، لمْ أذكرْ فيه إلا ما جزمَ بصحتِهِ أهلُ التصحيحِ والعرفانِ، وعليه الفتوى فيما بينَ أَهْلِ الترجيحِ والْإتقانِ، وسميتُهُ بـ(دليلِ الطالبِ، لنيلِ المطالبِ). واللهَ أسألُ أنْ ينفعَ بهِ منِ اشتغلَ به، وَأنْ يرحمني والمسلمينَ، إنه أرْحمُ الراحمينَ .

Purification

Purification implies lifting a state of ritual impurity (*ḥadath*) and removing physical filth (*khabath*).

Water is of three categories: (i) purifying (*ṭahūr*), (ii) pure (*ṭāhir*), and (iii) impure (*najis*).

Purifying water refers to water which remains in its natural state as it was created. This type of water can lift ritual impurities and remove physical filth. Purifying water is of four types:

- Water that's prohibited (*ḥarām*) to use and cannot lift ritual impurities but can remove physical filth. It refers to waters that are not permissible to use.
- Water that lifts ritual impurities of women but not of mature men or of hermaphrodites. It refers to the water used and leftover by a responsible woman (*mukallafa*) after performing a full purification to remove a state of ritual impurity.[2]
- Water that's reprehensible (*makrūh*) to use when there is no need to use such water.[3] It refers to water from wells in graveyards; very hot and cold waters; water that has been heated up using filth (*najāsa*) as fuels or with something usurped; water already used for non-obligatory purifications; water used and leftover by non-Muslims after baths; water changed with sea salt; and water which has been mixed with insoluble substances such as agarwood, camphor, and oil.

  Zamzam water is not reprehensible to use unless it is used to remove physical filth.

---

2 This is a unique opinion of the Ḥanbalī school.

3 It becomes reprehensible when there is other purifying water available besides the aforementioned listed.

كتاب الطهارة

وهي: رفعُ الحدثِ وزوالُ الخبثِ.

وأقسامُ الماءِ ثلاثةٌ:

أحدُها: طهورٌ وهو الباقي على خلقتِه؛ يرفعُ الحدثَ ويزيلُ الخبثَ.
وهو أربعةُ أنواعٍ:

- ماءٌ: يحرمُ استعمالُه، ولا يرفعُ الحدثَ ويزيلُ الخبثَ وهو ما ليس مباحاً.
- وماءٌ: يرفعُ حدثَ الأنثى لا الرجلِ البالغِ والخنثى، وهو ما خلتْ به المرأةُ المكلفةُ لطهارةٍ كاملةٍ عن حدثٍ.
- وماءٌ: يكرَهُ استعمالُه مع عدمِ الاحتياجِ إليه، وهو ماءُ بئرٍ بمقبرةٍ وما اشتدَّ حرُّه أو بردُه أو سخنَ بنجاسةٍ، أو سخنَ بمغصوبٍ، أو استعملَ في طهارةٍ لم تجبْ، أو في غسلِ كافرٍ، أو تغيرَ بملحٍ مائيٍّ، أو بما لا يمازجُه كتغيرِه بالعودِ القماريِّ، وقطعِ الكافورِ، والدهنِ.

ولا يكرَه ماءُ زمزمَ إلا في إزالةِ الخبثِ.

- Water that's not reprehensible to use. This includes water from seas, wells, springs, and rivers, public bath houses and that which is heated using the sun. Likewise, water that has changed because of the effects of standing too long, owing to the smell of carcasses reaching the water, or because of something that's difficult to prevent, for example, the growth of algae and falling leaves from trees, so long as they were not placed intentionally by humans.

Pure water refers to waters, which are permissible to use, but neither for lifting states of ritual impurity nor for removing physical filth. It is water which has changed in its colour, taste, and smell notably owing to it being mixed with something pure. If the water's change disappears by itself, the water regains its purifying nature (i.e. it can be used for purification).

Forms of pure water: If its quantity is 'little' and it is utilised to lift a state of ritual impurity, or if the entire hand of a responsible Muslim is immersed in it after waking from a night's sleep which nullifies one's ablution before washing them thrice with an intention and mention of Allāh's name. Washing of the hands is obligatory in this scenario (i.e. when waking from a night's sleep).

Impure water refers to waters which are prohibited to use unless it was out of necessity. This type of water does not lift ritual impurities nor remove physical filth. It is 'little' water that has come in contact with filth; it also refers to a 'lot' of water mixed with filth which has changed one of the water's three characteristics. If the impure water's change disappears by itself or by adding more purifying water to it or by filtering out some whilst [ensuring] a 'lot' of it remains, then in such cases, the water will regain its purifying nature.

A 'lot' of water is what's approximately contained in two 'great jars' (*qullatān*), whereas a 'little' water is considered to be less than the aforementioned. A 'lot' of water is equivalent to five hundred Baghdad *riṭl* (pl. *arṭāl*) and eighty 2.5/7 Jerusalem *riṭl*.[4] Their volume is one and a quarter *dhirāʿ* in

4 This is roughly equivalent to one hundred and ninety-one liters. It is worth mentioning that Islamic societies of the past used varying ratios for weights and measurements at different times of their history. Hence, measures and weights were not unified across the Islamic

- وماءٌ: لا يكرَه كماءِ البحرِ، والآبارِ، والعيونِ، والأنهارِ، والحمامِ، والمسخنِ بالشمسِ، والمتغيرِ بطولِ المكثِ، أو بالريحِ من نحوِ ميتةٍ، أو بما يشقُّ صونُ الماءِ عنهُ كطحلبٍ، وورقِ شجرٍ ما لم يوضعا.

الثاني: طاهرٌ يجوزُ استعمالُه في غيرِ رفعِ الحدثِ وزوالِ الخبثِ، وهو ما تغيرَ كثيرٌ من لونِه، أو طعمِه، أو ريحِه بشيءٍ طاهرٍ، فإن زالَ تغيرُه بنفسِه عادَ إلى طهوريتِه.

ومن الطاهرِ: ما كان قليلا واستعملَ في رفعِ حدثٍ، أو انغمست فيه كلُّ يدِ المسلمِ المكلفِ، النائمِ ليلا نوما ينقضُ الوضوءَ، قبلَ غسلِها ثلاثًا بنيةٍ، وتسميةٍ، وذلك واجبٌ.

الثالثُ: نجسٌ يحرمُ استعمالُه إلا لضرورةٍ، ولا يرفعُ الحدثَ، ولا يزيلُ الخبثَ؛ وهو ما وقعتْ فيه نجاسةٌ وهو قليلٌ، أو كان كثيرا وتغيرَ بها أحدُ أوصافِه. فإن زالَ تغيرُه بنفسِه، أو بإضافَة طهورٍ إليه، أو بنزحٍ منه ويبقى بعدَه كثيرٌ طهرَ.

والكثيرُ: قلتانِ تقريباً، واليسيرُ: ما دونهُما وهُما خمسمائةِ رطلٍ بالعراقي وثمانونَ رطلاً وسبعانِ ونصفُ سبعِ بالقدسيِّ، ومساحتُهُما: ذراعٌ وربعٌ [...]

height, width, and length.[5]

If the quantity of purifying water was a 'lot' and it did not change because of filth falling in, it is considered as purifying water even if the filth remained in the water. If there is doubt regarding whether there was sufficient water for it to be a 'lot', it should be considered to be impure.

If water which is permissible to utilise for purification is indistinguishable from water which is impermissible to utilise, it is not permitted to inspect.[6] Rather, a person should perform the dry ablution without tipping the water out of the containers.

If one knows something to be impure, it becomes binding for the person to inform others who will use that thing.

---

economies. A good reference work in this field is Hinz's *Islamische Mase und Gewichte: Umgerechnet ins metrische System,* (Leiden, 1970). It has been translated into English, entitled, *Measures and Weights in the Islamic World,* (Malaysia IIUM, 2003) by M. Ismail Marcinkowski.

5 This is roughly equivalent to sixty centimetres in depth, width, and height. S'ad al-Khathlān, *Al-Salsabīl fī sharḥ al-dalīl* (Riyadh: Dār Aṭlās, 2019), vol.1 p.72

6 It not obligatory upon a person to inspect as to which one of the two can be the purifying water and thus can be used for purification. In fact it is not permissible for a person to do that in order to perform purification.

طولاً وعرضاً وعمقاً.

فإذا كان الماءُ الطهورُ كثيراً، ولم يتغيرْ بالنجاسةِ؛ فهو طهورٌ ولو مع بقائِها فيهِ، وإنْ شُكَّ في كثرتِهِ فهو: نجسٌ.

وإنْ اشتبَهَ ما تجوزُ بِهِ الطهارةُ بما لا تجوزُ؛ لمْ يتحرَّ ويتيممُ بلا إراقةٍ.

ويلزمُ مَن علمَ بنجاسةِ شيءٍ إعلامُ مَن أرادَ أنْ يستعملَهُ.

Containers and Utensils

It is permissible to acquire and utilise all kinds of pure containers, even if they happen to be very expensive, except for gold and silver. Similarly, gold and silver-plated[7] containers are not permitted to acquire nor use.

Purification performed using stolen containers and containers made from gold and silver will be deemed correct.

It is permissible to solder containers with small amounts of silver as long as the soldering was not done for decoration.

Containers, utensils, and clothes of non-Muslims are regarded to be pure.

Things are not considered to be impure as a result of being doubtful; all things are deemed to be pure as long as it's not known to be filthy.[8]

Bones, horns, claws and talons, hooves, tendons, and the hides of dead (non-slaughtered) animals are considered to be filthy. They (i.e. hides) are not purified through tanning.

Fur, wool, and feathers are regarded to be pure. That is, if the dead (non-slaughtered) animal or bird was deemed to be pure when it was alive. This also applies to animals, which are not consumed; for example cats, mice, and rats.

It is recommended (*masnūn*) to cover utensils and seal water bottles.

---

7 This refers to melting gold or silver and then the pouring it over utensils made of copper and other metals. The process helps to gain the colour of the gold and silver; and to the onlookers it seems like the utensils are made of real gold and silver.

8 This is because the default rule for things is of purity and this does cease because of doubt.

باب الآنية

يباحُ اتخاذُ كلِّ إناءٍ طاهرٍ واستعمالُهُ ولو ثمينًا إلا آنيةَ الذهبِ والفضةَ والمموهَ بهِما.

وتصحُّ الطهارةُ بهِما، وبالإناءِ المغصوبِ.

ويباحُ إناءٌ ضببَ بضبةٍ يسيرةٍ مِن الفضةِ لغيرِ زينةٍ.

وآنيةُ الكفارِ وثيابُهُم طاهرةٌ.

ولا ينجسُ شيءٌ بالشكِّ ما لم تعلمْ نجاستُهُ.

وعظمُ الميتَةِ، وقرنُها، وظفرُها، وحافرُها، وعصبُها، وجلدُها: نجسٌ، ولا يطهرُ بالدباغِ.

والشعرُ، والصوفُ، والريشُ طاهرٌ إذا كان مِن ميتةٍ طاهرةٍ في الحياةِ، ولو كانتْ غيرَ مأكولةٍ، كالهرِّ والفأرِ.

ويسنُّ تغطيةُ الآنيةِ، وإيكاءُ الأسقيةِ.

Istinjā' and Lavatory Etiquettes

Istinjā' refers to cleaning one's private parts of waste matter with purifying water; it also denotes cleaning using stones, which are pure, permissible, and have the ability to remove filth.

As for cleaning with stones and similar materials: one cleans to an extent that the remaining traces cannot be removed except with water. It is not sufficient unless a minimum of three wipes is applied. Each wipe should cover the whole area generally (i.e. the private parts). Cleaning with water entails returning the affected area to how it was (before the filth came out). If a person washed and presumed it was done thoroughly, it will suffice.

It is recommended to clean oneself with stones and then follow it with water. If it is done in the opposite order, it is considered reprehensible. It is sufficient to confine oneself to either of the two ways; however, using water to clean oneself is better.

It is reprehensible to clean the private parts while facing one's front or back towards the direction of prayer (*qibla*).

It is prohibited to clean with dung, bones, and foodstuff – even if it was for animals. If a person used the aforementioned to clean one's private parts, it will not suffice unless water was used. Similarly, if the filth moves beyond its normal area, water should be used for cleaning.[9]

It is obligatory (*wājib*) to clean the private parts for all types of substances (exiting the private parts) unless it was something pure. Likewise impure filth, which does not soil the area, is not obligatory to clean.

---

9 This includes, for example, dry pinworms. They are considered to be impure filth but since they are dry and do not spread beyond its normal place (i.e. the anus), there is no need for it to be cleaned with water or to be wiped. However, a person must perform the ablution because something has exited from his private part.

باب الاستنجاء وآداب التخلي

الاستنجاءُ هو إزالةُ ما خرج مِن السبيلَين بماءٍ طهورٍ، أو حجرٍ طاهرٍ مباحٍ منقٍ.

فالإنقاءُ بالحجرِ ونحوِهِ: أَن يبقَى أثرٌ لا يزيلُهُ إلا الماءُ، ولا يجزئُ أقلُّ مِن ثلاثِ مسحاتٍ تعمُّ كلُّ مسحةٍ المحلَّ. والإنقاءُ بالماءِ: عودُ خشونةِ المحلِّ كما كان وظَنُّهُ كافٍ.

ويسنُّ الاستنجاءُ بالحجرِ، ثم بالماءِ، فإنْ عكس كرِهَ، ويجزئُ أحدُهُما والماءُ أفضلُ.

ويكرَهُ استقبالُ القبلةِ، واستدبارُها في الاستنجاءِ.

ويحرمُ بروثٍ، وعظمٍ، وطعامٍ، ولو لبهيمةٍ، فإنْ فعل لمْ يجزِئهِ بعدَ ذلك إلا الماءُ، كما لو تعدَّى الخارجُ موضعَ العادةِ.

ويجبُ الاستنجاءُ لكلِّ خارجٍ، إلا الطاهرَ، والنجسَ الذي لم يلوثِ المحلَّ.

Subsection

When entering the lavatory, it is recommended to enter with the left foot and say: 'In the name of Allāh, I seek refuge in Allāh from male and female demons.' Upon leaving the lavatory, the person should exit using his right foot and say: 'I seek Your forgiveness. All praise belongs to Allāh, who has removed harm from me and gave me health.'

Whilst using the lavatory, it is reprehensible to face towards the sun, the moon, and the direction of the wind. It is reprehensible to speak whilst using the lavatory. Similarly, it is reprehensible to urinate into containers, holes, fires, and ashes.

It is not reprehensible to urinate standing.

It is prohibited to face one's front or back towards the direction of prayer while relieving oneself in open areas, that is, if there was no barrier between the person and the direction of prayer. It is sufficient to place a garment or some barrier between the person and the direction of the prayer.[10]

It is prohibited to urinate and defecate in: (i) Pathways which are in use, (ii) useful shaded areas, (iii) under fruit trees, (iv) and near the graves of Muslims.

It is prohibited to remain in lavatories for more than what's required.

---

10 The word *dhayl* (lit. border or lower end of something) is referring to clothing or a sort of barrier, which is placed between the person and the direction of prayer. It seems as if the Ḥanbalī scholars considered facing the direction of the prayer to be reprehensible while a person's nakedness is exposed.

فصل

يسنُّ لداخلِ الخلاءِ: تقديمُ اليسرى وقولُ: (بسمِ اللَّهِ)، (أعوذُ باللَّهِ مِن الخُبثِ والخَبائِثِ). وإذا خرج قَدَّمَ اليمنَى وقال: (غُفرانَكَ)، (الحمدُ لِلَّهِ الذي أذهَبَ عَني الأذَى وعافاني).

ويكرَهُ في حالِ التخلِّي استقبالُ الشمسِ، والقمرِ، ومهبِّ الريحِ، والكلامُ، والبولُ في إناءٍ، وشقٍّ، ونارٍ، ورمادٍ.

ولا يكرَهُ البولُ قائمًا.

ويحرمُ: استقبالُ القبلةِ واستدبارُها في الصحراءِ بلا حائلٍ. ويكفي إرخاءُ ذيلِهِ.

وأن يبولَ أو يتغوطَ: بطريقٍ مسلوكٍ وظلٍّ نافعٍ وتحت شجرةٍ عليها ثمرٌ يُقصدُ وبينَ قبورِ المسلِمينَ.

وأنْ يلبثَ فوق قدرِ حاجتِهِ.

Brushing one's Teeth

It is recommended to use a soft-moist twig, which does not break up into small fragments.

Using the tooth-stick is recommended at all times except after the sun passes the zenith for the fasting person; for whom it's reprehensible to use the tooth-stick. For the fasting person, it is recommended to use a dry tooth-stick before the sun passes the zenith; although it is permissible to use a moist tooth-stick.

Whoever used anything else besides a tooth-stick (i.e. a twig), they will not attain the Prophetic Sunna.

It is emphasised to use the tooth-stick for the following:

- Performing ablution
- Nearing the prayer
- Reciting the Qurʿān
- Waking up from sleep
- Change of the mouth's odour
- Similarly, when entering mosques and entering one's residence
- After prolonged silence
- Yellowing of teeth

There is no harm if two or more people share the same tooth-stick.

باب السواك

يسنُّ بعودٍ رطبٍ لا يتفتتُ.

وهو مسنونٌ مطلقًا، إلا بعدَ الزوالِ للصائمِ، فيكرَهُ، ويسنُّ له قبلَهُ بعودٍ يابسٍ، ويباحُ برطبٍ.

ولَم يصبِ السنةَ مَن استاكَ بغيرِ عودٍ.

ويتأكدُ عند:

- وضوءٍ
- وصلاةٍ
- وقراءةٍ
- وانتباهٍ من نومٍ
- وتغيرِ رائحةِ فمٍ
- وكذا عند دخولِ مسجدٍ ومنزلٍ
- وإطالةِ سكوتٍ
- وصفرةِ أسنانٍ

ولا بأسَ أنْ يتسوكَ بالعودِ الواحدِ اثنانِ فصاعدا.

Subsection

It is recommended to: (i) Shave pubic hairs, (ii) pluck armpit hairs, (iii) clip the nails, (iv) look in the mirror, (v) perfume oneself, (vi) apply kohl every night three times in each eye, (vii) trim the moustache and (vii) grow the beard.

It is prohibited to shave the beard; however there is no problem if a person trims what is beyond a fist's length. Circumcision is obligatory for males and females upon reaching puberty; however it is best to do it before.

فصل

يسنُّ: حلقُ العانةِ، ونتفُ الإبطِ، وتقليمُ الأظافرِ، والنظرُ في المرآةِ، والتطيبُ بالطيبِ، والاكتحالُ كلَّ ليلةٍ في كلِّ عينٍ ثلاثًا، وحفُّ الشاربِ، وإعفاءُ اللحيةِ.

وحرمَ حلقُها ولا بأسَ بأخذِ ما زادَ على القبضةِ منها. والختانُ واجبٌ على الذكرِ والأنثى عند البلوغِ، وقبلَهُ أفضلُ.

Ablution

It is obligatory to say *bismillāh* when performing *wuḍū'*; the obligation rescinds with forgetfulness. But, if a person remembered that he forgot to say it during the *wuḍū'* itself, one restarts the *wuḍū'*.

There are six compulsory acts of *wuḍū'*:

- To wash the face, which includes rinsing the mouth (*maḍmaḍa*) and snuffing water (*istinshāq*)
- To wash the arms, including the elbows
- To wipe the whole head, including the ears
- To wash the feet, including the ankles
- To wash the limbs in their sequential order
- To avoid long intervals between the acts of *wuḍū'*

There are eight pre-requisites (*shurūṭ*) of *wuḍū'*:

- To be free from things which obligate the *wuḍū'*
- Intention
- Islam
- Intellect
- Discernment
- To use purifying water that's permissible
- To remove any barrier which prevents the water from reaching the skin

باب الوضوء

تجبُ فيهِ التسميةُ، وتسقطُ سهوًا، وإن ذكرَها في أثنائِهِ ابتدأَ.

وفروضُهُ ستةٌ:

- غسلُ الوجهِ، ومنهُ المضمضةُ والاستنشاقُ
- وغسلُ اليدَينِ مع المرفقَينِ
- ومسحُ الرأسِ كلهِ، ومنهُ الأذنانِ
- وغسلُ الرجلَينِ مع الكعبَينِ
- والترتيبُ
- والموالاةُ

وشروطُهُ ثمانيةٌ:

- انقطاعُ ما يوجبُهُ
- والنيةُ
- والإسلامُ
- والعقلُ
- والتمييزُ
- والماءُ الطهورُ المباحُ
- وإزالةُ ما يمنعُ وصولَهُ

- To clean one's private parts with purifying water or stones

- والاستنجاءُ أو الاستجمارُ

Subsection

Here, the intention refers to lifting a state of ritual impurity; or when a person intends to do things which require purification, for example: Prayer, circumambulation (*ṭawāf*), touching the printed Qur'ān.

It also refers to when one intends to do things for which purification is recommended, for example: recitation, remembrance (*dhikr*), sleeping, lifting doubt regarding one's *wuḍū'*, abating anger, when falling into prohibited speech, sitting in the mosque, teaching knowledge and when eating food.

If a person intends any of the aforementioned, it will lift the person's state of ritual impurity.

There is no problem if a person's tongue slipped regarding what was intended, or if a person fell into doubt about his intention or about an obligatory element after an act of worship.[11] However, if a person doubts during the course of the worship, it must be restarted.

---

11 For instance after purification [he ignores the doubts] because the default rule has been fulfilled, namely, the person did what was legislated, accompanying the intention. Hence, the purification is not nullified owing to doubts. Likewise is the case if a person was certain about his purification but doubted the state of his ritual impurity.

فصل

فالنيةُ هنا: قصدُ رفعِ الحدثِ، أو قصدُ ما تجبُ له الطهارةُ كصلاةٍ، وطوافٍ، ومس مصحفٍ.

أو قصدُ ما تسنُّ له كقراءةٍ، وذكرٍ، ونومٍ، ورفعِ شكٍّ، وغضبٍ، وكلامٍ محرمٍ، وجلوسٍ بمسجدٍ، وتدريسِ علمٍ، وأكلٍ.

فمتى نوى شيئًا من ذلك، ارتفعَ حدثُهُ.

ولا يضرُّ سبقُ لسانِهِ بغيرِ ما نوَى، ولا شكُّهُ في النيَّةِ، أو في فرضٍ بعدَ فراغِ كلِّ عبادةٍ. وإن شكَّ فيها في الأثناءِ، استأنفَ.

Description of *Wuḍū'*

The way to perform *wuḍū'* is as follows:

The person begins by making the intention and then mentions the name of Allāh. Thereafter, the hands are washed, which is followed by rinsing the mouth and snuffing water into the nostrils. Following this, the person washes the face from where the hairline usually begins. It is insufficient to wash the outer part of the beard unless the skin beneath it cannot be seen. Thereafter, the person washes the hands up to and including the elbows – if there is a little dirt under the nails etc., it's not a problem. After this, the person wipes the top part of the whole head from the forelock to the nape – the hairless skin above the ears (i.e. between the hairline and ears) is considered to be part of the 'head' (i.e. needs to be wiped). This is followed with the wiping of the ear canals using the index fingers, and the outer part of the ears using the thumbs. Finally, the person washes the feet up to and including the anklebones; they are the two bones which bulge outwards.

فصل في صفة الوضوء

وهي:

أنْ ينويَ ثمَّ يسمي، ويغسلُ كفيهِ، ثمَّ يتمضمضُ، ويستنشقُ، ثمَّ يغسلُ وجهَهُ مِن منابتِ، شعرِ الرأسِ المعتادِ، ولا يجزِئ غسلُ ظاهرِ شعرِ اللحيةِ، إلا أن لا يصفَ البشرةَ، ثمَّ يغسلُ يدَيهِ مع مرفقيهَ، ولا يضرُّ وسخٌ يسيرٌ تحتَ ظفرِهِ ونحوِهِ، ثمَّ يمسحُ جميعَ ظاهرِ رأسِهِ مِن حدِّ الوجهِ إلى ما يسمى قفًا، والبياضُ فوق الأذنَينِ مِنهُ، ويدخِلُ سبابتَيهِ في صِماخَي أذنَيهِ، ويمسحُ بإبهامَيهِ ظاهرهُما، ثمَّ يغسلُ رجلَيهِ مع كعبَيهِ؛ وهما: العظمانِ الناتئانِ.

Subsection

There are eighteen recommended acts of *wuḍūʾ*:

- Facing the direction of prayer (*qibla*)
- Cleaning the teeth
- Washing the hands three times
- Rinsing the mouth (*maḍmaḍa*) and snuffing water (*istinshāq*) before washing the face
- Exaggerating in rinsing the mouth and snuffing water unless one is fasting
- Exaggerating in washing all the limbs unrestrictedly
- Being plentiful in the water used upon the face.
- Permeating water between the thick beard (by combing it with wet fingers)
- Saturating water between the fingers
- Wiping the ears with new water
- Precedency in washing the right before the left
- Washing the limbs beyond the places wherein it is obligatorily required
- The second and third washings of the limbs
- Intention accompanying one's washing until the end of *wuḍūʾ*
- Existing of the intention upon washing the hands
- Pronouncing the intention quietly

فصل

وسننُهُ ثمانيَّةَ عشرَ:

- استقبالُ القبلةِ
- والسواكُ
- وغسلُ الكفَّين ثلاثًا
- والبداءةُ قبلَ غسلِ الوجهِ بالمضمضةِ والاستنشاقِ
- والمبالغةُ فيهما لغيرِ الصائمِ
- والمبالغةُ في سائرِ الأعضاءِ مطلقاً
- والزيادةُ في ماءِ الوجهِ
- وتخليلُ اللحيةِ الكثيفةِ
- وتخليلُ الأصابعِ
- وأخذُ ماءٍ جديدٍ للأذنينِ
- وتقديمُ اليمنى على اليسرى
- ومجاوزةُ محلِّ الفرضِ
- والغسلةُ الثانيةُ والثالثةُ
- واستصحابُ ذكرِ النيةِ إلى آخرِ الوضوءِ
- والإتيانُ بها عند غسلِ الكفَّيْنِ
- والنطقُ بها سرًّا

- Saying: 'I bear witness that there is no god except Allāh alone, without any partners, and I bear witness that Muḥammad is His servant and messenger.' [Doing so] whilst raising one's gaze towards the sky, after completing the *wuḍū'*
- Arranging to do the *wuḍū'* by oneself, without any assistance.

- وقولُ: (أشهَدُ أن لّا إلَهَ إلّا اللّهُ وحدَهُ لا شريكَ لهُ، وأشهَدُ أنَّ محمداً عَبدُهُ ورَسُولُهُ) مع رفعِ بصرِهِ إلى السماءِ بعد فراغِهِ
- وأن يتولى وضوءَهُ بنفسِهِ من غيرِ معاونةٍ.

Wiping over Leather Socks

It is permissible to wipe over leather socks if seven pre-requisites are met:

- They are worn after complete purification using water
- It covers the obligatory areas which require washing – even if this is achieved through tying
- A person is able to walk around in them, in a manner concordant to custom
- Being robust enough for them stay on the feet by themselves
- Being permissible to use
- Being of pure material
- The footgear does not describe the skin beneath (owing to it being so thin etc.)

The residential person and the person who travelled to commit sins can wipe over their leather socks for a day and a night from the time one's *wuḍū'* breaks after wearing them. The travelling person can wipe over his leather socks for three days and three nights.

One does not wipe more than a day and a night (i.e. a residential person's concession) in the following cases: a person who wiped while travelling and then reached his residential place; a person who wiped while being a residential person and then travels; a person who is doubtful regarding when he started wiping.

It is obligatory to wipe over most of the top of the leather socks. It is not sufficient to wipe only the bottom and heel of the leather socks; it's not recommended either.

باب مسح الخفين

يجوزُ بشروطٍ سبعةٍ:

- لبسُهُما بعدَ كمالِ الطهارةِ بالماءِ
- وسترُهُما لمحلِّ الفرضِ ولو بربطِهِما
- وإمكانُ المشي بهِما عرفًا
- وثبوتُهُما بنفسِهِما
- وإباحتُهُما
- وطهارةُ عينِهِما
- وعدمُ وصفِهِما البشرَةَ.

فيمسحُ المقيمُ، والعاصي بسفرِهِ من الحدثِ بعدَ اللبسِ يومًا وليلةً، والمسافرُ ثلاثةَ أيامٍ بلياليهِنَّ.

فلو مسح في السفرِ ثمَّ أقامَ، أو في الحضرِ ثمَّ سافرَ، أو شكَّ في ابتداءِ المسحِ، لم يزد على مسحِ المقيمِ.

ويجبُ مسحُ أكثرِ أعلى الخفِّ ولا يجزئُ مسحُ أسفلِهِ وعقبِهِ، ولا يسنُّ.

The *wuḍū'* becomes nullified (*baṭal*) in the following cases: when it becomes obligatory to do a major-ritual ablution (*ghusl*); when some of the obligatory areas that require washing show; and when the wiping duration ends.

ومتى حصل ما يوجبُ الغسلَ، أو ظهر بعضُ محلِّ الفرضِ، أو انقضتِ المدةُ، بطل الوضوءُ.

Subsection

Bandages and casts: providing that it was placed after purification and the bandage applied did not go beyond the affected areas, it will be sufficient to wash the unaffected areas and wipe over the bandage with water. If this is not the case, it becomes obligatory to combine between washing and doing the dry ablution (*tayammum*).

It is impermissible for a person to wipe over a bandage which was placed prior to having purification, and which is applied beyond the wound affected areas. In such a case the person must: wash (the unaffected parts), wipe (the affected areas over the bandage), and do the dry ablution (owing to the bandage covering the extra area).[12]

---

12 In reality, bandages and casts fall into four scenarios: (i) it's placed after purification and does not exceed beyond the affected area, here the unaffected areas are washed (i.e. the limbs), the affected area is wiped over, and no dry ablution is required; (ii) it's placed after purification and exceeds beyond the affected area, here the unaffected areas are washed and dry ablution is required; (iii) it's placed without purification and does not exceed beyond the affected area; and (iv) it's placed without purification and exceeds beyond the affected area – for these two last scenarios, the unaffected areas must be washed and dry ablution is also required; but no wiping is to be done.

فصل

وصاحبُ الجبيرةِ إنْ وضعَهَا على طهارةٍ، ولم تتجاوزْ محلَّ الحاجةِ، غسل الصحيحَ ومسح عليها بالماءِ: وأجزأَ، وإلَّا: وجبَ - مع الغسلِ - أن يتيممَ لها.

ولا مسحَ ما لم توضعْ على طهارةٍ وتتجاوزِ المحلَّ: فيغسلُ، ويمسحُ، ويتيممُ.

Nullifiers of *Wuḍū'*

There are eight nullifiers of *wuḍū'*:

- Anything that exits from the front or rear private parts; whether little or large in quantity and whether it happened to be pure or filth.
- Filth that exits from other than the front or rear private parts; if it was urine or feces, the *wuḍū'* will be nullified unrestrictedly. However, if the filth was other than urine and feces, such as blood and vomit, the *wuḍū'* will be nullified if the amount was a lot – and the judgment of this returns to each person's understanding.
- Loss of intellect or loss of ability to distinguish because of unconsciousness or sleep – that is, unless it was a light sleep according to custom, while sitting or standing.
- Touching (*mass*) unsevered front private parts or the anus of a human being with one's hand, in the absence of a barrier; though 'touching' does not include contact with nails. Touching the testicles or the root segment of a severed penis[13] does not nullify the *wuḍū'*.
- Touching (*lams*) skin of the opposite gender with sexual arousal in the absence of a barrier – even if the touched skin was that of a corpse, an aged person, or one's unmarriageable kin (*maḥram*). Touching the skin of a child (of the opposite gender) under the age of seven does not nullify the *wuḍū'*. Similarly, the *wuḍū'* will not be rendered null by touching a person's teeth, nail, or hair. Contact made with them is not counted as 'touching'.

---

13 The penis consists of three main parts: the root, the body, and the glans penis. The root is attached to the abdominal and pelvic wall. If the penis was severed off totally and the person touched the remaining root segment of the penis, the *wuḍū'* will not be nullified. Even if the root segment was used to pass urine, it will not be considered as a 'penis' (*dhakar*) or a 'private part' (*farj*).

باب نواقض الوضوء

وهي ثمانيةٌ:

- أحدُها: الخارجُ من السبيلَينِ، قليلًا كان أو كثيرًا، طاهرًا أو نجسًا.
- الثاني: خروجُ النجاسةِ من بقيةِ البدنِ؛ فإن كان بولاً أو غائطًا، نقضَ مطلقًا، وإنْ كان غيرَهُما، كالدمِ والقيءِ، نقض إنْ فحشَ في نفسِ كلِّ أحدٍ بحسبِهِ.
- الثالثُ: زوالُ العقلِ، أو تغطيتُهُ بإغماءٍ أو نومٍ، ما لم يكنِ النومُ يسيرًا عرفًا من جالسٍ وقائمٍ.
- الرابعُ: مسُّهُ بيدِهِ - لا ظفرِهِ - فرجَ الآدميِّ المتصلَ بلا حائلٍ، أو حلقةَ دبرِهِ لا مسُّ الخصيتَينِ، ولا مسُّ محلِّ الفرجِ البائنِ.
- الخامسُ: لمسُ بشرةِ الذكرِ لأنثى أو الأنثى الذكرَ؛ لشهوةٍ من غيرِ حائلٍ. ولو كان الملموسُ ميتًا أو عجوزًا أو محرمًا، لا لمسُ مَن دونَ سبعٍ، ولا لمسُ سنٍّ، وظفرٍ، وشعرٍ، ولا اللمسُ بذلك.

The person's *wuḍū'* will not become nullified if his private parts are touched or if the rest of the body is touched, even if sexual arousal is experienced.

- Washing the human corpse or parts of it; the diener is a person who is responsible for moving, handling, and washing the corpse. So, the person who assists with pouring the water for cleaning is not considered as a diener.
- Consumption of camel meat, even if it was raw. Consumption of other organs and parts will not nullify the *wuḍū'*; this includes its liver, heart, spleen, stomach, fat, kidneys, head, tongue, hump, hooves, intestine, and the broth from its meat. Whomsoever made an oath not to eat camel meat will not break his oath by consuming any of the aforementioned.
- Apostasy

Everything that obligates the *ghusl* similarly obligates the *wuḍū'* except for the case of death.

ولا ينتقضُ وضوءُ الممسوسِ فرجُهُ، والملموسِ بدنُهُ، ولو وجد شهوةً.

- السادسُ: غسلُ الميتِ أو بعضِهِ؛ والغاسلُ هو: من يقلبُ الميتَ ويباشرُهُ، لا من يصبُّ الماءَ.
- السابعُ: أكلُ لحمِ الإبلِ، ولو نيئًا، فلا نقضَ ببقيةِ أجزائِها، ككبدٍ وقلبٍ، وطحالٍ، وكرشٍ، وشحمٍ، وكليةٍ، ورأسٍ، ولسانٍ، وسنامٍ، وكوارعَ، ومصرانٍ، ومرقِ لحمٍ، ولا يحنثُ بذلك مَن حلفَ لا يأكلُ لحمًا.
- الثامنُ: الردةُ.

وكلُّ ما أوجبَ الغسلَ: أوجبَ الوضوءَ، غيرَ الموتِ.

Subsection

If a person was certain about having ritual purity, but then doubted whether ritual impurity had occurred, or if a person was certain that ritual impurity had occurred, but later doubted whether purification for it was performed, the person goes by what is certain.

The following actions are prohibited for someone in a state of minor ritual impurity:

- Performing the prayer
- Circumambulating the Kaʿba
- Touching the printed Qurʾān with one's skin, without any barriers.

If *ghusl* was obligatory upon someone, these additional actions will be prohibited:

- Reading the Qurʾān
- Remaining in mosques before performing *wuḍūʾ*.

فصل

ومَن تيقنَ الطهارةَ وشكَّ في الحدثِ، أو تيقنَ الحدثَ وشكَّ في الطهارةِ، عمل بما تيقنَ.

ويحرمُ على المحدثِ:

- الصلاةُ
- والطوافُ
- ومسُّ المصحفِ ببشرتِهِ، بلا حائلٍ.

ويزيدُ مَن عليهِ غسلٌ:

- بقراءةِ القرآنِ
- واللبثِ في المسجدِ بلا وضوءٍ.

Things that obligate the major ritual ablution

Seven things obligate the major ritual ablution *(ghusl)*:

- Movement of semen (*manī*);[14] now, if a person managed to stop the semen from coming out after sensing its movement, the *ghusl* becomes obligatory regardless of an absence of emission. There is no need to repeat the *ghusl* if the semen emitted again without feeling any sexual pleasure.
- Exiting of sexual fluids from its orifice, even if it is mixed with blood. Here, sensation of sexual pleasure is a pre-requisite for the *ghusl* to be obligatory, providing the person was not asleep etc.
- When the head of the penis completely enters a vagina or to its equivalent measure without a barrier – even if the orifice was an anus of a dead being, an animal, or a bird – the ruling applies. The *ghusl* is not obligatory (if a minor had sexual intercourse) unless the boy was a ten year old and the girl was a nine year old.
- A non-Muslim accepting Islam; even if the person was an apostate
- After a woman's menstrual period
- When a woman's postnatal lochia stops
- Death; in this case, the *ghusl* is performed devotionally.

---

14 The Arabic term '*manī*' refers to the sexual fluid that exits during orgasm, referring to males and females. It will be translated as 'semen' in reference to males only, and 'sexual fluid' in reference to males and females. We ought to mention the difference between semen and sperm as often they are used interchangeably in translations. Semen is emitted from the male reproductive tract and it contains the sperm cells, which are capable of fertilising the female eggs. The sperm is the microscopic male reproductive cell while semen refers to the seminal fluid that contains the millions of sperm cells. The semen is a viscous liquid and easily visible to the naked eye, unlike the sperm cells.

باب ما يوجب الغسل

وهو سبعةٌ:

- أحدُها: انتقالُ المنيِّ؛ فلو أحسَّ بانتقالِهِ فحبسَهُ، فلم يخرجْ، وجبَ الغسلُ، فلوِ اغتسلَ لَهُ، ثمَّ خرج بلا لذةٍ، لم يعدِ الغسلَ.
- الثاني: خروجُهُ مِن مخرجِهِ ولو دمًا، ويشترطُ أَن يكونَ بلذةٍ، ما لم يكنْ نائمًا، ونحوَهُ.
- الثالثُ: تغييبُ الحشفةِ كلِّها، أو قدرِها بلا حائلٍ في فرجٍ، ولو دبرًا لميتٍ، أو بهيمةٍ، أو طيرٍ، ولكن لا يجبُ الغسلُ، إلا على ابنِ عشرٍ وبنتِ تسعٍ.
- الرابعُ: إسلامُ الكافرِ، ولو مرتدًّا.
- الخامسُ: خروجُ الحيضِ.
- السادسُ: خروجُ دمِ النفاسِ.
- السابعُ: الموتُ، تعبدًا.

Subsection

The pre-requisites of the *ghusl* are seven:

- Cessation of the things which obligate the *ghusl*
- Intention
- Islam
- Intellect
- Discernment
- Purifying water which is permissible for usage
- Removal of anything which prevents the water from reaching the body

Its mandatory act (*wājib*): mentioning the name of Allāh; it rescinds with forgetfulness.

Its obligatory act (*farḍ*): pouring water over the entire body with water reaching the mouth and nose. The water should even reach the private parts of a woman which are normally apparent when she squats to relieve herself; and similarly, the water should saturate her hair roots.

It is obligatory to unbraid the hair for bathing after menstruation and post-natal lochia, but not for bathing to lift a state of major ritual impurity (*janāba*).

If a person preponderantly thinks that the necessary steps were taken to wash properly, then it will suffice.

Its recommended acts include:

- Performing *wuḍū'* prior to the *ghusl*

فصل

وشروطُ الغسلِ سبعةٌ:

- انقطاعُ ما يوجبُهُ
- والنيةُ
- والإسلامُ
- والعقلُ
- والتمييزُ
- والماءُ الطهورُ المباحُ
- وإزالةُ ما يمنعُ وصولَهُ.

وواجبُهُ: التسميةُ، وتسقطُ سهوًا.

وفرضُهُ: أنْ يعمَّ بالماءِ جميعَ بدنِهِ، وداخلَ فمِهِ وأنفِهِ، حتى ما يظهرُ من فرجِ المرأةِ عندَ القعودِ لحاجتِها، وحتَّى باطنَ شعرِها.

ويجبُ نقضُهُ في الحيضِ والنفاسِ لا الجنابَةِ.

ويكفي الظنُّ في الإسباغِ.

وسننُهُ:

- الوضوءُ قبلَهُ

- Removing any unclean matter
- Pouring water over the head thrice and then over the rest of the body thrice
- Beginning the washes with the right side
- Avoiding long intervals (between washing parts of the body)
- Using the hands to rub water on the body
- Washing the two feet again in another place

If someone intended a recommended or an obligatory *ghusl,* one would suffice for the other. If a person intended to lift states of major and minor ritual impurity or lift ritual impurity without any specifications or wanted to do an action that's not permitted to do except with *wuḍū'* and *ghusl* (e.g. prayer), the intention will suffice to lift both states of ritual impurity (i.e. the major and minor).

It is recommended to perform *wuḍū'* with a *mudd* of water, and the *ghusl* with a *ṣā'* of water. [15]

It is reprehensible to waste water. It is not reprehensible to use less than what's been mentioned to perform one's *wuḍū'* or *ghusl* properly.

It is permissible to perform *ghusl* in mosques providing no harm is done.

It is permissible to perform *ghusl* in bathhouses (*ḥammām*) if someone felt safe from falling into prohibited matters. However, if a person feared falling into prohibited matters, it becomes reprehensible to perform *ghusl* therein. If prohibited matters were renowned therein, performing *ghusl* therein becomes prohibited.

15 The units preserved in the translation are the units that were used during the Prophet's lifetime. A *mudd* is roughly equivalent to 687 milliliters, and a *ṣā'* is roughly equivalent to 2.75 liters of water. It is worth mentioning that Islamic societies of the past used varying ratios for weights and measurements at different times of their history. A good reference work in this field is Hinz's *Islamische Mase und Gewichte: Umgerechnet ins metrische System,* (Leiden, 1970). It has been translated into English, entitled, *Measures and Weights in the Islamic World,* (Malaysia IIUM, 2003) by M. Ismail Marcinkowski.

- وإزالةُ ما لوثَهُ من أذى
- وإفراغُهُ الماءَ على رأسِهِ ثلاثًا وعلى بقيةِ جسدِهِ ثلاثًا
- والتيامنُ
- والموالاةُ وإمرارُ اليدِ على الجسدِ
- وإعادةُ غسلِ رجلَيْهِ بمكانٍ أخرَ.

ومَن نوَى غسلاً مسنوناً أو واجبًا، أجزأَ عنِ الآخرِ. وإنْ نوى رفعَ الحدثَيْنِ أو الحدثَ وأطلقَ، أو أمراً لا يباحُ، إلا بوضوءٍ وغسلٍ، أجزأ عنهُما.

ويسنُّ: الوضوءُ بمدٍّ؛ وهو: رطلٌ وثلثٌ بالعراقيِّ، وأوقيتانِ وأربعةُ أسباعٍ بالقدسيِّ، والاغتسالُ بصاعٍ؛ وهو: خمسةُ أرطالٍ وثلثٌ بالعراقيِّ، وعشرُ أواقٍ وسبعانِ بالقدسيِّ.

ويكرَهُ: الإسرافُ، لا الإسباغُ بدونِ ما ذكرَ.

ويباحُ الغسلُ في المسجدِ ما لم يؤذِ بِهِ، وفي الحمامِ إنْ أمنَ الوقوعَ في المحرمِ، فإنْ خيفَ كرهَ، وإنْ علم حرمَ.

Recommended *Ghusls*

There are sixteen recommended *ghusls*, performed for the following:

- Friday prayer (*jumu'a*); this *ghusl* is the most emphasised, namely for males attending the congregation and it's performed during the day itself
- Washing the dead; being the next most emphasised
- The festive prayer (*'īd*) is the next emphasised, and it is performed during the day
- Eclipse prayer (*kusūf*)
- Drought prayer (*istisqā'*)
- Regaining sanity
- Regaining consciousness
- Women with chronic vaginal discharge; she performs *ghusl* for each prayer
- Entering into the state of sanctification for pilgrims (*iḥrām*)
- Entering Mecca
- Entering Mecca's sanctuary
- Standing in 'Arafa
- Performing the going-forth circumambulation (*ṭawāf al-ziyāra or ṭawāf al-ifāḍa*)
- Performing the farewell circumambulation (*ṭawāf wadā'*)
- Spending the night in Muzdalifa
- Symbolic stoning of the Devil at Mina

فصل في الأغسال المستحبة

وهي ستةَ عشرَ:

- آكدُها لصلاةِ جمعةٍ في يومِها، لذكرٍ حضرَها
- ثم لغسلِ ميتٍ
- ثم لعيدٍ في يومِهِ
- ولكسوفٍ
- واستسقاءٍ
- وجنونٍ
- وإغماءٍ
- ولاستحاضةٍ لكل صلاةٍ
- ولإحرامٍ
- ولدخولِ مكةَ
- وحرمِها
- ولوقوفٍ بعرفةَ
- وطوافِ زيارةٍ
- وطوافِ وداعٍ
- ومبيتٍ بمزدلفةَ
- ورميِ جمارٍ.

For all acts wherein recommended *ghusl*s have been legislated, a person can perform the dry ablution instead, when necessary. It similarly applies to acts for which recommended *wuḍū'*s have been legislated.

ويتيممُ للكلِّ لحاجةٍ، ولما يسنُّ له الوضوءُ: إنْ تعذرَ.

Dry Ablution

The dry ablution (*tayammum*) is valid with eight pre-requisites:

- Intention
- Islam
- Intellect
- Discernment
- To clean one's private parts with water or stones
- Entry of prayer times; therefore, the dry ablution will be invalid if it was done prior to the prayer times. The dry ablution is not valid if done for voluntary prayers during the forbidden time periods.
- Inability to use water; whether it's due to a lack of water or one fears that using it will cause harm. It is obligatory to use (one's excess) water to quench the thirst of worthy humans and animals. If someone found insufficient water to perform his purification, it becomes obligatory for the person to use the water and then perform the dry ablution.

  If a travelling person located water and the prayer time was very tight or he knew that the efforts to fetch the water would result in the prayer time finishing, then in such a circumstance, the travelling person resorts to doing the dry ablution. The ruling does not apply to non-travellers, even if the prayer time ends.

  It is prohibited to pour out one's water after the prayer time has entered; similarly, passing *wuḍū'* places understanding that there will be no other *wuḍū'* places ahead. Following such circumstances, if the person resorted to the dry ablution and prayed, he will not be required to repeat the prayer (despite being sinful).

باب التيمم

ويصحُّ بشروطٍ ثمانيةٍ:

- النيةُ
- والإسلامُ
- والعقلُ
- والتمييزُ
- والاستنجاءُ أو الاستجمارُ.
- السادسُ: دخولُ وقتِ الصلاةِ؛ فلا يصحُّ التيممُ لصلاةٍ قبلَ وقتِها، ولا لنافلةٍ وقتَ نَهْيٍ.
- السابعُ: تعذرُ استعمالِ الماءِ؛ إما لعدمِهِ، أو لخوفِهِ باستعمالِهِ الضررَ. ويجبُ بذلُهُ لعطشانَ مِن آدميٍّ أو بهيمةٍ محترمَينِ. ومَن وجد ماءً لا يكفي لطهارتِهِ استعملَهُ فيما يكفي وجوبًا ثم تيممَ.

وإنْ وصل المسافرُ إلى الماءِ، وقد ضاقَ الوقتُ، أو علم أنَّ النوبةَ لا تصلُ إليهِ إلا بعد خروجِهِ: عدل إلى التيممِ، وغيرُهُ لا، ولو فاتَهُ الوقتُ.

ومَن في الوقتِ أراقَ الماءَ، أو مرَّ بِهِ وأمكنَهُ الوضوءُ، ويعلمُ أنَّهُ لا يجدُ غيرَهُ حرم، ثم إنْ تيممَ وصلى، لم يُعِدْ.

If one is in a state of ritual impurity and finds filth on his body and clothes but has insufficient water, it becomes obligatory to do the following in sequential order: (i) wash filth from clothes; (ii) if any water remains, wash filth from the body; (iii) if any water remains, perform purification with it; (iv) and if not, perform the dry ablution.

Dry ablution is valid for everything which causes a state of ritual impurity. Similarly, it's valid for all filth on the body, that is, after the filth has been lightened. If someone performed dry ablution before lightening the filth on the body, the dry ablution will be invalid.

- The dry ablution must be performed with permissible purifying earth containing dust particles that attach to the hand; scorched earth cannot be used. If such earth is unavailable, the person offers only the obligatory prayers in his given state. In performing the prayer, the person does not exceed beyond the minimal required elements of the prayer. Repetition of the prayer is not needed later.

وإنْ وجد محدثٌ ببدنِهِ وثوبِهِ نجاسةً ماءً لا يكفِي، وجب غسلُ ثوبِهِ، ثم إنْ فضل شيءٌ غسل بدنَهُ، ثم إنْ فضل شيءٌ تطهرَ به، وإلا تيممَ.

ويصحُّ التيممُ لكلِّ حدثٍ، وللنجاسةِ على البدنِ بعدَ تخفيفِها ما أمكنَ، فإن تيممَ لها قبلَ تخفيفِها لم يصحَّ.

- الثامنُ: أن يكونَ بترابٍ طهورٍ مباحٍ غيرِ محترقٍ، له غبارٌ يعلقُ باليدِ. فإن لَّم يجدْ ذلك، صلى الفرضَ فقطْ على حسبِ حالِهِ، ولا يزيدُ في صلاتِهِ على ما يجزئُ، ولا إعادةَ.

Subsection

Mentioning the name of Allāh (i.e. to say, *bismillāh*) for the dry ablution is an obligatory act but it rescinds with forgetfulness.

The dry ablution composes of five obligatory acts:

- Wiping of the face;
- Wiping of the hands up to the wrists;
- Performing the above in its sequential order when performing the dry ablution for a state of minor ritual impurity. Therefore, if some of the limbs of *wuḍū'* are wounded, one performs dry ablution for that limb or part of it at its stage of being washed if it was healthy during the *wuḍū'*.[16]
- To avoid long intervals between the wipes; every time someone renews the dry ablution, it becomes binding to rewash the unaffected limbs.
- To specify the intention for what the dry ablution is being performed – whether it was for a state of ritual impurity or filth. If someone specified for the former, it would not suffice for the latter and vice versa. However, if the intention was specified for both, it would suffice.

Five things nullify the dry ablution:

- Things which nullify the *wuḍū'*
- Obtaining water

16 For example, if an arm was wounded – the person must wash the face, then perform the dry ablution for the injured arm, and then wash the remaining uninjured limbs. In this way, the obligation of the sequence is maintained. However, Ibn Taymiyya considered preforming the dry ablution between washings as an act of innovation; he preferred the dry ablution to be done at the end of *wuḍū'* when the limbs have dried up.

فصل

واجبُ التيممِ: التسميةُ، وتسقطُ سهوًا.

وفروضُهُ خمسةٌ:

- مسحُ الوجْهِ
- ومسحُ اليدَيْنِ إلى الكوعينِ.
- الثالثُ: الترتيبُ في الطهارةِ الصغرى؛ فيلزمُ مَن جرحُهُ ببعضِ أعضاءِ وضوئِهِ إذا توضأَ، أن يتيممَ له عند غسلِهِ لو كان صحيحًا.
- الرابعُ: الموالاةُ؛ فيلزمُهُ أن يعيدَ غسلَ الصحيحِ، عند كلِّ تيممٍ.
- الخامسُ: تعيينُ النيةِ لما تيممُ له مِن حدثٍ أو نجاسةٍ؛ فلا تكفي نيةُ أحدِهِما عنِ الآخرِ، وإن نواهُما أجزأَ.

ومبطلاتُهُ خمسةٌ:

- ما أبطلَ الوضوءَ
- ووجودُ الماءِ

- When the time period ends[17]
- The permitting factor (*mubīḥ*) for the dry ablution ceases[18]
- By removing what was wiped over[19]

If someone found water while in prayer, the prayer becomes nullified. However, it is not obligatory to repeat the prayer if a person found water after performing the prayer.

Description of the dry ablution:

The person begins by making the intention and then mentions the name of Allāh. Having removed rings and similar things, the person strikes the earth once with his two hands, although two strikes is a better precautionary measure; the fingers should be spread apart. Thereafter, the person wipes the face with the fingers, and the hands with the palms.

It is recommended to delay the dry ablution to the endings of the prayers' preferred timings, that is, if someone anticipated finding water.

It is permissible for someone to perform the obligatory and the voluntary prayers with one dry ablution. However, if a person performed the dry ablution intending to pray voluntary prayers, then it will not be permissible to perform the obligatory prayer with that dry ablution.

---

17 The expiration of the time period predominantly is connected to the prayer timings. However, it can include other time frames that are not connected to the prayers. For example, if someone in a state of sexual impurity performed the dry ablution to dwell in a mosque or read some Qur'ān for a specified time, the dry ablution will be nullified when the time period finishes.

18 For example, if someone performed the dry ablution because of an illness. The 'illness' is considered as a 'permitting factor' for making it possible for the person to do the dry ablution. If the person is cured, the dry ablution becomes nullified. In other words, the 'permitting factor' for the person's dry ablution has ceased, resulting in the nullification.

19 This is a unique opinion of the Ḥanbalī school (*mufradāt*); since removing something that's wiped over nullifies the *wuḍū'*; it similarly nullifies the dry ablution.

- وخروجُ الوقتِ
- وزوالُ المبيحِ له
- وخلعُ ما مسحَ عليْهِ.

وإن وجدَ الماءَ وهو في الصلاةِ؛ بطلتْ. وإنِ انقضتْ؛ لمْ تجبِ الإعادةُ.

وصفتُهُ: أن ينويَ، ثم يسمِّي، ويضربُ الترابَ بيديْهِ، مفرجتَي الأصابعِ ضربةً واحدةً، والأحوطُ ثنتان، بعد نزعِ خاتمٍ ونحوِهِ؛ فيمسحُ وجهَهُ بباطنِ أصابعِهِ، وكفَيْهِ براحتَيْهِ.

وسنَّ لمَن يرجو وجودَ الماءِ تأخيرُ التيممِ إلى آخرِ الوقتِ المختارِ.

وله أن يصليَ بتيممٍ واحدٍ ما شاءَ مِنَ الفرضِ والنفلِ، لكنْ لو تيممَ للنفلِ لم يستبحِ الفرضَ.

Removing Filth

It is a pre-requisite for all things affected with filth to be washed seven times; one of the washes must be with pure and purifying earth or the like of soap when something becomes impure with impurities of dogs or swine.

If the taste from the filth remains (after washing), it affects the spot's purity. However, if the colour or the odour remained, or both remained owing to difficulties in removing them, then it will not affect a spot's purity.

The spot affected by the urine of a baby boy who does not consume food out of desire can be purified sufficiently by sprinkling water, and that is namely to douse the spot with water.

When rocks and boulders, watering-troughs (generally constructed of stones cemented with mud), and grounds are affected by liquid filth, even from dogs and swine – it will be sufficient to drench the place with water until the filth's colour and odour are removed.

Grounds are not purified with the effects of the sun, wind, and desiccation; nor can fire purify filth.

When wine turns into vinegar by itself in vessels, it becomes pure.

If someone was unsure about the spot affected by filth, the person washes until he becomes certain about removing the filth.

باب إزالة النجاسة

يشترطُ لكلِّ متنجسٍ سبعُ غسلاتٍ: وأن يكونَ أحدُها بترابٍ طاهرٍ طهورٍ - أو صابونٍ ونحوِهِ - في متنجسٍ بكلبٍ، أو خنزيرٍ.

ويضرُّ بقاءُ طعمِ النجاسةِ لا لونِها، أو ريحِها، أو هما عجزًا.

ويجزئُ في بولِ غلامٍ لم يأكلْ طعاماً لشهوةٍ، نضحُهُ - وهو غمرُهُ بالماءِ.

ويجزئُ في تطهيرِ صخرٍ، وأحواضٍ، وأرضٍ تنجستْ بمائعٍ - ولو مِن كلبٍ، أو خنزيرٍ -: مكاثرتُها بالماءِ، حتى يذهبَ لونُ النجاسةِ، وريحُها.

ولا تطهرُ الأرضُ بالشمسِ، والريحِ، والجفافِ، ولا النجاسةُ بالنارِ.

وتطهرُ الخمرةُ بإنائِها إنِ انقلبتْ خلاً بنفسِها.

وإذا خفيَ موضعُ النجاسةِ، غسلَ حتى يتيقنَ غسلُها.

Subsection

Liquid intoxicants, hashish,[20] birds and animals which are not eaten and are larger than the size of a cat, are considered to be filth; creatures that are smaller than the size of a cat like snakes and mice are pure; and non-liquid intoxicants are similarly considered pure.[21]

All unslaughtered dead animals are considered as filth; however, dead humans, fish, and locusts are regarded to be pure. Creatures such as scorpions, beetles, bed bugs, lice, and fleas, which do not have flowing blood, are all considered pure.

The following things are considered pure if they came from edible animals which were not nourished mainly on filth: its urine; excrement; vomit; pre-ejaculate (*madhy*); prostatic fluid (*wady*); semen (*manī*); and its milk. If the above-mentioned was from animals which are not eaten, then it's considered as filth. However, human semen and milk are deemed pure.

Pus, blood, and matter (a combination of pus and blood) are filth. If it was on someone during prayer, little amounts of it are disregarded, and they do not nullify one's ablution. That is, providing the substance was emitted from pure living beings (whether from animals or humans).[22] The same applies for little amounts from menstruation.

Little amounts of the substance in different areas of the same garment are considered as a whole (i.e. combined); but not when the substances are on different garments.[23]

20 The cannabis plant itself is considered pure. What is intended here by filth is the actual cannabis resin after it has been processed.

21 This would include intoxicating plants and herbs.

22 If the substances were from living impure animals, for example, the excrements of predatory animals, the aforementioned substances would be considered as filth, and thus the prayer will be nullified.

23 For example, if a person had a little patch of blood on his trousers and another patch on

فصل

المسكرُ المائعُ، وكذا الحشيشةُ، وما لا يؤكلُ مِنَ الطيرِ، والبهائمِ، مما فوقَ الهرِّ خلقةً، نجسٌ. وما دونَهما في الخلقةِ كالحيةِ، والفأرِ، والمسكرِ غيرِ المائعِ، فطاهرٌ.

وكلُّ ميتةٍ نجسةٌ، غيرَ ميتةِ الآدميِّ، والسمكِ، والجرادِ، وما لا نفسَ له سائلةٌ، كالعقربِ، والخنفساءِ، والبقِّ، والقملِ، والبراغيثِ.

وما أكلَ لحمُهُ، ولم يكنْ أكثرُ علفِهِ النجاسةَ: فبولُهُ، وروثُهُ، وقيئُهُ، ومذيُهُ، ووَدْيُهُ، ومَنِيُّهُ، ولبنُهُ، طاهرٌ. وما لا يؤكلُ: فنجسٌ، إلا منيَّ الآدميِّ، ولبنَهُ، فطاهرٌ.

والقيحُ والدمُ والصديدُ نجسٌ، لكن يعفَى في الصلاةِ عن يسيرٍ مِنهُ لم ينقضْ، إذا كان مِن حيوانٍ طاهرٍ في الحياةِ، ولو مِن دمِ حائضٍ.

ويضمُّ يسيرٌ متفرقٌ بثوبٍ، لا أكثرَ.

Mud on the streets is treated to be pure unless it's known to be filthy; sweat and saliva from pure beings are regarded to be pure.

If a cat or similar pure creatures such as a mongoose, mouse, hedgehog, or a child scoffed filth and then drank fluid (from containers etc.,) it will not affect the liquid's purity.

The remnants from pure animals are not reprehensible to use; remnants are the leftover of their food and drink.[24]

---

his shirt, the patches should not be considered as a whole because they are on separate garments. However, if someone had around six patches of blood just on his shirt, this should be considered together as it's on the same garment. This will consequently determine whether it can be regarded as a 'little amount' of impure substance on the body according to one's own account.

24 For example, if a camel or a sheep drank from a container, the remaining water therein is considered to be pure and it's not reprehensible to use such water.

وطينُ شارعٍ ظنتْ نجاستُهُ، وعرقٌ، وريقٌ من طاهرٍ، طاهرٌ.

ولو أكلَ هرٌّ، ونحوُه مِن الحيواناتِ الطاهراتِ كالنمسِ، والفأر، والقُنفُذِ، أو طفلٌ نجاسةً، ثم شربَ مِن مائعٍ، لم يضرَّ.

ولا يكرهُ سؤرُ حيوانٍ طاهرٍ؛ وهو: فضلةُ طعامِهِ، وشرابِهِ.

Menstruation

Menstruation (*ḥayḍ*) does not occur before the age of nine years or after the age of fifty years; similarly, when a woman becomes pregnant. The minimal menstrual period is a day and a night and the maximum menstrual period is fifteen days; but for most women it generally lasts for six or seven days. The minimal interval of purity between two menstruations is thirteen days. There is no maximum limit between two menstruations; however, the interval of purity is normally what remains of a lunar month after a menstrual period.[25]

Things that are prohibited during the menstruation include:

- Vaginal sexual intercourse
- To divorce
- Performing prayers
- Observing fasts
- Performing circumambulations
- Reading the Qur'ān
- Touching printed copies of the Qur'ān
- Remaining in mosques
- Passing through mosques when she fears polluting its vicinity

Occurrence of menstruation enacts the following:

- Obligation to perform *ghusl*

25 This is referring to when a woman has her period and the interval of purity without any complications. If a woman's menstrual period lasted seven days, the interval of purity will be for twenty-three days, the remaining days of the month.

باب الحيض

لا حيضَ قبلَ تمامِ تسعِ سنينَ، ولا بعدَ خمسينَ سنةً، ولا مع حملٍ، وأقلُّ الحيضِ: يومٌ وليلةٌ، وأكثرُهُ خمسةَ عشرَ يومًا، وغالبُهُ: ستٌّ أو سبعٌ. وأقلُّ الطهرِ بين الحيضتَينِ: ثلاثةَ عشرَ يومًا، وغالبُهُ بقيةُ الشهرِ، ولا حدَّ لأكثرِهِ.

ويحرمُ بالحيضِ أشياءُ، منها:

- الوطءُ في الفرجِ
- والطلاقُ
- والصلاةُ
- والصومُ
- والطوافُ
- وقراءةُ القرآنِ
- ومسُّ المصحفِ
- واللبثُ في المسجدِ
- وكذا المرورُ فيهِ، إنْ خافتْ تلويثَهُ.

ويوجبُ:

- الغسلَ

- Indication of reaching puberty
- Expiation (*kaffāra*) for vaginal sexual intercourse. This applies whether it occurred compellingly, absentmindedly or whilst ignorant of the period or the prohibition. Likewise, for a woman who conformed to the act.

  The expiation is to pay a whole *dīnār* or half of a *dīnār*, being a matter of choice.[26]

When a woman's bleeding ceases, the aforementioned things remain impermissible for her to do until she performs the *ghusl* or the dry ablution. However, the following are permitted prior to doing *ghusl* or dry ablution:

- To observe fast
- To be divorced
- To remain in mosques if the *wuḍū'* was performed

When a sanitary pad or ball of cotton placed in her private part does not change colour during the menstrual period (i.e. it remains white), it suggests the blood has ceased and she has entered into her interval of purity.

Women undergoing menstruation and postnatal lochia make up the missed fasts but not the missed prayers.

26 This is a unique opinion of the Ḥanbalī school. The other three Imams considered such a person to be sinful; hence, the person must repent but no further expiation is required. A full *dīnār* is roughly equivalent to the value of 4.25 grams of pure gold. Therefore, in monetary value, a *dīnār* in GBP is equivalent to £130.05, that is, with the value of gold priced at £30.60 per gram – which was the case during the time of this calculation.

- والبلوغَ
- والكفارةَ بالوطءِ فيهِ ولو مكرهًا، أو ناسيًا، أو جاهلَ الْحيضِ والتحريمِ.

  وهي: دينارٌ، أو نصفُهُ على التخييرِ، وكذا هي إنْ طاوعَتْ.

ولا يباحُ بعد انقطاعِهِ، وقبل غسلِها، أو تيممِها غيرُ:

- الصومِ
- والطلاقِ
- واللبثِ بوضوءٍ في المسجدِ.

وانقطاعُ الدمِ: بأن لا تتغيرَ قطنةٌ احتشتْ بها في زمنِ الحيضِ، طهرٌ.

وتقضي الحائضُ، والنفساءُ: الصومَ، لا الصلاةَ.

Subsection

If a woman surpasses fifteen days of bleeding per month, she has chronic vaginal discharge (*mustaḥāḍat*). For each month, she counts her menstrual period to be six or seven days when she is unable to differentiate. Thereafter, she performs the *ghusl*; she can pray and observe fast after the private area has been washed and padded using an absorbable dressing. She performs *wuḍū'* at the time of each obligatory prayer; and every time she performs *wuḍū'*, she intends permission (to perform the obligation of prayers). This type of intention applies to all who are constantly in a state of ritual impurity. It is impermissible to have sexual intercourse with her, but if one did, there will be no expiation.

Postnatal bleeding (*nifās*) has no minimum limit; it's maximum is forty days. If a woman gave birth to a foetus when the human body structures are in a recognisable form, the ruling of *nifās* applies. If there were non-bleeding intervals within the forty days, they are times of purity, but it's reprehensible to have sexual intercourse therein. If a woman gave birth to twins or more, postnatal bleeding will be counted from the first child; so, even if there is a forty-day gap between the two births, the blood for the second will not be counted. The expiation for vaginal sexual intercourse during menstruation applies to *nifās*.

It is acceptable for men to take permissible medication for preventing sexual intercourse; similarly, it is permissible for women to use medication to bring on and stop menstrual periods.

فصل

ومَن جاوزَ دمُها خمسةَ عشرَ يومًا، فهي مستحاضةٌ؛ فتجلسُ مِن كلِّ شهرٍ ستًّا، أو سبعًا، حيثُ لا تمييزَ، ثم تغتسلُ، وتصومُ، وتصلِّي بعدَ غسلِ المحلِّ وتعصيبِهِ، وتتوضأُ في وقتِ كلِّ صلاةٍ، وتنوِي بوضوئِها الاستباحةَ. وكذا يفعلُ كلُّ مَن حدثُهُ دائمٌ. ويحرمُ وطءُ المستحاضةِ، ولا كفارةَ.

والنفاسُ: لا حدَّ لأقلِّهِ، وأكثرُهُ أربعونَ يومًا، ويثبتُ حكمُهُ: بوضعِ ما يتبينُ فيهِ خلقُ إنسانٍ. فإنْ تخللَ الأربعينَ نقاءٌ، فهو طهرٌ، لكن يكرَهُ وطؤُها فيهِ. ومَن وضعتْ ولدَين فأكثرَ، فأولُ مدةِ النفاسِ مِن الأولِ؛ فلو كان بينهُما أربعونَ يومًا، فلا نفاسَ للثاني. وفي وطءِ النفساءِ، ما في وطءِ الحائضِ.

ويجوزُ للرجلِ شربُ دواءٍ مباحٍ يمنعُ الجماعَ، وللأنثَى شربُهُ لحصولِ الحيضِ ولقطعِهِ.

The call to prayer and the call for its imminent beginning

The *adhān* and *iqāmah* are communal obligations, i.e. on free men residing in permanent settlements. It is recommended to do them during travels as well as when one prays alone. They are reprehensible for women to do – even without raising the voice. The *adhān* and *iqāmah* are incorrect unless they are recited in the correct order, free from long intervals – according to custom. And one person, with intention, must complete each of them."[27]

The pre-requisites for giving the calls are that the person must be:

- Muslim
- Male
- Sane
- A person who has reached the age of discernment (*mumayyiz*)
- Able to articulate
- An upright person – even if that's the case outwardly

The *adhān* and the *iqāmah* will be considered incorrect if done before a prayer's entry time, with the exemption of the dawn prayer. The call for the dawn prayer is correct from the middle of the night onwards.

Raising one's voice for the *adhān* is an integral element unless it was being done for those present.

It is recommended for the person:

---

27 It will be incorrect for a person to complete the call of another person. So, if one person recited the first half of the call to prayer, and another person completed the second half, such calls to prayer will be considered incorrect. For the prayer call to be correct, one person, having intended to do the call, must complete the call to prayer from the beginning to the end, reciting all the phrases. The same pre-requisite applies to the call for the prayer's imminent beginning.

باب الأذان والإقامة

وهما فرضُ كفايةٍ في الحضرِ على الرجالِ الأحرارِ، ويسنانِ للمنفردِ، وفي السفرِ، ويكرهانِ للنساءِ، ولو بلا رفعِ صوتٍ. ولا يصحانِ إلا مرتبينِ متواليينِ عرفًا، وأن يكونا مِن واحدٍ بنيةٍ منه.

وشرطَ كونُهُ:

- مسلمًا
- ذكرًا
- عاقلًا
- مميزًا
- ناطقًا
- عدلًا ولو ظاهرًا

ولا يصحانِ قبلَ الوقتِ إلا أذانَ الفجرِ، فيصحُّ بعد نصفِ الليلِ.

ورفعُ الصوتِ ركنٌ، ما لم يؤذِّنْ لحاضرٍ.

وسنَّ:

- To have a strong voice
- To be trustworthy
- To be acquainted with the prayer times
- To be in a state of purification
- To be standing when doing the calls

It is not reprehensible for someone in a state of minor ritual impurity to give the *adhān*. However, it is reprehensible for them to do the *iqāmah*.

The following things are also recommended:

- To do the *adhān* at the beginning of a prayer's entry time
- To recite the *adhān* slowly
- To make it from a high place
- To raise one's face
- To put one's forefingers in the ears
- To face the direction of prayer (*qibla*)
- To turn towards the right when saying, 'Come to the prayer' (*ḥayyā 'alā al-ṣalāt*)
- To turn towards the left when saying, 'Come to success' (*ḥayyā 'alā al-falāḥ*)
- Keeping one's feet stationary – providing it was not done from a minaret
- To say, 'Prayer is better than sleep' (*al-ṣalāt khayr min al-nawm*) twice during the *adhān* of dawn prayer, after the sayings, 'Come to prayer' and 'Come to success' (*al-ḥay'alat*). This additional phrase in the dawn *adhān* is termed: *al-tathwīb*.

It is recommended for the same person to do the *adhān* and the *iqāmah* – providing it is not difficult to do so.

- كونُهُ صيتًا
- أمينًا
- عالمًا بالوقتِ
- متطهرًا
- قائمًا فيهِما

لكن لا يكرهُ أذانُ المحدثِ بل إقامتُهُ.

ويسنُّ:

- الأذانُ أولَ الوقتِ
- والترسلُ فيه
- وأن يكونَ على علوٍّ
- رافعًا وجهَهُ
- جاعلًا سبابتَيهِ في أذنيهِ
- مستقبلَ القبلةِ
- ويلتفتُ يمينًا بـ(حيَّ على الصلاةِ)
- وشمالا بـ(حيَّ على الفلاحِ)
- ولا يزيلُ قدمَيهِ ما لم يكنْ بمنارةٍ
- وأنْ يقولَ بعدَ حيعلةِ أذانِ الفجرِ: (الصلاةُ خَيرٌ مِّنَ النَومِ) مرتينِ، ويسمى التثويبَ.

ويسنُّ أَن يتولى الأذانَ والإقامةَ واحدٌ، ما لمْ يشقَّ.

When combining between prayers or making up missed prayers, the person gives the *adhān* for the first, but does the *iqāmah* for each one.

It is recommended for the person who hears the *adhān* and the *iqāmah* to repeat each phrase after the muezzin except the following:

- When the muezzin says, 'Come to prayer' and 'Come to success', one says, 'There is no power and might except in God'
- When the muezzin says, 'Prayer is better than sleep', the person should say, 'You have spoken the truth and piously'
- During the *iqāmah*: when the phrase, 'The prayer is commencing' is recited, one says, 'May Allāh establish it and make it regular'

Thereafter, the person sends salutation and blessing to the Prophet and says, 'Allāh! Lord of this perfect call and of the prayer being established – grant Muḥammad the highest status in paradise, the most honourable place, and resurrect him to the exemplary position that you have promised him.' Having sent the salutation and blessing, the person can supplicate; supplication can also be made after the *iqāmah*.

Once the *adhān* has been made, it is prohibited to leave the mosque unless someone had an excuse or had the intention of returning to the mosque.

ومن جمعَ، أو قضى فوائِتَ، أذنَ للأولى، وأقامَ للكلِّ.

وسنَّ لمَن يسمعُ المؤذنَ، أو المقيمَ أن يقولَ مثلَهُ إلا:

- في الحيعلةِ فيقولُ: (لا حَولَ ولا قُوَّةَ إلا باللَّهِ)
- وفي التثويبِ: (صَدَقتَ وَبَرِرتَ)
- وفي لفظِ الإقامةِ: (أَقَامَها اللَّهُ وأدامَها)

ثم يصلِّي على النبيِّ صلى الله عليه وسلم إذا فرغَ ويقولُ: (اللهمَّ رَبَّ هَذِهِ الدَّعوَةِ التَّامَّةِ، والصَّلاةِ القَائِمَةِ، آتِ محمدًا الوَسيلَةَ والفَضِيلَةَ، وَابْعَثهُ مَقَامًا محمودًا الَّذِي وَعَدتَّهُ). ثم يدعُو هُنا وعندَ الإقامةِ.

ويحرمُ بعدَ الأذانِ الخروجُ منَ المسجدِ بِلا عذرٍ، أو نيةِ رجوعٍ.

Pre-requisites of the Prayer

The pre-requisites of the prayer are nine in number:

- Islam
- Intellect
- Discernment
- Purification from ritual impurities, with ability
- Entry of prayer times

The noon prayer starts when the sun passes its zenith, and ends when the length of an object's shadow becomes equal to the object's height, after dismissing its length at the zenith. Thereafter follows the preferable timing of the mid-afternoon prayer. Its timing ends when the length of an object's shadow equals twice as long as the object's height – after dismissing the length at the zenith. Then the timing of necessity enters and lasts up to sunset. Thereafter follows the timing of the sunset prayer, and it ends when the red twilight in the sky disappears. Then follows the preferable timing of the nightfall prayer. Its timing lasts until the third of the night. Thereafter, the timing of necessity enters, and it lasts up to 'true dawn'. The timing of the dawn prayer then follows and lasts until sunrise.

The prayer is caught on time by stating the initial exclamation of 'Allāh is the greatest!'

It is prohibited to delay the prayer beyond its permissible timing. However, it is acceptable to delay performing the prayer within its proper timing when someone has a firm will to perform the prayer later. It is best to perform all the prayers in their earliest times; preparing and getting oneself ready at its earliest time achieves the virtues.

باب شروط الصلاة

وهي تسعةٌ:

- الإسلامُ
- والعقلُ
- والتمييزُ
- وكذا الطهارةُ مع القدرةِ
- الخامسُ: دخولُ الوقتِ.

فوقتُ الظهرِ مِنَ الزوالِ إلى أَن يصيرَ ظِلُّ كل شيءٍ مثلَهُ، سوى ظلِّ الزوالِ. ثم يليهِ الوقتُ المختارُ للعصرِ، حتى يصيرَ ظلُّ كلِّ شيءٍ مثلَيهِ، سوى ظلِّ الزوالِ. ثمَّ هو وقتُ ضرورةٍ إلى الغروبِ. ثم يليهِ وقتُ المغربِ، حتى يغيبَ الشفقُ الأحمرُ. ثم يليهِ الوقتُ المختارُ للعشاءِ إلى ثلثِ الليلِ، ثم هو وقتُ ضرورةٍ إلى طلوعِ الفجرِ ثم يليه وقتُ الفجرِ إلى شروقِ الشمسِ.

ويدركُ الوقتُ بتكبيرةِ الإحرامِ.

ويحرمُ تأخيرُ الصلاةِ عن وقتِ الجوازِ. ويجوزُ تأخيرُ فعلِها في الوقتِ مع العزمِ علَيهِ. والصلاةُ أولَ الوقتِ أفضلُ، وتحصلُ الفضيلةُ بالتأهبِ أولَ الوقتِ.

It is obligatory to make up missed prayers immediately, in order; any unrestricted recommended prayers done will be incorrect. The order rescinds with forgetfulness or when the time is very tight to catch a current prayer – even for catching it in its preferable timing.

- Clothing one's nakedness (*'awra*)

A person's nakedness must be covered when able to do so with something that renders the skin imperceptible.

The area between the navel and knees is the nakedness of a mature male over ten, a free female at the age of discernment, and a woman slave – even if she happens to be part free and part slave. The area of the private parts is the nakedness of a boy aged between seven and ten years. And the nakedness of a free mature woman, during prayers, is her entire body except for her face.[28] For the obligatory prayers, it is conditional for a mature man to cover at least one of his shoulders, using some part of his garments.

The prayer will be incorrect if someone deliberately and mindfully[29] prayed using a stolen or a silk garment. If someone only had a stolen garment, the person must perform the prayer naked,[30] whereas if a person had no clothes other than a silk garment, the prayer can be performed using that garment. For the two scenarios, the prayer does not need to be repeated. However, if a person had no clothes other than a garment soiled with filth, the prayer needs to be repeated later.

---

28 Womens' *'awra* is of two types: in prayer and out of prayer. In prayer; whether she performs an obligatory or a voluntary prayer, it is obligatory for her to cover her entire body except the face. All of the body is considered as *'awra* but the face has been exempted owing to scholarly consensus. Out of prayer; all of her body is considered as *'awra* when in front of men. As for her being in front of other women, whether they happen to be Muslims or non-Muslims, her *'awra* becomes the area between her navel and knees – being the same as men.

29 This is in reference to the materials and its legal ruling. The prayer will be correct if the person in prayer happens to be ignorant or forgot about the nature of the two materials and the prohibition of praying in them.

30 This is from the unique opinions of the Ḥanbalī school – stolen garments cannot be used in any case to perform the prayer unlike silk, it can be used out of necessity, for example when someone suffers from itching and etc.

ويجبُ قضاءُ الصلاةِ الفائتةِ مرتبةً فورًا، ولا يصحُّ النفلُ المطلقُ إذًا. ويسقُطُ الترتيبُ بالنسيانِ، وبضيقِ الوقتِ ولو للاختيارِ.

- السادسُ: سترُ العورةِ مع القدرةِ بشيءٍ لا يصفُ البشرةَ.

فعورةُ الذكرِ البالغِ عشرًا، والحرةِ المميزةِ، والأمةِ ولو مبعضةً: ما بين السرةِ والركبةِ، وعورةُ ابنِ سبعٍ إلى عشرٍ: الفرجانِ، والحرةُ البالغةُ: كلُّها عورةٌ في الصلاةِ إلا وجهَهَا. وشرطَ في فرضِ الرجلِ البالغِ: سترُ أحدِ عاتقيهِ بشيءٍ مِنَ اللباسِ.

ومَن صلى في مغصوبٍ أو حريرٍ عالمًا ذاكرًا: لم تصحَّ. ويصلي عُريانًا مع غصبٍ، وفي حريرٍ؛ لعدمٍ ولا يعيدُ، وفي نجسٍ؛ لعدمٍ ويعيدُ.

It is prohibited for males to wear clothing woven and embroidered with gold and silver; the prohibition does not extend to females. It is similarly prohibited for males to wear garments which are purely or predominantly made from silk. However, it is permissible to embroider a garment with silk thread (i.e. for patching) and use it to join other fibres. Likewise, when a fabric is mixed with silk and the silk appears to be the same in amount."[31]

- Absence of filth

The body, clothes, and the place of the prayer must be free from filth, with ability. If someone is held in an impure place but prays therein, the prayer will be considered correct. However, if the filth therein was moist and wet, the person must make gestures (of bowing and prostrating) to the furthest points as possible; he also sits on his feet for such a scenario.

The prayer will be correct in the following scenarios: firstly, if a person's garment touched another garment that was filthy; secondly, if a person's garment touched a filthy wall without the person leaning on it; thirdly, if someone prayed on a pure section of something and its sides or ends were affected with some filth; and finally, if some filth fell on him, but went away swiftly or the filth was removed straight away. The prayer is rendered invalid if someone was incapable of removing the filth straight away or remembered about the filth after forgetting.

The prayer will be incorrect in the following places: stolen lands; graveyards; abattoirs; rubbish dumps; toilet areas; camel pens; in the middle of a path; bathhouses; and on the roof of these places.

Obligatory prayers performed inside the Kaʿba will be incorrect, including within the Ḥijr area. Similarly, it will be incorrect on top of the Kaʿba, unless nothing remains behind the person.[32] A vowed prayer performed inside and on top of the Kaʿba will be correct. This is also the case with voluntary prayers, in fact, it is recommended to do voluntary prayers inside the Kaʿba.

31 Ibn ʿAqīl (d. 513/1119) mentioned that it is not reprehensible to wear silk garments that are mixed with animal fur; however, the fur content must be more than the silk. Similarly, garments with more cotton content than silk are not reprehensible for men to wear.

32 In order for the obligatory prayer to be correct on top of the Kaʿba, the person will need to stand on its edge, with the Kaʿba being in front of the person.

ويحرمُ على الذكورِ لا الإناثِ لبسُ منسوجٍ ومموهٍ بذهبٍ، أو فضةٍ، ولبسُ ما كلُّهُ أو غالبُهُ حريرٌ. ويباحُ ما سديَ بالحريرِ وألحمَ بغيرِهِ، أو كان الحريرُ وغيرُهُ في الظهورِ سيانِ.

- السابع: اجتنابُ النجاسةِ.

اجتنابُ النجاسةِ لبدنِهِ وثوبِهِ، وبقعتِهِ مع القدرةِ. فإنْ حبسَ ببقعةٍ نجسةٍ وصلى، صحتْ، لكن يومئُ بالنجاسةِ الرطبةِ غايةَ ما يمكنُهُ، ويجلسُ على قدمَيهِ.

وإنْ مسَّ ثوبُهُ ثوبًا نجسًا، أو حائطًا لم يستنِدْ إليه، أو صلى على طاهرٍ طرفُهُ متنجسٌ، أو سقطتْ علَيهِ النجاسةُ فزالتْ، أو أزالها سريعًا: صحتْ. وتبطلُ إنْ عجزَ عن إزالتِها في الحالِ، أو نسيَها، ثم علمَ.

ولا تصحُّ الصلاةُ في الأرضِ المغصوبةِ، وكذا المقبرةِ، والمجزرةِ، والمزبلةِ، والحشِّ، وأعطانِ الإبلِ، وقارعةِ الطريقِ، والحمامِ، وأسطحةُ هذِهِ مثلُها.

ولا يصحُّ الفرضُ في الكعبةِ والحجرُ منهَا ولا على ظهرِها، إلا إذا لَم يبقَ وراءَهُ شيءٌ. ويصحُّ النذرُ فيها وعليها، وكذا النفلُ، بل يسنُّ فيها.

- Facing the direction of prayer, with ability

If a person did not find an informant to provide him the direction of prayer with certainty, the person employs personal diligence and performs the prayer. And if he got the direction wrong, the prayer will not need to be repeated later.

- Intention

The intention does not rescind in any circumstance. The place for the intention is the heart; and the reality of intention is to have a firm resolution to carry something out. The intention's pre-requisites are: Islam, intellect, and discernment. It is made at the start of an act of worship or shortly before. It is best for the intention to be made simultaneously while pronouncing the initial exclamation of 'Allāh is the greatest!' in prayer.

With the intention of prayer, it is a pre-requisite that a person specifies what prayer he will be performing whether it is the noon, mid-afternoon, odd-unit, or regular voluntary prayer; otherwise the general intention of prayer will suffice (i.e. for non-specific prayers). It is not a pre-requisite to specify whether it is a current performance, a make-up prayer or obligatory.

It is a pre-requisite for the imam to intend leading the prayer, and the follower to intend following him. If the imam or the follower had an excuse which permitted them to leave the congregation prayer, then intending separation (from the congregation) will be considered correct. If the follower intends to pray alone during the standing (i.e. before the imam's al-Fātiḥa), then he must recite or complete its recitation. However, if he intended to pray alone after al-Fātiḥa, then he has a choice to go into the bowing position.

If someone intended to pray an obligatory prayer but then decided to change it to a voluntary prayer, it will be considered correct providing there was sufficient time (i.e. to pray both). Otherwise, the voluntary prayer will be incorrect and the obligatory prayer will be nullified.

- الثامنُ: استقبالُ القبلةِ مع القدرةِ.

فإن لَّم يجدْ مَن يخبرُهُ عنها بيقينٍ صلَّى بالاجتهادِ، فإنْ أخطأَ فلا إعادَةَ.

- التاسعُ: النيةُ.

ولا تسقطُ بحالٍ؛ ومحلُها: القلبُ. وحقيقتُها: العزمُ على فعلِ الشيءِ وشرطُها: الإسلامُ، والعقلُ، والتمييزُ. وزمنُها: أولَ العبادةِ، أو قبيلَها بيسيرٍ، والأفضلُ قرنُها بالتكبيرِ.

وشرطَ - مع نيةِ الصلاةِ - تعيينُ ما يصلِّيهِ من ظهرٍ، أو عصرٍ، أو وترٍ، أو راتبةٍ، وإلا أجزأتْهُ نيةُ الصلاةِ. ولا يشترطُ تعيينُ كونِ الصلاةِ حاضرةً، أو قضاءً، أو فرضًا.

وتشترطُ نيةُ الإمامةِ للإمامِ، والإئْتِمامِ للمأمومِ. وتصحُّ نيةُ المفارقةِ لكلٍّ منهما لعذرٍ يبيحُ تركَ الجماعةِ، ويقرأُ مأمومٌ فارقَ في قيامٍ أو يكملُ وبعدَ الفاتحةِ، له الركوعُ في الحالِ.

ومَن أحرمَ بفرضٍ ثم قلبَهُ نفلاً صحَّ، إن اتسعَ الوقتُ وإلا لم يصحَّ، وبطل فرضُهُ.

Ritual Prayer

The prayer is obligatory for accountable Muslims except women experiencing menstruation and postnatal lochia.

If a person of discernment offered the prayer, it will be correct and one will be rewarded - he is a minor, aged seven. The guardian orders the child to pray when seven; and when ten, the child is disciplined for neglecting the prayer.

Whoever denies the obligation of prayer and neglects it, the person becomes an unbeliever. The legal proceedings for apostasy are applied.

The prayer consists of fourteen integrals; they cannot be omitted deliberately, absent-mindedly, or out of ignorance. They are as follows:

- Standing upright in all obligatory prayers for anyone who is capable

The prayer will be incorrect if someone without any excuse stands inclining forward or bowing down to the extent that he is not considered to be 'standing'; there is no harm if a person bowed his head. It's reprehensible to stand on one foot without excuse.

- The initial exclamation of 'Allāh is the greatest!' (*takbīrat al-iḥrām*)

It's to say the phrase, *allāhu akbar* – nothing besides this phrase will suffice. It must be done standing. If someone did not stand while initiating or completing it, the prayer will be correct but as a voluntary prayer.

If one lengthened the *lām* in *allāhu*, the prayer will be considered to have begun validly. The following will not begin it validly: if one prolonged the *hamza* in *allāhu* or *akbar*, or replaced *akbar* with *akbār* or *al-akbar*. It's obligatory to utter the *takbīrat al-iḥrām* to the extent that one can hear oneself; likewise the integrals and obligatory elements.

كتاب الصلاة

تجبُ على كلِّ مسلمٍ مكلفٍ غيرَ الحائضِ، والنفساءِ.

وتصحُّ مِن المميزِ؛ وهو مَن بلغَ سبعًا، والثوابُ له. ويلزمُ وليَّهُ أمرُهُ بها لسبعٍ، وضربُهُ على تركِها لعشرٍ.

ومَن تركَها جحودًا فقدِ ارتدَّ، وجرتْ عليهِ أحكامُ المرتدينَ.

وأركانُ الصلاةِ أربعةَ عشرَ: لا تسقطُ عمداً، ولا سهوًا، ولا جهلًا.

- أحدُها: القيامُ في الفرضِ على القادرِ منتصبًا.

فإن وقفَ منحنيًا، أو مائِلًا بحيثُ لا يسمى قائمًا لغيرِ عذرٍ، لم تصحَّ، ولا يضرُّ خفضُ رأسِهِ، وكرِهَ قيامُهُ على رجلٍ واحدةٍ، لغيرِ عذرٍ.

- الثاني: تكبيرةُ الإحرامِ.

وهي: (اللَّهُ أكبَرُ) لا يجزئُهُ غيرُها، يقولُها قائمًا، فإن ابتدأَها، أو أتمَّها غيرَ قائمٍ، صحتْ نفلًا.

وتنعقدُ إنْ مدَّ اللامَ، لا إنْ مدَّ همزةَ (اللَّه)، أو همزةَ (أكبَرُ) أو قال أكبار، أو الأكبر. وجهرُهُ بها، وبكلِّ ركنٍ، وواجبٍ، بقدرِ ما يُسمعُ نفسَهُ فرضٌ.

- Recitation of al-Fātiḥa's verses in order

Al-Fātiḥa contains eleven doubled letters. If one fails to double a letter or omits a letter, the prayer will be incorrect unless it's recited again without the omissions. If someone only knew one verse, he should repeat that verse to the extent of covering the full reading of al-Fātiḥa. Whoever was prevented from reciting al-Fātiḥa standing, he must pray sitting and recite.

- Bowing

The minimum requirement is to bow so that a person can touch his knees with his hands. The optimal way is to extend one's back straight and to make one's head aligned.

- Rising from the bowing position

While rising,the rising must be for the prayer; so, if a person rose being terrified of something, then it will not suffice.

- Straightening up and being upright

If someone prolonged the standing, it will not nullify the prayer.

- Prostration

The optimal way is to firmly position one's forehead, nose, hands, knees, and the bottom of the toes of each foot upon the place of prostration. The minimum requirement is to place some parts of the aforementioned limbs. It is binding for the limbs of prostration to press against the place of prostration; therefore, if someone merely placed (i.e. touched) his forehead upon fluffy cotton without pressing firmly against it, the prayer will be incorrect. If a person prostrated upon his sleeves or upon the end parts of his clothing, such prostrations are regarded to be correct. However, it is reprehensible to do this without excuse. If someone is incapable of performing the prostration with one's forehead, then it will not be binding for him to do the prostration with the other limbs. In such a case, gestures are made as much as possible.

- الثالثُ: قراءةُ الفاتحةِ مرتبةً.

وفيها إحدى عشرةَ تشديدةً، فإن تركَ واحدةً، أو حرفًا ولم يأتِ بما تركَ لم تصحَّ، فإن لم يعرفِ إلا آيةً كررها بقدرِها. ومَنِ امتنعتْ قراءتُهُ قائمًا، صلى قاعدًا، وقرأ.

- الرابعُ: الركوعُ.

وأقلُّهُ أن ينحنيَ، بحيثُ يمكنُهُ مسُّ ركبتَيهِ بكفَّيهِ، وأكملُهُ أن يمدَّ ظهرَهُ مُستَوِيًا ويجعلَ رأسَهُ حيالَهُ.

- الخامسُ: الرفعُ منهُ.

ولا يقصدُ غيرَهُ، فلو رفعَ فزعًا مِن شيءٍ، لم يكْفِ.

- السادسُ: الاعتدالُ قائمًا.

ولا تبطلُ إن طالَ.

- السابعُ: السجودُ.

وأكملُهُ تمكينُ جبهتِهِ، وأنفِهِ، وكفيهِ، وركبتيهِ وأطرافِ أصابعِ قدمَيهِ مِن محلِّ سجودِهِ، وأقلُّهُ وضعُ جزءٍ مِن كلِّ عضوٍ، ويعتبرُ المقرُّ لأعضاءِ السجودِ، فلو وضعَ جبهتَهُ على نحوِ قطنٍ منفوشٍ، ولم ينكبِسْ لم تصحَّ، ويصحُّ سجودُهُ على كمِّهِ وذيلِهِ، ويكرَهُ بلا عذرٍ، ومَن عجزَ بالجبهةِ لم يلزمْهُ بغيرِها، ويومئُ ما يمكنُهُ.

- Rising from prostration
- Sitting between prostrations

Whatever way a person sits between prostrations, it will suffice. The recommended way for the sitting is to spread one's left foot (on its side) and sit upon it while the right foot is raised (resting on the bottom of its toes) and facing the direction of the prayer.[33]

- Reposefulness

It is namely to remain motionless – even for a short time. Reposefulness is required for all movement-based integrals.[34]

- The final Testification of Faith supplication (*al-tashahhud al-akhīr*)

That is, to say, 'O Allāh, bless Muḥammad'[35] after saying the minimal amount required from the first Testification of Faith supplication. And the minimum required amount is as follows: 'Exaltedness is for Allāh. Allāh's peace and mercy be upon you O Prophet! Peace be upon us and upon the pious servants of Allāh! I testify there is no god but Allāh and I testify Muḥammad is Allāh's messenger.' The optimal way to say the final Testification of Faith supplication is well known.

- Sitting for the final Testification of Faith supplication and the two invocations of peace

If a person said the final Testification of Faith supplication without sitting down, the prayer will be incorrect. Similarly, if someone did the first invocation of peace sitting and the second standing, the prayer will be incorrect.

- The two invocations of peace (*al-salām ʿalaykum wa raḥmatullāh*)

---

33 This sitting posture is known as the *iftirāsh* position. The left foot remains spread out under one's buttocks.

34 The movement-based integrals include: bowing; rising from bowing; prostration; rising from prostration; and sitting between prostrations.

35 The Ḥanbalī scholars have differed about whether the invocation of peace and blessing for the Prophet is a completely separate integral or a part of the final Testification of Faith supplication; the author adopted the former view.

- الثامنُ: الرفعُ مِن السجودِ.
- التاسعُ: الجلوسُ بينَ السجدتَينِ.

وكيف جلسَ كفَى، والسنةُ: أنْ يجلسَ مفترشًا على رجلِهِ اليسرى، وينصبَ اليمنَى، ويوجهَهُما إلى القبلةِ.

- العاشرُ: الطمأنينةُ.

وهي السكونُ - وإنْ قلَّ - في كلِّ ركنٍ فعليٍّ.

- الحادِي عشرَ: التشهدُ الأخيرُ

وهو: (اللَّهُمَّ صلِّ على مُحَمَّدٍ) بعدَ الإتيانِ بما يجزئُ مِن التشهدِ الأولِ، والمجزئُ مِنهُ: (التَّحِيَّاتُ للهِ، سَلَامٌ عَلَيكَ أَيُّهَا النَّبيُّ وَرَحْمَةُ اللهِ، سَلَامٌ عَلَيْنَا وعَلَى عِبَادِ اللَّهِ الصَّالِحِينَ أَشْهَدُ أَنْ لَّا إِلَهَ إِلَّا اللَّهُ وَأَنَّ مُحَمَّدًا رَّسُولُ اللَّهِ) والكاملُ مشهورٌ.

- الثانِي عشرَ: الجلوسُ له وللتسليمتَينِ.

فلو تشهدَ غيرَ جالسٍ، أو سلمَ الأولى جالسًا، والثانيةَ غيرَ جالسٍ: لم تصحَّ.

- الثالثَ عشرَ: التسليمتانِ.

It is to say, 'Peace and mercy of Allāh be upon you' twice. It is better not to add the phrase, 'and his blessings' to the aforementioned. For voluntary and funeral prayers, it is sufficient to say, 'Peace and mercy of Allāh be upon you', once.

- Doing the aforementioned integral components in their systematic order

So for instance, if someone prostrated before bowing and it was done intentionally, the prayer will be nullified. But if it occurred absent-mindedly, it will be obligatory for the person to get up to do the bowing and then prostrate afterwards.

وهو أنْ يقولَ مرتَينِ: (السَّلَامُ عَلَيكُم وَرَحمَةُ اللَّهِ) والأولى أنْ لا يزِيدَ: (وَبَرَكَاتُهُ). ويكفي في النفلِ تسليمةٌ واحدةٌ، وكذا في الجنازةِ.

- الرابعَ عشرَ: ترتيبُ الأركانِ كما ذكرنَا.

فلو سجدَ - مثلًا - قبلَ ركوعِهِ عمدًا، بطلتْ، وسهوًا، لزمَهُ الرجوعُ، ليركعَ ثُمَّ يسجدُ.

Obligatory elements in the Prayer

There are eight obligatory elements; the prayer becomes nullified if they are omitted intentionally, and rescind if left out absent-mindedly or ignorantly:

- Exclamations of 'Allāh is the greatest' except the initial one. The latecomer's one after the initial is recommended.[36]
- To say, 'Allāh hears whoever praises Him' for the imam and one praying alone; but not for a follower of a group prayer.
- To say, 'Our Lord, all praise belongs for you' for everyone.
- To say, 'Exalted be Allāh, the Great' once in the bowing position.
- To say, 'Exalted be Allāh, the High' once in prostration.
- To say, 'My Lord, forgive me' once sitting between prostrations.
- The first Testification of Faith supplication; if the imam omits it forgetfully, the obligation rescinds for the imam's followers.
- To sit for the first Testification of Faith supplication.

36 This is when a latecomer to a group prayer attempts to catch the prayer while the imam is in the bowing position. Once the initial exclamation of 'Allāh is the greatest!' has been done, another is made to catch the imam in the bowing position (*takbīrat al-masbūq*). The former is an integral component, whereas the latter is a recommended act.

فصل

وواجباتُها ثمانيةٌ: تبطلُ الصلاةُ بتركِها عمدًا، وتسقطُ سهوًا وجهلًا:

- التكبيرُ لغيرِ الإحرامِ، لكن تكبيرةُ المسبوقِ التِي بعدَ تكبيرةِ الإحرامِ سنةٌ
- وقولُ (سَمِعَ اللَّهُ لِمَنْ حَمِدَهُ) للإمامِ والمنفردِ لا للمأمومِ
- وقولُ (رَبَّنَا وَلَكَ الْحَمْدُ) للكلِّ
- وقولُ: (سُبْحَانَ رَبِّيَ العَظِيمِ) مرةً في الركوعِ
- و(سُبْحَانَ رَبِّيَ الأَعْلَى) مرةً في السجودِ
- و(ربِّ اغْفِر لي) بين السجدتينِ
- والتشهدُ الأولُ على غيرِ مَن قامَ إمامُهُ سهوًا
- والجلوسُ لهُ.

Recommended actions in the Prayer

The recommended elements include statements and actions. Prayer is not nullified by omitting them - even on purpose. If they were left out forgetfully, one can do the forgetfulness prostrations.

There are eleven recommended statements:

- The saying after *takbirat al-iḥrām*, 'Glorification and laudation belongs to you O Allāh, blessed be your name and your greatness exalted, there is no god but Allāh.'
- To say, 'I seek refuge in Allāh from the accursed Satan'
- To say, 'In the name of Allāh, the merciful, the compassionate'
- To say, *'āmīn'* (O Allāh, accept our prayers)
- To recite a chapter of the Qur'ān (*sūrat*) after reciting al-Fātiḥa
- For the imam to recite the Qur'ān audibly (for those prayers recited aloud), but it's reprehensible for the followers. The person praying alone can choose between reciting audibly or quietly.
- It is recommended for the imam and the person praying alone to say the subsequent statement after the saying, 'Our Lord, all praise belongs for you': 'The heavens, the earth, and whatever else you will abounds with your praise and laudation.'
- To say, 'Exalted be Allāh, the Great' more than once in the bowing
- To say, 'Exalted be Allāh, the High' more than once in the prostrations
- To say, 'My Lord, forgive me' more than once (between prostrations)
- To supplicate for the Prophet and his family to be blessed (*ṣalāt*) and to be shown grace (*barakat*) during the final Testification of Faith

سنن الصلاة

وسُنَنُها: أقوالٌ وأفعالٌ، ولا تبطلُ بتركِ شيءٍ منها ولو عمدًا، ويباحُ السجودُ لسهوِهِ.

فسننُ الأقوالِ أحدَ عشرَ:

- قولُهُ - بعدَ تكبيرةِ الإحرامِ - (سُبْحانَكَ اللَّهُمَّ وَبِحَمْدِكَ، وَتَبَارَكَ اسْمُكَ، وَتَعَالَى جَدُّكَ، وَلَا إِلَهَ غَيْرُكَ)
- والتعوذُ
- والبسملةُ
- وقولُ (آمِين)
- وقراءةُ السورةِ بعدَ الفاتحةِ
- والجهرُ بالقراءةِ للإمامِ، ويكرهُ للمأمومِ، ويخيرُ المنفردُ
- وقولُ غيرِ المأمومِ - بعدَ التحميدِ - (مِلْءَ السَّمَاءِ وَمِلْءَ الْأَرْضِ ومِلءَ ما شِئْتَ مِنْ شَيْءٍ بَعْدُ)
- وما زادَ على المرةِ في تسبيحِ الركوعِ والسجودِ
- و(رَبِّ اغْفِر لِي)
- والصلاةُ - في التشهدِ الأخيرِ - على آلِهِ عليهِ السلامُ [...]

supplication. Once a person completes the final Testification of Faith supplication, it is recommended to do additional supplications

The recommended actions are namely the 'external features' of the prayer.

[In relation to the hands,] it includes: raising the hands during the initial exclamation; when going into the bowing position; when straightening up from it; and putting them down once finished doing these elements. Also, it is recommended to put the right hand over the left and position them under one's navel.

It is recommended to keep one's gaze at the place of prostration; and while standing erect, it's recommended to have a gap between the two feet.

[For bowing and prostration, the recommended acts include:] to grab hold of the knees with one's hands with the fingers being apart; to extend one's back straight and to make one's head aligned; while prostrating, to put down the knees first and then followed by the hands, forehead, and finally the nose (i.e. the limbs of prostration); to firmly position the limbs on the place of prostration; for the limbs to make direct contact with the place of prostration except the knees – for which, it is reprehensible. It is recommended to spread the forearms out from one's sides; keep one's stomach apart from one's thighs; and one's thighs apart from one's calves; to keep a gap between the knees; to erect one's feet; to place the bottom of the toes of each foot spread out on the ground; to prostrate with the hands being spread out directly under one's shoulders; and for the fingers to be together.

[For standing up,] it includes: to bring up one's hands first when moving to the next unit; to stand up using the soles of the feet; and by depending on one's knees with the support of one's hands.

[For sitting down, the recommended acts include:] to sit in the *iftirāsh* position between prostrations and during the first Testification of Faith supplication; and to sit in the *tawarruk* position[37] during the final Testification of Faith supplication. It is recommended to put the hands on the thighs, with

37 It is to spread one's left foot on its side and then bring it towards the right and placed under the right shin. The buttocks are on the ground. The right foot is raised, resting on the bottom of its toes, and facing the direction of the prayer.

والبركةُ عليهِ وعليهِم والدعاءُ بعدَهُ.

وسننُ الأفعالِ - وتسمى الهيئاتِ:

رفعُ اليدينِ مع تكبيرةِ الإحرامِ، وعند الركوعِ، وعندَ الرفعِ مِنهُ. وحطُّهُما عقبَ ذلك. ووضعُ اليمينِ على الشمالِ، وجعلُهُما تحتَ سرتِهِ.

ونظرُهُ إلى موضعِ سجودِهِ. وتفرقتُهُ بين قدمَيهِ قائمًا.

وقبضُ ركبتيهِ بيدَيْهِ مفرجتَي الأصابعِ في ركوعِهِ، ومدُّ ظهرِهِ فيهِ، وجعلُهُ رأسَهُ حيالَهُ. والبداءةُ في سجودِهِ بوضعِ ركبتَيهِ، ثم يديْهِ، ثم جبهتِهِ وأنفِهِ، وتمكينُ أعضاءِ السجودِ مِنَ الأرضِ، ومباشرتُها لمحلِّ السجودِ سوى الركبتَينِ، فيكرَهُ، ومجافاةُ عضدَيْهِ عن جنبَيْهِ، وبطنِهِ عَنْ فخذَيْهِ وفخذَيْهِ عن ساقَيْهِ، وتفريقُهُ بين ركبتَيهِ، وإقامةُ قدميْهِ، وجعلُ بطونِ أصابعِهُما على الأرضِ مفرقةً، ووضعُ يدَيْهِ حذوَ منكبَيْهِ مبسوطةً مضمومةَ الأصابعِ.

ورفعُ يديهِ أولًا في قيامِهِ إلى الركعةِ، وقيامُهُ على صدورِ قدمَيْهِ، واعتمادُهُ على ركبتَيْهِ بيدَيْهِ.

والافتراشُ في الجلوسِ بين السجدتَينِ، وفي التشهدِ الأولِ، والتوركُ في الثاني، ووضعُ اليدينِ على الفخذَينِ [...]

the palms spread out, and the fingers together when sitting between prostrations and when sitting for the Testification of Faith supplications. However, during the latter, the person closes the two right small fingers, forms a circle with one's thumb and middle finger, and points with the index finger when one mentions the word, 'Allāh' in the supplication.

[For the invocations of peace, the recommendations include:] to turn to the right and left when saying the invocations of peace; to have the intention of ending one's prayer when doing the invocations of peace; and when turning, to give more preference (i.e. to turn more) towards the left side over the right side.

مبسوطتَينِ مضمومتَيِ الأصابعِ بين السجدتَينِ وكذا في التشهدِ، إلا أنَّهُ يقبضُ مِن اليمنى الخنصرَ والبنصرَ، ويلحقُ إبهامَها مع الوسطَى، ويشيرُ بسبابتِها عند ذكرِ اللهِ.

والتفاتُهُ يمينًا وشمالاً في تسليمِهِ، ونيتُهُ بِهِ الخروجَ مِن الصلاةِ، وتفضيلُ الشمالِ على اليمينِ في الالتفاتِ.

Reprehensible actions in the Prayer

The following things are reprehensible (*makrūh*) for a person to do during the ritual prayer: to offer the prayer by reciting al-Fātiḥa only; to repeat it (in the same unit); to turn without a pressing need; to shut one's eyes; to bear something which will preoccupy the person; to spread one's forearms on the floor while prostrating; to fiddle; to put one's hands on the hips; to stretch; to open one's mouth; and to place something in one's mouth.

It is reprehensible to pray in the direction of pictures, a person's face, someone speaking, someone sleeping, fires, or something distracting.

Touching and moving little stones and levelling the ground's earth (in the place of prayer) without an excuse are reprehensible actions. Other reprehensible actions include: fanning oneself with a fan; popping knuckles; interlacing fingers; touching one's beard; and gathering one's clothes.

If the above are done a lot according to custom, the prayer will be nullified.

It is reprehensible to single out the forehead for it to prostrate on a specific place[38] and to wipe the dust from one's forehead after prostrating. Similarly, supporting oneself on something (such as a stick while standing) without a need; however, if the person depended on the item to the extent that if it ceased, the person would fall down – the prayer will be nullified.

It's reprehensible to say, 'All praise belongs to Allāh' after sneezing or upon receiving some good news. Likewise, to say, 'To Allāh we belong, and to him is our return' if something filled one with sadness and pain.

---

38 The Ḥanbalī scholars listed it as a reprehensible action as it is a practice of the Rafidites (*al-Rawāfiḍ*), a Shiitic sect.

فصل فيما يكره في الصلاة

يكرهُ للمصلِّي اقتصارُهُ على الفاتحةِ، وتكرارُها، والتفاتُهُ بلا حاجةٍ، وتغميضُ عينيهِ، وحملُ مشغلٍ له، وافتراشُ ذراعَيْهِ ساجدًا، والعبثُ، والتخصرُ، والتمطِّي، وفتحُ فمِهِ، ووضعُهُ فِيهِ شيئًا.

واستقبالُ صورةٍ، ووجهِ آدميٍّ، ومتحدثٍ، ونائمٍ، ونارٍ، وما يلهِيهِ.

ومسُّ الحصَى، وتسويَةُ الترابِ بلا عذرٍ، وتروحٌ بمروحةٍ، وفرقعةُ أصابعِهِ وتشبيكُهُا، ومسُّ لحيتِهِ، وكفُّ ثوبِهِ.

ومتى كثرَ ذلك عرفًا بطلتْ.

وأنْ يخصَّ جبهتَهُ بما يسجدُ علَيْهِ، وأنْ يمسحَ فيها أثرَ سجودِهِ، وأنْ يستندَ بلا حاجةٍ، فإنْ استندَ بحيثُ يقعُ لو أزيلَ ما استندَ إلَيْهِ بطلتْ.

وحمدُهُ إذا عطسَ، أو وجدَ ما يسرُّهُ واسترجاعُهُ إذا وجدَ ما يغمُّهُ.

Things that invalidate the Prayer

The following invalidates the prayer:

- Anything that invalidates the ritual purification, invalidates the prayer
- Uncovering of one's nakedness (*'awra*) on purpose during the prayer

But not if it was uncovered, for example, owing to a gust of wind and one concealed it straight away, or if one did not [conceal it straight away] but the uncovering was not considered obscene in sight.[39]

- Turning away from the direction of prayer; since it is a pre-requisite to face the direction of prayer
- Filth being attached to the performer of prayer; unless it was removed straight away
- Doing a lot of actions according to custom; that is, actions which neither are from the actions of the prayer (*jins*) or done out of necessity
- Depending and supporting oneself heavily on something (while standing) without an excuse
- Returning to sit for the Testification of Faith supplication after beginning to recite (i.e. al-Fātiḥa while standing); that is, if it was done deliberately and while remembering
- To add a movement-based integral to the prayer deliberately
- To put forth some of the integrals of prayer before others on purpose
- To say the invocations of peace on purpose before the prayer is com-

39 It is understood from the statement that if a large area of a person's nakedness was exposed and this lasted for a 'long' period, it will invalidate the prayer. But, if the exposure was for a 'short' period, it will not – that is, if any of the two cases occurred unintentionally. Determining the length of time is in accordance to custom since no specific time for it has been specified.

فصل فيما يبطل الصلاة

يبطلُها:

- ما أبطلَ الطهارةَ
- وكشفُ العورةِ عمدًا

لا إنْ كشفَها نحوُ ريحٍ فسترَها في الحالِ، أو لَا، وكانَ المكشوفُ لا يفحشُ في النظرِ

- واستدبارُ القبلةِ حيثُ شرطَ استقبالُها
- واتصالُ النجاسةِ بِهِ إنْ لم يزلها في الحالِ
- والعملُ الكثيرُ عادةً مِنْ غيرِ جنسِها لغيرِ ضرورةٍ
- والاستنادُ قويًّا لغيرِ عذرٍ
- ورجوعُهُ عالمًا ذاكرًا للتشهدِ بعدَ الشروعِ في القراءةِ،
- وتعمدُ زيادةِ ركنٍ فعليٍّ
- وتعمدُ تقديمِ بعضِ الأركانِ على بعضٍ
- وتعمدُ السلامِ قبلَ إتمامِها

plete

- To deliberately change the meanings of the Qur'ān when reciting
- A naked person (in prayer) finding something to cover himself but the item is far from him[40]
- Nullifying the intention; to hesitate in nullifying it or not; to resolve to nullify the intention; or to be in doubt as to whether or not the intention was made in the first place, but regardless of the doubt, the person continued – all the aforementioned cases invalidate the prayer
- By supplicating for worldly pleasures and delights (in the prayer)
- Directly addressing someone (in prayer) other than Allāh and his messenger, Aḥmad[41]
- Laughing aloud
- Speaking; even if it was done absent-mindedly
- Followers preceding the imam's actions (in a group prayer)
- Nullification of the imam's prayer (invalidates the followers' prayer)
- To say the invocations of peace purposely before the imam's invocations of peace or when it was said absent-mindedly, but the follower did not repeat the invocations of peace after the imam's one
- Eating and drinking; unless it was a little according to custom and was consumed by an absent-minded or uninformed person

40 This is because the performer of the prayer in such a scenario will not be able to cover his body with the item at a distance unless he does numerous actions in his prayer or puts some time into attaining the item to cover the body. In such a scenario, the person conceals his body with the item and does the prayer again. If the item happens to be near according to custom, he covers the mandatory parts, and continues his prayer.

41 This is when the performer of the prayer addresses someone in his supplication or etc., using the second person pronouns such as 'you'. In a Prophetic report, it is said that when the Satan came to the Prophet and attempted to disturb him in his prayer, the Prophet cursed the Satan and said: 'I seek refuge in Allāh from *you* and I curse *you* with the curse of Allāh.' This is an example of a direct address. The scholars mentioned that it was an action specific to the Prophet only; therefore, it is prohibited for others to do so unless it was a direct address towards Allāh and his messenger, Muḥammad.

- وتعمدُ إحالةِ المعنَى في القراءةِ
- وبوجودِ سترةٍ بعيدةٍ وهو عريانُ
- وبفسخِ النيةِ وبالترددِ في الفسخِ، وبالعزمِ علَيْهِ، وبشكِّهِ هل نوَى فعملَ مع الشكِّ عملًا
- وبالدعاءِ بملاذِّ الدنيا
- وبالإتيانِ بكافِ الخطابِ لغيرِ اللَّهِ ورسولِهِ أحمدَ
- وبالقهقهةِ
- وبالكلامِ ولو سهوًا
- وبتقدمِ المأمومِ على إمامِهِ
- وببطلانِ صلاةِ إمامِهِ
- وبسلامِهِ عمدًا قبلَ إمامِهِ، أو سهوًا، ولم يعدْهُ بعدَهُ
- وبالأكلِ، وبالشربِ سوى اليسيرِ عرفًا لناسٍ وجاهلٍ

The prayer is not nullified if someone swallowed foodstuff stuck between one's teeth without chewing on it.

- The following things are like speaking (i.e. in its legal ruling): clearing one's throat unnecessarily; crying (with noise) resulting from other than the fear of God; and whistling – if the aforementioned produced two phonemes, the prayer will be invalidated.

The following cases do not invalidate the prayer (even if two or more sounds were produced): speaking during sleep; accidentally saying something during one's recitation; or when coughing, sneezing, yawning, and crying overwhelms an individual.

ولا تبطلُ إنْ بلعَ ما بينَ أسنانِهِ بلا مضغٍ.

- وكالكلامِ إن تنحنحَ بلا حاجةٍ، أو انتحبَ لا خشيةً، أو نفخَ فبانَ حرفانِ.

لا إنْ نامَ فتكلمَ، أو سبقَ على لسانِهِ حالَ قراءتِهِ، أو غلبَهُ سعالٌ، أو عطاسٌ، أو تثاؤبٌ أو بكاءٌ.

Prostrations of Forgetfulness

It's recommended to do the prostrations of forgetfulness if one forgetfully says a prescribed dictum in the wrong place. If one omitted a recommended act, it's permissible to do the prostrations of forgetfulness.

It's obligatory to do the prostrations of forgetfulness for the following: if one forgetfully added an action of bowing; prostrating; standing; or sitting – even if it's the length of the brief sitting. Similarly, if one said the invocations of peace before the prayer's completion; made errors in reciting the Qur'ān which distorted its meaning; omitted an obligatory element; or when one is uncertain whether a surplus action has been added at the time of doing that particular action.[42]

The prayer is nullified if the obligatory prostrations of forgetfulness are left out on purpose. However, if someone left them out (on purpose) because of stating the invocations of peace early and before the prayer's completion, it will not nullify the prayer.[43]

A person can choose to do the prostrations of forgetfulness before or after the invocations of peace. Nevertheless, if the prostrations of forgetfulness are done after the invocations of peace, the person must do the final Testification of Faith supplication and utter the invocations of peace (again).

---

42 This would include, for instance, if someone was in the prostration position and felt uncertain whether the prostration is a surplus action or not – in such a case, the prostrations of forgetfulness become obligatory to do at the end.

43 If someone uttered the invocations of peace early in a prayer, for example, after two units when praying a four unit prayer – in such a case, it's recommended to do the prostrations of forgetfulness for the mistake after the final invocations of peace (once the prayer has been made-up and corrected). Therefore, if a person leaves out the prostrations of forgetfulness, on purpose, to do it after the final invocations of peace, it will not nullify the prayer.

باب سجود السهو

يسنُّ: إذا أتى بقولٍ مشروعٍ في غيرِ محلِّهِ سهوًا، ويباحُ: إذا تركَ مسنونًا.

ويجبُ: إذا زادَ ركوعًا، أو سجودًا، أو قيامًا، أو قعودًا، ولو قدرَ جلسةِ الاستراحةِ، أو سلمَ قبلَ إتمامِها، أو لحنَ لحنًا يحيلُ المعنَى، أو تركَ واجبًا، أو شكَّ في زيادةٍ وقت فعلِها.

وتبطلُ الصلاةُ: بتعمدِ تركِ سجودِ السهوِ الواجبِ، لا إنْ تركَ ما وجبَ بسلامِهِ قبلَ إتمامِها.

وإنْ شاءَ سجدَ سجدتَي السهوِ قبلَ السلامِ، أو بعدَهُ، لكنْ إنْ سجدَهُما بعدَهُ، تشهدَ وجوبًا وسلمَ.

The prostrations of forgetfulness rescind because of the following things: when someone forgot to do them but remembered to do so after a long interval according to custom; after becoming ritually impure (i.e. losing one's *wuḍū'*); or when one has left the mosque.

A follower who joins a group prayer at its start does not need to prostrate for forgetfulness for any personal errors he commits. If the imam errs out of forgetfulness, the followers must adhere to the imam's leadership and prostrate with him. And if the imam does not prostrate (after erring), it becomes obligatory for the followers to prostrate.

If someone stood up for a unit of prayer, but then remembers that it is a surplus unit, one must sit down.

If one begins to rise (for the third unit) after forgetting to do the first Testification of Faith supplication, it becomes binding for the person to return for the first Testification of Faith supplication. However, it is reprehensible to return to it if the person was already fully standing; in this regard, the followers must adhere to the imam's leadership. If someone begins to recite the Qur'ān (in the third unit), it becomes prohibited for the person to return to do the first Testification of Faith supplication.

In prayer, if someone was uncertain whether an integral component was missed or uncertain about the number of units prayed, one proceeds on the assumption of certainty; namely, to proceed by the smaller number; thereafter, the person prostrates for forgetfulness. Once the prayer has been completed, uncertainties about the prayer are ineffective.

وإنْ نسيَ السجودَ حتى طالَ الفصلُ عرفًا، أو أحدثَ، أو خرجَ مِن المسجدِ سقطَ.

ولا سجودَ على مأمومٍ دخلَ أولَ الصلاةِ، إذا سها في صلاتِهِ. وإنْ سها إمامُهُ: لزمَهُ متابعتُهُ في سجودِ السهوِ، فإنْ لم يسجدْ إمامُهُ: وجبَ عليهِ هو.

ومَن قامَ لركعةٍ زائدةٍ: جلسَ متَى ذكرَ.

وإنْ نهضَ عن تركِ التشهدِ الأولِ ناسيًا: لزمَهُ الرجوعُ ليتشهدَ، وكرِهَ: إن استتمَّ قائمًا، وتلزمُ: المأمومَ متابعتُهُ، ولا يرجعُ إنْ شرعَ في القراءةِ.

ومَن شكَّ في ركنٍ أو عددِ ركعاتٍ وهو في الصلاةِ، بنى على اليقينِ؛ وهو الأقلُّ، ويسجدُ للسهوِ، وبعدَ فراغِها لا أثرَ للشكِّ.

Voluntary Prayers

Voluntary prayer is the best form of voluntary devotion pertaining to the body after warfare and sacred knowledge; and the best of voluntary prayers are those recommended to be performed in groups. The most emphasised prayers (in groups) are the eclipse prayer, the rain prayer, the night prayer in Ramadan, and then the odd-unit night prayer.

Odd-unit night prayer (*witr*)

One unit (*rakʿa*) is its minimum, and the maximum is eleven units. The lowest optimal form is to perform three units with two invocations of peace. It is permissible to perform them by serially joining the units and then stating the invocations of peace once in the last unit. The time period for *witr* is between the nightfall prayer and the appearance of dawn.

It's recommended to supplicate after the bowing.[44] If one did the *takbīr* and then raised his hands to supplicate before the bowing, it will be permissible. One can use any supplications he wishes; one can similarly use the following reported petition:

> Allāh! Guide us among those you have guided; grant us safety among those who you have granted safety; take care of us among those who you have taken care of; and bless us among those you have bestowed. Allāh! Protect us from the bad you have ordained – you certainly decree things and none decrees for you! None can be humiliated whom you have supported and none can be dignified whom you have showed hostility towards. Our Lord! Blessed and exalted be you. Allāh! We seek refuge in your pleasure from your anger; in your forgiveness from your punishment; and we seek safety in you from you. We are incapable of enumerating your praise; you are as you have praised yourself.

44 This is in reference to the *qunūt*-supplication; it is offered in prayer while standing. It is recommended to utter the supplications audibly if the person is praying alone or if he is the imam of a group prayer.

باب صلاة التطوع

وهي: أفضلُ تطوعِ البدنِ، بعد الجهادِ، والعلمِ. وأفضلُها: ما سنَّ جماعةً. وآكدُها: الكسوفُ، فالاستسقاءُ، فالتراويحُ، فالوترُ.

[الوتر]

وأقلُه ركعةٌ، وأكثرُهُ إحدى عشرةَ، وأدنى الكمالِ ثلاثٌ بسلامينِ، ويجوزُ بواحدٍ سردًا ووقتُهُ ما بينِ صلاةِ العشاءِ وطلوعِ الفجرِ.

ويقنتُ فيهِ بعدَ الركوعِ ندبًا، فلو كبرَ ورفعَ يديهِ، ثمَّ قنتَ قبلَ الركوعِ جازَ. ولا بأسَ أنْ يدعوَ في قنوتِهِ بما شاءَ، وممَّا وردَ:

(اللَّهُمَّ اهدِنا فِيمَنْ هَدَيْتَ، وَعَافِنَا فِيمَنْ عَافَيْتَ، وَتَوَلَّنَا فِيمَنْ تَوَلَّيْتَ، وَبَارِكْ لَنَا فِيمَا أَعْطَيْتَ، وَقِنَا شَرَّ ما قَضَيْتَ، إنَّكَ تَقْضِي وَلَا يُقْضَى عَلَيْكَ، إنَّهُ لَا يَذِلُّ مَنْ وَالَيْتَ، وَلَا يَعِزُّ مَنْ عَادَيْتَ، تَبَارَكْتَ رَبَّنا وَتَعَالَيْتَ)، (اللَّهُمَّ إنَّا نَعُوذُ بِرِضَاكَ مِنْ سَخَطِكَ، وَبِعَفْوِكَ مِنْ عُقُوبَتِكَ، وَبِكَ مِنكَ، لا نُحْصِي ثَنَاءً عَلَيْكَ، أَنْتَ كَمَا أَثْنَيْتَ عَلَى نَفْسِكَ).

Thereafter, the person invokes salutations for the Prophet and ends by wiping the face with his hands; similarly, the act of wiping of the face can be done when one is not performing a ritual prayer. During the supplication, the followers should utter the dictum, *āmīn*.[45] It is reprehensible to do *qunūt*-supplications in other than the *witr* prayer.

Voluntary prayers before and after the obligatory (*rawātib*)

The best *rawātib* prayer is the voluntary prayer affiliated with the dawn prayer and then the one affiliated with the sunset prayer. Thereafter, the remaining *rawātib* prayers are identical in their excellence.

The emphasised *rawātib* prayers are ten units: two units before and two units after the midday prayer; two units after the sunset prayer; two units after the nightfall prayer; and two units before the dawn prayer.

It is recommended to make up the *witr* and the *rawātib* prayers if someone missed them. However, if a person missed them as well as the obligatory prayers and its numbers became a lot, then it's better to leave making them up.

It is superior to perform all the voluntary prayers in one's residence. It is recommended to have a short cut off period between the obligatory prayer and its affiliated voluntary prayers – either by standing or speaking.

The night payer in Ramadan (*tarāwīḥ*)

The night prayer in Ramadan consists of twenty units. Its timing is between the nightfall prayer and the *witr* prayer.[46]

---

45 It's recommended to utter the dictum, *āmīn*, for everything the imam says, whether the imam is praising Allāh or supplicating to him; it is even uttered when salutations are sent to the Prophet. The earliest commentator of *Dalīl al-ṭālib* (Al-Maqdiṣī, *Sharḥ*, vol.1 p. 369) mentioned: 'The followers say the dictum during the requests and supplications but remain silent when Allāh is being praised.' According to the apparent opinion of the Ḥanbalī school: the followers do not utter the dictum, *subḥānank*, when Allāh is being praised and exalted.

46 It is performed after praying the two units affiliated with the nightfall prayer. If the *tarāwīḥ* prayer was performed straight away after the nightfall prayer, it will be correct but it is preferred to perform the two units first.

ثمَّ يصلِّي على النبيِّ صلى الله عليه وسلم ويؤمنُ المأمومُ، ثمَّ يمسحُ وجهَهُ بيديهِ هنا، وخارجَ الصلاةِ. وكرهَ القنوتُ في غيرِ الوترِ.

[الرواتب]

وأفضلُ الرواتبِ: سنةُ الفجرِ، ثمَّ المغربِ، ثمَّ سواءٌ.

والرواتبُ المؤكدةُ عشرٌ: ركعتانِ قبلَ الظهرِ، وركعتانِ بعدَها، وركعتانِ بعد المغربِ، وركعتانِ بعد العشاءِ، وركعتانِ قبل الفجرِ.

ويسنُّ: قضاءُ الرواتبِ والوترِ، إلَّا ما فاتَ مع فرضِهِ وكثرَ، فالأولى تركُهُ.

وفعلُ الكلِّ ببيتٍ أفضلُ. ويسنُّ الفصلُ بينَ الفرضِ وسنتِهِ، بقيامٍ أو كلامٍ.

[التراويحُ]

والتراويحُ عشرونَ ركعةً برمضانَ، ووقتُها ما بينَ العشاءِ والوترِ.

Subsection

The night vigil prayers (*ṣalāt al-layl, tahajjud, qiyām al-layl*)

The night prayers are more superior to the daytime prayers and the second-half of the night is better than the first-half for praying. The *tahajjud* prayer is the one performed after sleep. The night vigil prayer is encouraged, and it is recommended to commence it with two short units. When someone goes to bed, it is recommended to have an intention to wake up for the night vigil prayer. If someone performed one unit, it will be considered correct.[47] The reward for a sitting person in prayer is half that of a standing person, that is, if the sitting person was not exempted. It is more superior to do lots of bowing and prostrating than to prolong one's standing in prayer.

The mid-morning prayer (*ḍuḥā*)

It is recommended to perform the *ḍuḥā* prayer every other day or so. The *ḍuḥā* prayer minimally consists of performing two units and its maximum consists of eight units. Its timing begins after the end of the forbidden time, and lasts until shortly before the noon prayer. The optimal time to perform the *ḍuḥā* prayer is when the sun has risen high and become very hot.

Other voluntary prayers

It is recommended to perform the prayer for greeting the mosque (*taḥiyyat al-masjid*)[48] and after doing ablution (*sunnat al-wuḍū'*). It is equally recommended to pray between the sunset prayer and the nightfall prayer; doing voluntary prayers within this time period is counted to be part of the night vigil prayer.

---

47 Likewise, if a person did three units, five units, and etc., it will be correct, based on analogical deductions to the *witr* prayer.

48 The *taḥiyyat al-masjid* prayer is recommended for anyone who enters a mosque, whether he intends to sit down or not – a person can pray two or more units.

فصل

[صلاةُ الليلِ]

وصلاةُ الليلِ أفضلُ مِن صلاةِ النهارِ، والنصفُ الأخيرُ أفضلُ مِن الأولِ، والتهجدُ ما كانَ بعدَ النومِ. ويسنُّ: قيامُ الليلِ وافتتاحُهُ بركعتينِ خفيفتينِ، ونيتُهُ عند النومِ. ويصحُّ: التطوعُ بركعةٍ. وأجرُ القاعدِ غيرِ المعذورِ، نصفُ أجرِ القائمِ. وكثرَةُ الركوعِ والسجودِ، أفضلُ مِن طولِ القيامِ.

[صلاةُ الضحَى]

وتسنُّ: صلاةُ الضحَى غبًّا، وأقلُّها: ركعتانِ، وأكثرُها ثمانٍ، ووقتُها: مِن خروجِ وقتِ النهيِ إلى قبيلِ الزوالِ، وأفضلُهُ: إذا اشتدَّ الحرُّ.

[غيرها]

وتسنُّ: تحيَّةُ المسجدِ، وسنةُّ الوضوءِ، وإحياءُ ما بينَ العشاءينِ؛ وهو مِن قيامِ الليلِ.

Subsection

Prostrations for Qur'ān recital (*sujūd al-tilāwat*)

It is recommended for the person reciting and listening to do the prostration for Qur'ān recital while keeping the interval brief.[49] The prostration for Qur'ān recital is similar to a voluntary prayer in terms of what it requires to be correct.

While prostrating, one exclaims, 'Allāh is the greatest' – here, there is no initial exclamation; likewise, one exclaims the dictum when rising up from the prostration. One sits and utters the invocation of peace - the Testification of Faith supplication is not recited.

If a follower performed a prostration, on purpose, for his own recital or recital of someone other than his imam, his prayer will be invalidated. It's obligatory for a follower to adhere to the imam's leadership for audible prayers; and if one did not, on purpose,[50] his prayer will be invalidated.

The Qur'ān reciter is required to be fitting as an imam for the listener (to do the prostration). The listener must not prostrate if the reciter does not prostrate. Likewise, the listener does not prostrate in the following cases: when positioned in front of the reciter; when standing by the reciter's left side while there is no one on his right side; and when a man is listening to a woman's or a hermaphrodite's recital.[51] The listener can prostrate for the recital of the following: one who cannot recite al-Fātiḥa properly; one incapable of standing; and a person of discernment.[52]

49 The performance of the prostration must closely follow the recital or the listening and if there is a long interval, the prostration is not performed.

50 This implies that if one did not follow the imam, on purpose, in audible prayers, for the prostration of Qur'ān recital, the follower's prayer will be nullified.

51 This is namely because the imamate of these three individuals is not fitting for the listeners.

52 These three reciters of the Qur'ān are fitting for the listeners to be regarded as an imam

فصل

[سجودُ التلاوةِ]

ويسنُّ: سجودُ التلاوةِ مع قصرِ الفصلِ للقارئِ، والمستمعِ. وهو كالنافلةِ فيما يعتبرُ لها.

يكبِّرُ إذا سجدَ بلا تكبيرةِ إحرامٍ، وإذا رفعَ، ويجلسُ ويسلمُ بلا تشهدٍ.

وإنْ سجدَ المأمومُ لقراءةِ نفسِهِ، أو لقراءةِ غيرِ إمامِهِ عمدًا بطلتْ صلاتُهُ. ويلزمُ: المأمومَ متابعةُ إمامِهِ في صلاةِ الجهرِ؛ فلو تركَ متابعتَهُ عمدًا، بطلتْ.

ويعتبرُ كونُ القارئِ يصلحُ إمامًا للمستمعِ؛ فلا يسجدُ إنْ لم يسجدْ، ولا قدامَهُ، ولا عن يسارِهِ مع خلوِّ يمينِهِ، ولا يسجدُ رجلٌ لتلاوةِ امرأةٍ، وخنثَى، ويسجدُ لتلاوةِ أميٍّ، وزمنٍ، ومميزٍ.

Prostration of thanks (*sujūd al-shukr*)

It is recommended to prostrate out of thanks to Allāh whenever blessings manifest anew or when afflictions are averted. If one did the prostration of thanks in prayer deliberately while remembering, the prayer will be nullified. Its description and rulings are akin to the prostration of Qur'ān recital.

---

and so their imamate is correct. Recitation of al-Fātiḥa and standing in prayer is not a pre-requisite for the prostration. Similarly, the imamate of a person of discernment (i.e. a child) is correct for voluntary prayers; and since the prostration of Qur'ān recital is a voluntary act, it's not problematic. So if the listeners of the Qur'ān recital happen to be a man, woman, or a hermaphrodite – they can prostrate for the Qur'ān recital of the second aforementioned group.

[سجودُ الشكرِ]

ويسنُّ سجودُ الشكرِ عندَ تجددِ النعمِ، واندفاعِ النقمِ. وإنْ سجدَ لَهُ عالمًا ذاكرًا في صلاتِهِ، بطلتْ. وصفتُهُ، وأحكامُهُ كسجودِ التلاوةِ.

The Forbidden Times

The times when the prayer is forbidden are: (i) From dawn until the sun is a spear's length (above the horizon), (ii) from the mid-afternoon prayer until sunset, and (iii) from the time the sun is at its zenith (i.e. highest point) until it moves on.

It is prohibited to perform voluntary prayers in the forbidden times. The voluntary prayers within these times will not be considered to have begun validly, that is, even if someone was uninformed about the forbidden times or about the prohibition of praying therein.

The following voluntary prayers will be correct in the forbidden times:

- The two units before dawn prayer
- The two units after circumambulation (*ṭawāf*)
- The two units associated with the noon prayer, that is, when the noon prayer is joined (with the mid-afternoon prayer)
- Repeating a prayer with a group that's about to pray it while one is present in a mosque

During the forbidden times, it is permissible to make-up missed obligatory prayers and the prayers one has vowed to do – even if someone vowed to perform them in one of the forbidden times.

The prohibition after the mid-afternoon prayer is in relation to finishing the actual prayer; it is not related to when one begins to pray in the forbidden time. So, if a person started to perform the mid-afternoon prayer in the forbidden time but changed it to a voluntary prayer, he will not be prevented from performing further voluntary prayers.[53]

---

53 As long as the mid-afternoon prayer has not been performed, it will be permissible to do voluntary prayers in the forbidden times. However, once the mid-afternoon prayer has

فصل في أوقات النهي

وهي:

- مِن طلوعِ الفجرِ إلى ارتفاعِ الشمسِ قيدَ رمحٍ
- ومِن صلاةِ العصرِ إلى غروبِ الشمسِ
- وعندَ قيامِها حتَّى تزولَ.

فتحرمُ: صلاةُ التطوعِ في هذهِ الأوقاتِ، ولا تنعقدُ ولو جاهلًا للوقتِ والتحريمِ، سوى:

- سنةِ الفجرِ قبلَها
- وركعتَي الطَّوافِ
- وسنةِ الظهرِ إذا جمعَ
- وإعادةِ جماعةٍ أقيمتْ، وهو في المسجدِ.

ويجوزُ فيها: قضاءُ الفرائضِ، وفعلُ المنذورةِ، ولو نذرَها فيها.

والاعتبارُ في التحريمِ بعدَ العصرِ بفراغِ صلاةِ نفسِهِ، لا بشروعِهِ فيها؛ فلو أحرمَ بها، ثمَّ قلبَها نفلًا، لم يمنَعْ مِن التطوعِ.

It is permissible to recite the Qur'ān while on paths and roads. Likewise, it is permissible to recite when someone is in a state of minor ritual impurity or when someone has filth attached to one's clothes, body, or mouth. It is a collective obligation to memorise the Qur'ān. However, it becomes a personal obligation to memorise parts of the Qur'ān that are required for the prayer.[54]

---

been performed, the prohibition to perform voluntary prayers comes into action.

54 According to the Ḥanbalī school only al-Fātiḥa from the Qur'ān is an obligatory requirement in the prayer.

وتباحُ: قراءةُ القرآنِ في الطريقِ، ومع حدثٍ أصغرَ ونجاسةِ ثوبٍ، وبدنٍ، وفمٍ. وحفظُ القرآنِ، فرضُ كفايةٍ. ويتعينُ حفظُ ما يجبُ في الصلاةِ.

The Group Prayer

The group prayer is obligatory for free and able men, whether in residence or on a journey. The minimum participants for a group prayer is an imam and a follower – even if the follower is a woman. An obligatory prayer is not considered to have begun validly if the imam was a person of discernment. It's recommended to perform it in a mosque, and for women to do it separated from men.

When a mosque has an assigned imam, it's prohibited to lead a group prayer (before him). If the assigned imam reprehended others leading (before him), one's imamate will be incorrect unless permission was sought beforehand or if the prayer time became constricted.[55]

Whoever exclaims, 'Allāh is the greatest' before the imam's first invocation of peace, has caught the group prayer. Whoever catches the imam in the bowing position, without being doubtful, one attains that unit; the person remains motionless a moment and follows the imam thereafter.[56] It's recommended for the latecomer to do what he catches the imam doing. If a latecomer stands up before the imam's second invocation of peace and then does not sit back down, the obligatory prayer will change to a voluntary.

If the *iqāma* is given for a prayer that one intended to do with the imam, then any voluntary prayers started thereafter will not be considered to have begun validly. But if someone is already in a voluntary prayer, one should complete it briefly.

55 The author presented two scenarios when the imamate of another person is considered correct: firstly, if the assigned imam does not find it reprehensible for others to lead the group prayer before him; secondly, if the assigned imam arrives late to the extent that the present prayer time becomes too constricted.

56 While trying to catch the imam in the bowing position, it is sufficient for the latecomer to exclaim, 'Allāh is the greatest' once providing the intention was made for entering the prayer (i.e. *takbīrat al-iḥrām*). However, its best to exclaim 'Allāh is the greatest' twice; the first for entering the prayer and the second for going into the bowing position.

باب صلاة الجماعة

تجبُ: على الرجالِ الأحرارِ القادرينَ، حضرًا وسفرًا. وأقلُّها: إمامٌ ومأمومٌ ولو أنثَى. ولا تنعقدُ بالمميزِ في الفرضِ. وتسنُّ الجماعَةُ بالمسجدِ، وللنساءِ منفرداتٍ عن الرجالِ.

وحرمَ: أنْ يؤمَّ بمسجدٍ له إمامٌ راتبٌ؛ فلا تصحُّ إلا مع إذنِهِ إنْ كرِهَ ذلكَ، ما لم يضقِ الوقتُ.

ومَن كبرَ قبلَ تسليمةِ الإمامِ الأولَى، أدركَ الجماعةَ. ومَن أدركَ الركوعَ - غيرَ شاكٍّ - أدركَ الركعةَ، واطمأنَّ، ثمَّ تابعَ. وسنَّ: دخولُ المأمومِ مع إمامِهِ، كيف أدركَهُ. وإنْ قامَ المسبوقُ قبلَ تسليمَةِ إمامِهِ الثانيةِ ولم يرجعِ، انقلبتْ نفلًا.

وإذا أقيمتِ الصلاةُ التي يريدُ أنْ يصلىَ مع إمامِها، لم تنعقدْ نافلةٌ، وإنْ أقيمتْ وهو فيها، أتمَّها خفيفةً.

If one has already performed an obligatory prayer and the *iqāma* is given for it, it's recommended to repeat the prayer; the first prayer is one's obligatory.

The imam shoulders responsibility for: recitation of al-Fātiḥa; prostrations of forgetfulness; prostration for Qur'ān recital; the barrier (*sutra*); *qunūt*-supplication; and the first Testification of Faith supplication, namely when a latecomer has missed the first unit of a four-unit prayer.

In audible prayers, it's recommended for a follower to say the opening supplication and the dictum for seeking refuge in God. Likewise, to recite al-Fātiḥa and a chapter of the Qur'ān for the units it's legislated during an imam's intermissions. The intermissions occur before his recitation of al-Fātiḥa, after it, and when he finishes reading an additional chapter. During the imam's inaudible recitations, a follower can recite when he wants.

ومَن صلَّى ثمَّ أقيمتِ الجماعةُ، سنَّ أنْ يعيدَ؛ والأولى فرضُهُ.

ويتحملُ الإمامُ عن المأمومِ: القراءةَ، وسجودَ السهوِ، وسجودَ التلاوةِ، والسترةَ، ودعاءَ القنوتِ، والتشهدَ الأولَ، إذا سبقَ بركعةٍ في رباعيةٍ.

وسنَّ: للمأمومِ أنْ يستفتحَ، ويتعوذَ في الجهريةِ، ويقرأَ الفاتحةَ، وسورةً حيثُ شرعتْ في سكتاتِ إمامهِ؛ وهي: قبلَ الفاتحةِ، وبعدَها، وبعدَ فراغِ القراءةِ. ويقرأُ فيما لا يجهرُ فِيهِ: متى شاءَ.

Subsection

If a follower uttered the initial 'Allāh is the greatest' with the imam or before the imam's completion, his prayer will not be considered to have begun validly. Followers ought to begin actions after the imam's. It's reprehensible if one concurs with the imam's actions or with his invocations of peace.[57] And it's prohibited to go ahead of the imam. Therefore, if one bowed, prostrated, or straightened up before the imam intentionally, it's binding to return and follow the imam's actions. If one refused to return, on purpose, being fully informed, the person's prayer will be nullified; but if one was forgetful or uninformed, it will not.

It's recommended for the imam to keep the prayer brief but at the same time complete[58] providing the followers don't mind lengthy prayers. Likewise, for the imam to wait for a latecomer to join the group prayer providing the wait will not be difficult upon the other followers.

It is reprehensible for a person to prevent his wife or his slave woman to attend the mosque if they sought permission; nonetheless, it is better for her to pray at home.

57 It is permissible for a follower to do the first invocation of peace once the imam has completed his first invocation of peace, and likewise for the second. However, it is better for a follower to do both once the imam has completed them. If the invocations of peace were done at the same time as the imam, it is reprehensible. And if the invocations of peace were uttered before the imam's on purpose, the follower's prayer will be nullified.

58 This is namely to perform the prayer including its integrals, obligations, and recommended elements. It is reprehensible for an imam to pray so swiftly, which causes followers to miss out doing recommended elements of the prayer.

فصل

ومَن أحرمَ مع إمامِهِ أو قبلَ إتمامِهِ لتكبيرةِ الإحرامِ، لم تنعقدْ صلاتُهُ. والأولى: للمأمومِ أنْ يشرعَ في أفعالِ الصلاةِ بعدَ إمامِهِ، فإنْ وافقَهُ فيها، أو في السلامِ كرِهَ، وإنْ سبقَهُ حرمَ. فمَن ركعَ، أو سجدَ، أو رفعَ قبلَ إمامِهِ عمدًا، لزِمَهُ أنْ يرجعَ ليأتيَ بِهِ مع إمامِهِ، فإنْ أبى عالمًا عمدًا، بطلتْ صلاتُهُ لا صلاةُ ناسٍ وجاهلٍ.

ويسنُّ: للإمامِ التخفيفُ مع الإتمامِ، ما لم يؤثرِ المأمومُ التطويلَ، وانتظارُ داخلٍ إنْ لم يشقَّ على المأمومِ.

ومَن استأذنتْهُ امرأتُهُ أو أمتُهُ إلى المسجدِ كرِهَ منعُها، وبيتُها خيرٌ لها.

Imamate

The one most worthy of being an imam (in order of preference) is as follows:

- The best reciter of the Qur'ān and the most learned in Islamic law

A proficient reciter who is not acquainted with the legal rulings of the prayer is given preference to the learned who is unable to recite al-Fātiḥa properly.

- Thereafter, the eldest in age
- Thereafter, the most noble in lineage
- Thereafter, the most god-fearing and pious
- Thereafter, lots are drawn (i.e. when equal in the aforementioned)

A person residing in a house where the group prayer takes place and the mosque's assigned imam have the most right to lead the prayer – even if they happen to be slaves.

A free person is more worthy of being an imam over a slave. Similarly, the sighted person is more worthy than a blind person; a non-traveller more worthy than a traveller; and the one who performed *wūḍū'* is more worthy over someone who has performed the dry ablution (*tayammum*).

The imamate of a less worthy person is reprehensible without consent.

The imamate of an immoral person is incorrect except in the Friday and Festive prayers (*'īd*) which an individual cannot pray behind someone else (i.e. behind an upright imam).

The imamate of the following are correct but reprehensible at the same time: one who is deaf and blind; one who is uncircumcised; one who commits a lot of inconsequential mistakes in the Arabic vowelling which do not change the word's meaning; and someone who stutters over the letter *t*.

فصل في الإمامة

الأولى بها:

- الأجودُ قراءةً الأفقَهُ

ويقدمُ قارئٌ لا يعلمُ فقْهَ صلاتِهِ على فقيهٍ أميٍّ.

- ثمَّ الأسنُّ
- ثمَّ الأشرفُ
- ثمَّ الأتقى والأورعُ
- ثمَّ يقرعُ.

وصاحبُ البيتِ، وإمامُ المسجدِ ولو عبدًا، أحقُّ.

والحرُّ أولى مِن العبدِ. والحاضرُ، والبصيرُ، والمتوضئُ، أولى مِن ضدِّهِم.

وتكرهُ: إمامةُ غيرِ الأولى بلا إذنِهِ.

ولا تصحُّ: إمامةُ الفاسقِ، إلا في جمعةٍ وعيدٍ تعذرَا خلفَ غيرِهِ.

وتصحُّ: إمامةُ الأعمى، والأصمِّ، والأقلفِ وكثيرِ لحنٍ لم يحلِ المعنَى، والتمتامِ الذي يكررُ التاءَ، مع الكراهةِ.

The imamate of a person who is incapable of fulfilling a pre-requisite or an integral component of the prayer is incorrect except over his like or if the incapability was related to the mosque's assigned imam but his problem was not expected to last long (e.g. unable to stand upright). In the latter case, the assigned imam can pray sitting and the followers pray behind him seated; and if the followers prayed behind him standing, their prayer will be correct.

If an imam omitted a pre-requisite or an integral which was differed over, one's prayer will be considered correct following the imam.[59] However, if one prayed behind the imam believing that his prayer was incorrect, he is to repeat the prayer; one is not reprehended in matters of diligent enquiry.

The imamate of a woman leading men in prayer is incorrect. Equally, the imamate of a person of discernment leading adults in obligatory prayers is incorrect; but it is correct for voluntary prayers. A discerning minor can lead others in obligatory prayers who are equal to him.

If the imam was in a state of ritual impurity or had filth on him, the imamate will be incorrect – that is, if the imam was aware. However, if the imam and the follower were unaware until concluding the prayer, then in such a case only the follower's prayer will be considered correct.

The imamate of a person who cannot recite al-Fātiḥa properly is incorrect unless he was leading someone equal to him. A voluntary prayer is correct behind an obligatory prayer but not vice versa. A follower's make-up prayer is valid when performed behind a current prayer of an imam or vice versa as long as both the prayers are termed the same.[60]

---

59 For example, the imam being a Ḥanafī and the follower being a Ḥanbalī – if the imam omitted reposefulness in prayer (which is not an integral component in the Ḥanafī school but it is in the Ḥanbalī school); the prayer of the Ḥanbalī as a follower of the Ḥanafī imam will be considered correct even though they differ on that particular integral.

60 An example of this scenario is when a follower performs one of his missed noon prayers behind the imam when he is performing the current noon prayer or vice versa. The group prayer between them will be correct since both are performing the same prayer (i.e. the noon prayer). However, if a follower was performing his noon prayer behind an imam who was performing the mid-afternoon prayer, it will be invalid – since the two prayers are different to each other.

ولا تصحُّ: إمامةُ العاجزِ عن شرطٍ، أو ركنٍ إلا بمثلِهِ، إلا الإمامُ الراتبُ بمسجدٍ المرجوَّ زوالُ علتِهِ؛ فيصلِّى جالسًا، ويجلسون خلفَهُ، وتصحُّ قيامًا.

وإنْ ترك الإمامُ ركنًا، أو شرطًا مختلفًا فيهِ مقلدًا، صحتْ ومَن صلَّى خلفَهُ معتقدًا بطلانَ صلاتِهِ، أعادَ، ولا إنكارَ في مسائلِ الاجتهادِ.

ولا تصحُّ: إمامةُ المرأةِ بالرجالِ، ولا إمامةُ المميزِ بالبالغِ في الفرضِ. وتصحُّ: إمامتهُ في النفلِ، وفي الفرضِ بمثلِهِ.

ولا تصحُّ: إمامةُ محدثٍ، ولا نجسٍ يعلمُ ذلك؛ فإنْ جهل هو والمأمومُ حتى انقضتْ، صحتْ صلاةُ المأمومِ وحدَهُ.

ولا تصحُّ [إمامةُ] الأميِّ - وهو مَن لا يحسنُ الفاتحةَ - إلا بمثلِهِ. ويصحُّ: النفلُ خلفَ الفرضِ، ولا عكسَ. وتصحُّ: المقضيةُ خلفَ الحاضرةِ وعكسُهُ؛. حيثُ تساوتَا في الاسمِ.

Subsection

It is correct for the imam to stand in the middle, between the followers but it is recommended for the imam to stand ahead of them. A single male follower stands on the imam's right, aligned to him. The prayer of a single male standing behind the imam will be incorrect. Similarly, if a follower stood on the left side of the imam while the right was empty, his prayer will be incorrect. A woman stands behind the imam.[61] If a man performed one unit of prayer alone behind a row of followers, his prayer will be invalid.

The group prayer is valid as long as the followers are able to follow the imam, even if the distance between the followers and the imam exceeded beyond 300 *dhirā'* (144 meters). The group prayer will be correct providing the followers can see the imam or those directly behind the imam.[62] If the imam and the followers were in a mosque, it is not a pre-requisite for the followers to see the imam (or those behind him) in order for the group prayer to be correct. In such a scenario, it will suffice to follow the imam's exclamations of 'Allāh is the greatest'. If there was a river in which boats flowed or a pathway between the imam and the followers, the prayer of the followers will not be valid. It is reprehensible for an imam to be in a more elevated position than a follower but not vice versa. It is reprehensible to attend the mosque if someone consumed the likes of onion, radish, and etc.

61 If a single female was praying with a male, she stands behind him – for example a man praying with his wife.

62 This is a pre-requisite for the validity of a follower's prayer when he is outside the mosque while the imam is in the mosque. He must be able to see the imam or those behind him – even if it was during some parts of the group prayer.

فصل

يصحُّ وقوفُ الإمامِ وسطَ المأمومينَ، والسنةُ: وقوفُهُ متقدمًا عليهِم. ويقفُ الرجلُ الواحدُ عن يمينِهِ محاذيًا له، ولا تصحُّ خلفَهُ، ولا عن يسارِهِ مع خلوِّ يمينِهِ. وتقفُ المرأةُ خلفَهُ. وإنْ صلى الرجلُ ركعةً خلفَ الصفِّ منفردًا، فصلاتُهُ باطلةٌ.

وإن أمكنَ المأمومَ الاقتداءُ بإمامِهِ، ولوْ كان بينهُما ثلاثِ مائَةِ ذراعٍ صحَّ، إن رأى الإمامَ، أو رأى مَن وراءَهُ، وإن كان الإمامُ والمأمومُ في المسجدِ، لم تشترطِ الرؤيةُ، وكفى سماعُ التكبيرِ، وإنْ كان بينهُما نهرٌ تجري فيهِ السفنُ، أو طريقٌ، لم تصحَّ. وكرِهَ: علوُّ الإمامِ عن المأمومِ، لا عكسُهُ. وكرِهَ: لمَن أكلَ بصلًا، أو فجلًا ونحوَهُ، حضورُ المسجدِ.

Subsection

One is excused from attending the Friday and the group prayers when a person is sick or fears falling sick and when one is holding back from urine or feces. Likewise, when someone hopes to find his lost property; when someone fears destruction, misplacement, or harm to one's property; or when someone fears harm to a property that's rented out which one is obliged to protect – for example, a warden overlooking an orchard. A person is similarly excused from attending the Friday and the group prayers if one is harmed due to rain; heavy mud; snow; ice; cold winds in dark nights; or if the imam prolonged the group prayer.

فصل

يعذرُ بتركِ الجمعةِ والجماعةِ: المريضُ، والخائفُ حدوثَ المرضِ، والمدافعُ أحدَ الأخبثَينِ، ومَن له ضائعٌ يرجوهُ، أو يخافُ ضياعَ مالِهِ، أو فواتَهُ، أو ضررًا فيهِ، أو يخافُ على مالٍ استؤجرَ لحفظِهِ، كنظارةِ بستانٍ، أو أذى بمطرٍ، ووحلٍ، وثلجٍ، وجليدٍ وريحٍ باردةٍ بليلةٍ مظلمةٍ، أو تطويلِ إمامٍ.

Prayer of people who have excuses

It is binding for a sick person to perform the obligatory prayers standing, even if it meant depending on something. However, if one is unable, then one prays seated. And if one is unable to pray seated, then one prays lying on his side; and the right side is better.

One bows and prostrates by nodding one's head; the nodding for prostrations is performed deeper than for bowings. If someone was unable to nod one's head, one gestures with one's eyes and calls to mind and heart the actions of bowing and prostrating. The same applies for dictums, namely, when an individual is unable to use his tongue.[63] The obligation of prayer does not rescind as long as a person's mind is intact.

If one becomes capable of standing or sitting during the prayer, one must shift to that position. If one is able to stand and pray alone or able to pray seated in a group prayer, then one can opt to do either.

The obligatory prayer is valid on a vehicle if one becomes harmed with the likes of rain, heavy mud, etc., or if someone fears for one's safety when coming out of the vehicle. In such scenarios, the person faces the direction of prayer and does what he is able to. One bows and prostrates by nodding one's head when one is (restrained) in water and mud.

---

63 This could even be a prisoner who fears that if he uttered the dictums of prayer or recited, he will be caught performing the prayer.

باب صلاة أهل الأعذار

يلزمُ المريضَ أنْ يصليَ المكتوبةَ قائمًا ولو مستندًا، فإنْ لم يستطعْ فقاعدًا، فإنْ لم يستطعْ فعلى جنبِهِ؛ والأيمنُ أفضلُ.

ويومئُ بالركوعِ وبالسجودِ ويجعلُهُ أخفضَ، فإنْ عجزَ أومأَ بطرفِهِ واستحضرَ الفعلَ بقلبِهِ، وكذا القولَ إنْ عجزَ عنْهُ بلسانِهِ، ولا تسقُطُ ما دامَ عقلُهُ ثابتًا.

ومَن قدرَ على القيامِ، أو القعودِ في أثنائِها انتقلَ إليهِ. ومَن قدرَ على أنْ يقومَ منفردًا ويجلسَ في الجماعةِ خيرَ.

وتصحُّ على الراحلةِ لمَن يتأذَّى بنحوِ مطرٍ، ووحلٍ، أو يخافُ على نفسِهِ مِن نزولِهِ، وعليهِ الاستقبالُ وما يقدرُ عليهِ. ويومئُ مَن بالماءِ والطينِ.

The Travel Prayer

It is best to shorten the four-unit prayers if one plans to make a lawful trip to a specified destination when the distance of the journey exceeds 16 *farsakh*.[64] It is around two days of travelling during moderate travel conditions, with animals carrying the goods, and one walking at a steady pace. One can shorten once one has passed the inhabited buildings of the town. A person does not need to repeat a prayer if one had shortened the prayer and then returned to his residence before completing the distance.

It is binding for one (i.e. the traveller) to pray the full number of units in the following cases:

- The prayer time enters and one is still in residence
- One prays behind someone who is praying the full number of units
- If one's intention to shorten the prayer did not coincide with the initial exclamation of 'Allāh is the greatest'
- If one intends to stay at the destination unlimitedly or for more than four days
- If one travels to a place for some need but believes it can be met or achieved only after four days

64 One *farsakh* is equivalent to 3 Hāshimite miles, making 16 *farsakh* a total of 48 Hāshimite miles. The Hāshimite mile is not equivalent to the British standard mile. The past scholars proposed different equivalent figures for one *farsakh*. In terms of its equivalence according to *dhirāʿ* (arm-lengths), the following figures have been proposed: (i) 10,500 'arm-lengths' according to Ibn 'Abd al-Barr and (ii) 18,000 'arm-lengths' according to al-Nawawī, Mūsā al-Ḥajjāwī, and others. If we consider each 'arm-length' to be 0.48 m, then according to the conversion factor of Ibn 'Abd al-Barr, the modern equivalence for 16 *farsakh* is 80.64 kilometers or 50.4 miles (i.e. 16 *farsakh* x 10,500 'arm-lengths' x 0.48 m = 80.64 km). However, according to al-Ḥajjāwī's conversion factor, the modern equivalence of 16 *farsakh* is 138.24 kilometers or 86.4 miles – making the distance greater for one to travel before one can shorten one's four-unit prayers.

فصل في صلاة المسافر

قصرُ الصلاةِ الرباعيةِ أفضلُ، لمَنْ نَوَى سفرًا مباحًا، لمحلٍّ معينٍ يبلغُ ستةَ عشرَ فرسخًا؛ وهي: يومانِ قاصدانِ في زمنٍ معتدلٍ بسيرِ الأثقالِ، ودبيبِ الأقدامِ، إذا فارقَ بيوتَ قريتِهِ العامرةِ. ولا يعيدُ مَن قصرَ، ثمَّ رجعَ قبلَ استكمالِهِ المسافةِ.

ويلزمُهُ: إتمامُ الصلاةِ إنْ

- دخلَ وقتُها، وهو في الحضرِ
- أو صلى خلفَ مَن يتمُّ
- أو لم ينوِ القصرَ عندَ الإحرامِ
- أو نوَى إقامةً مطلقةً، أو أكثرَ مِن أربعةِ أيامٍ
- أو أقامَ لحاجةٍ، وظنَّ أنْ لا تنقضيَ إلا بعدَ الأربعةِ

- If the prayer was delayed without an excuse to the extent that the time for performing the shortened prayer became constricted

If one travelled to a place for some need but had no intention of staying there for more than four days and did not know when his need could be accomplished by, then one can shorten the prayer. Correspondingly, one can shorten the prayers if one has been imprisoned unjustly or obstructed due to rain – even if one remained in such a scenario for several years.

- أو أخرَ الصلاةَ بلا عذرٍ حتى ضاقَ وقتُها عنها.

ويقصرُ إنْ أقامَ لحاجةٍ بلا نيةِ الإقامةِ فوقَ أربعةٍ، ولا يدرِي متى تنقضِي، أو حبسَ ظلمًا، أو بمطرٍ، ولو أقامَ سنينَ.

Joining Prayers

It's permissible to join prayers during a journey in which prayers can be shortened. The noon with the mid-afternoon prayer, and the sunset with the nightfall prayer; one can join in the time of either of them.[65]

It is permissible for the following to join prayers:

- A resident who is ill, for whom not joining prayers would cause difficulty
- A wet nurse who faces the difficulty of excessive impurity
- A person incapable of doing purification for each prayer
- A person who had some excuse or some work, which exempted him from attending the Friday and the group prayers

One can specifically join the sunset prayer and the nightfall prayer, even if one prays at home for the following factors: snow; ice; heavy mud; due to strong cold winds; and due to rain which drenches one's clothes and because of the hardship associated with it.[66]

It is best to do whatever is most convenient, whether performing both prayers in the time of the first or delaying them to the time of second.

If both prayers are performed in the time of the first, the following conditions are required for the joining to be correct:

- The intention to join coincides with the commencing of the first one.

---

65 Joining prayers during travels is permissible; it is neither reprehensible nor recommended. However, it is best to leave joining prayers during journeys in which prayers can be shortened.

66 If the clothes do not drench because of the rain, it is not permissible to join the prayers.

فصل في الجمع

يباحُ بسفرِ القصرِ: الجمعُ بينَ الظهرِ والعصرِ، والعشاءينِ، بوقتِ إحداهُما.

ويباحُ:

- لمقيمٍ مريضٍ يلحقُهُ بتركِهِ مشقةٌ
- ولمرضعٍ لمشقةِ كثرةِ النجاسةِ
- ولعاجزٍ عنِ الطهارةِ لكلِّ صلاةٍ
- ولعذرٍ أو شغلٍ يبيحُ تركَ الجمعةِ والجماعةِ.

ويختصُّ بجوازِ جمعِ العشاءينِ - ولو صلَّى ببيتِهِ - ثلجٌ، وجليدٌ، ووحلٌ، وريحٌ شديدةٌ باردةٌ، ومطرٌ يبلُّ الثيابَ، وتوجدُ معهُ مشقةٌ.

والأفضلُ: فعلُ الأرفقِ به مِن تقديمِ الجمعِ، أو تأخيرِهِ.

فإنْ جمع تقديمًا اشترطَ لصحةِ الجمعِ:

- نيتُهُ عندَ إحرامِ الأولَى

- One does not separate between them by performing a voluntary prayer, for example; rather, the gap between them should be no longer than the time to do a prayer's call for its imminent beginning or to perform a light ablution
- An excuse exists to join when the first and the second prayer begin
- The lawful excuse lasts until the second prayer ends

If both prayers are performed in the time of the second, the following conditions are required:

- One has the intention to join them at the time of the first prayer, that is, before the timing of the first prayer becomes very tight to perform
- The lawful excuse to join them must continue until the time of second prayer starts; besides these two conditions, no other is required

It is not a condition for the imam and the follower to be in agreement for the joining to be correct; accordingly, the following cases will be correct:

- If one performed each of the two prayers behind two different imams
- If one performed the first of the two prayers (as an imam) with a follower, and the second, with a different follower
- If one prayed behind someone who did not join the prayers
- If one performed one of the prayers alone, and the other with a group
- If one prayed (as an imam) with someone who did not join the prayers

- وأنْ لا يفرقَ بينهُما بنحوِ نافلةٍ، بل بقدرِ إقامةٍ، ووضوءٍ خفيفٍ،
- وأنْ يوجدَ العذرُ عندَ افتتاحِهِما
- وأنْ يستمرَّ إلى فراغِ الثانيةِ.

وإنْ جمعَ تأخيرًا اشترطَ:

- نيةُ الجمعِ بوقتِ الأولى، قبلَ أنْ يضيقَ وقتِ الثانيةِ عنها.
- وبقاءُ العذرِ إلى دخولِ وقتِ الثانيةِ لا غيرُ.

ولا يشترطُ للصحةِ اتحادُ الإمامِ والمأمومِ فلو:

- صلاهُما خلفَ إمامينِ
- أو بمأمومٍ الأولى وبآخرَ الثانيةَ
- أو خلفَ مَن لم يجمعْ
- أو إحدَاهُما منفردًا والأخرى جماعةً
- أو صلَّى بمَن لم يجمعْ، صحَّ.

The Prayer of Peril

The prayer of peril is valid whether performed in residence or during travels providing the fighting engaged in was permissible. The number of units of a prayer does not change and is unaffected due to the presence of peril; rather it affects the prayer's outward appearance and some of its pre-requisites.

When the peril is great, Muslims may perform the prayer while walking or riding, facing the direction of the prayer or otherwise. In such a state, it is not binding to commence the prayer while facing the direction of prayer. However, if the Muslims are able to face the direction of prayer, nodding is used (in place of bowing and prostrating) according to their capabilities.[67]

The prayer can be performed in the aforementioned manner if one is fleeing and escaping from: an enemy; a flood; a predatory animal; a fire; and an oppressive creditor. Likewise, when one fears that one will miss standing at ʿArafa; when one fears for oneself, one's family or one's wealth; or when one is in the process of defending oneself, one's family or one's wealth; or when defending someone else's life [or property.]

The person who lags behind his group and fears an enemy; if he ended up performing the peril prayer but it became clear later that the route was safe, the person does not need to repeat the prayer.

If one senses fear or feels safe during a prayer, one shifts and performs the prayer accordingly. It is permissible for the one performing the peril prayer to attack and retreat in battle for what dictates benefit.

The prayer will not be nullified due to lengthiness in attacking and retreating. It is permissible to carry filth due to some pressing need when performing the peril prayer; one is not required to repeat the prayer.

---

67 Nodding deeper for the prostrations than for the bowings.

فصل في صلاة الخوف

تصحُّ صلاةُ الخوفِ - إذا كان القتالُ مباحًا - حضرًا وسفرًا. ولا تأثيرَ للخوفِ في تغييرِ عددِ ركعاتِ الصلاةِ، بل في صفتِها وبعضِ شروطِها.

وإذا اشتدَّ الخوفُ، صلوا رجالًا وركبانًا، للقبلةِ وغيرِها، ولا يلزمُ افتتاحُها إليها يومئونَ طاقتَهُم.

وكذا في حالةِ الهربِ مِن عدوٍّ، أو سيلٍ، أو سبعٍ أو نارٍ أو غريمٍ ظالمٍ، أو خوفِ فواتِ وقتِ الوقوفِ بعرفةَ، أو خافَ على نفسِهِ، أو أهلِهِ، أو مالِهِ، أو ذبٍّ عِنْ ذلك، وعن نفسِ غيرِهِ.

وإنْ خافَ عدوًّا إنْ تخلفَ عن رفقتِهِ، فصلَّى صلاةَ خائفٍ، ثمَّ بانَ أمنُ الطريقِ، لم يعدْ.

ومَن خافَ أو أمنَ في صلاتِهِ، انتقلَ وبنَى. ولمصلٍّ كرٌّ وفرٌّ، لمصلحةٍ.

ولا تبطلُ بطولِهِ. وجازَ لحاجةٍ حملُ نجسٍ ولا يعيدُ.

The Friday Prayer

The Friday prayer is obligatory for male Muslims, who are accountable, free, and do not have a lawful excuse to forgo the Friday prayer.

It is equally obligatory for the traveller, that is, for whom it is not permissible to shorten the prayers. The Friday prayer is obligatory for one residing just outside the town; namely, when, at the time of the prayer, one is less than one *farsakh* away from where the Friday prayer is being established; the same rule applies to the traveller.[68]

The Friday prayer is not obligatory for one who can shorten prayers; slaves, part-slaves, or women. If any of them attended, it will suffice (from performing the noon prayer). The aforementioned and others who aren't local residents will not be counted among 'the forty' required for a valid Friday prayer. Their imamate will not be correct either.

There are four pre-requisites for the Friday prayer to be valid:

- Timing

It begins from the time when the Festive prayers (*ʿīd*) can be performed; it lasts until the noon prayer's timing ends. The Friday prayer becomes obligatory to establish when the sun passes its zenith; however, it is more preferred to do the Friday prayer at a later time.

- The Friday prayer site be located in villages – even if the dwelling therein were built up of stalks, canes, and etc.

In the village, there must be forty local residents living there who do not leave the village in the summer or in the winter. The Friday prayer will be valid if it's situated close to the desert areas, not being too far out from the village dwellings.

68 This is reference to the traveller who has not got far enough to shorten the prayers, or the traveller who is not permitted to shorten the prayers.

باب صلاة الجمعة

تجبُ: على كلِّ ذكرٍ مسلمٍ مكلفٍ حرٍّ، لا عذرَ لَهُ.

وكذا على مسافرٍ، لا يباحُ له القصرُ. وعلى مقيمٍ خارجَ البلدِ، إذا كان بينهُما وبين الجمعةِ وقتَ فعلِها فرسخٌ فأقلُّ.

ولا تجبُ على مَن يباحُ له القصرُ، ولا على عبدٍ، ومبعضٍ، وامرأةٍ. ومَن حضرَها مِنهم أجزأتْهُ، ولم يحسبْ هو، ولا مَن ليس مِن أهلِ البلدِ مِن الأربعينَ، ولا تصحُّ إمامتُهُم فِيها.

وشرطَ لصحةِ الجمعةِ أربعةُ شروطٍ:

- أحدُها: الوقتُ؛ وهو مِن أولِ وقتِ العيدِ إلى آخرِ وقتِ الظهرِ، وتجبُ بالزوالِ، وبعدَه أفضلُ.
- الثاني: أنْ تكونَ بقريةٍ ولو مِن قصبٍ، يستوطنُها أربعونَ، استيطانَ إقامةٍ؛ لا يظعنونَ صيفًا ولا شتاءً، وتصحُّ فيما قاربَ البنيانَ مِن الصحراءِ.

- A turnout of forty participants

If the number decreased before the Friday prayer finished, the attendees restart and perform the noon prayer instead.

- Presentation of two sermons before the prayer

There are five pre-requisites for them to be correct: the sermons to occur during the Friday prayer's timing; the presence of intention; they are presented in residence; the attendance of forty participants; and the sermons are delivered by someone whose imamate in the Friday prayer will be valid.

There are six integrals for the two sermons: to praise Allāh; to supplicate for the Prophet to be blessed; to recite one verse of the Qur'ān; enjoining to fear Allāh; their close preceding alongside the prayer; and their being presented in an audible voice loud enough for the required participants to hear – providing no factors prevent them from hearing the sermons.

The recommended elements include: to be in a state of purity; clothing one's nakedness; removing filth; to supplicate for the Muslims; for the same person to deliver the sermons and lead the Friday prayer; to raise one's voice according to ability; to deliver the sermons standing on an elevated place leaning on a sword or a staff; and for the speaker to sit down between the two for a short time. If a person refused to sit between the sermons or delivered the sermons seated, one should separate the two sermons with a short silence. It is recommended to keep the sermons short, making the second one shorter. There is no problem for one to read the sermons off a paper.

- الثالثُ: حضورُ أربعينَ؛ فإنْ نقصُوا قبلَ إتمامِها، استأنفُوا ظهرًا.
- الرابعُ: تقدُّم خطبتينِ.

مِن شرطِ صحتِهِما خمسةُ أشياءَ: الوقتُ، والنيةُ، ووقوعُهُما حضرًا، وحضورُ الأربعينَ، وأن يكونَا ممنْ تصحُّ إمامتُهُ فيها.

وأركانهُما ستةٌ: حمدُ اللهِ، والصلاةُ على رسولِ اللهِ صلى اللهُ عليهِ وسلمَ، وقراءةُ آيةٍ مِن كتابِ اللهِ، والوصيةُ بتقوى اللهِ، وموالاتُهُما مع الصلاةِ، والجهرُ؛ بحيثُ يسمعُ العددُ المعتبرُ، حيثُ لا مانعَ.

وسنتُهُما: الطهارةُ، وسترُ العورةِ، وإزالةُ النجاسةِ، والدعاءُ للمسلمينَ، وأنْ يتولاهُما مع الصلاةِ واحدٌ، ورفعُ الصوتِ بِهِما حسبَ الطاقةِ وأنْ يخطبَ قائمًا على مرتفعٍ، معتمدًا على سيفٍ أو عصًا، وأنْ يجلسَ بينهُما قليلًا. فإنْ أبى، أو خطبَ جالسًا، فصل بينهما بسكتةٍ. وسنَّ قصرُهما والثانيةُ أقصرُ. ولا بأسَ أنْ يخطبَ مِن صحيفةٍ.

Subsection

It is prohibited to speak while the imam is giving the sermon; that is, when one is close enough to the imam to the extent that he can hear him.[69] It is permissible for one to speak when the imam pauses between the two sermons and equally when he commences to supplicate.

It is prohibited to hold the Friday and Festive prayers in multiple locations of a town unless there is a pressing need; e.g. lack of space, being too far away, or fearing discord and friction. If the number of Friday prayers multiplied in a town without a pressing need, then the first of them to begin with the initial exclamation of 'Allāh is the greatest' will be the valid Friday prayer.

A latecomer who joins the Friday prayer within its timing and manages to bow with the imam for one unit, completes his prayer as a Friday prayer. However, if a latecomer could not bow for one unit with the imam, he intends to perform the noon prayer instead.

The minimum voluntary prayers after the Friday prayer is two units, and the maximum is six units.[70] It is recommended to recite al-Kahf (Qur'ān 18) during the daytime of Friday. It is recommended to recite al-Sajdat (Qur'ān 32) in the first unit of Friday's dawn prayer, and al-Insān (Qur'ān 72) in the second unit; however, it is reprehensible to do it continually.

---

69 If the imam was far away from the person speaking and cannot hear the individual talk, it will not be prohibited to speak.

70 There are no voluntary prayers before the Friday prayer as textually reported from Aḥmad. The recommended number of voluntary prayers after the Friday prayer is four units.

فصل

يحرمُ: الكلامُ والإمامُ يخطبُ، وهو مِنهُ بحيثُ يسمعُهُ، ويباحُ إذا سكتَ بينهُما، أو شرعَ في دعاءٍ.

وتحرمُ: إقامةُ الجمعةِ، وإقامةُ العيدِ في أكثرَ مِن موضعٍ مِن البلدِ، إلا لحاجةٍ؛ كضيقٍ، وبعدٍ، وخوف فتنةٍ، فإنْ تعددتْ لغيرِ ذلك فالسابقةُ بالإحرامِ هي الصحيحةُ.

ومَن أحرمَ بالجمعةِ في وقتِها، وأدركَ مع الإمامِ ركعةً، أتمَّ جمعةً، وإنْ أدركَ أقلَّ، نَوى ظهرًا.

وأقلُّ السنةِ بعدَها ركعتانِ، وأكثرُها ستةٌ. وسنَّ: قراءةُ سورةِ الكهفِ في يومِها وأنْ يقرأَ في فجرِها: ﴿الم﴾ السجدةَ وفي الثانيةِ ﴿هَلْ أَتَى﴾، وتكرَهُ مداومتُهُ عليهِما.

The Festive Prayers

The Festive prayers are a communal obligation. The pre-requisites are the same as the Friday prayer apart from the two sermons. It is recommended to perform the festive prayers outdoors. It is disliked to pray voluntary prayers before and after it, i.e. before leaving the prayer area. The time is the same as the mid-morning prayer. If the day of *ʿīd* is undetermined until it has passed, the festive prayer is performed the following day as a make-up prayer.

It is recommended for the followers to come early, and the imam to delay his arrival until the time of the actual prayer. If one used a particular route to attend the festive prayers, one should return home by a different route; the same applies for the Friday prayers.

The festive prayers consist of two units. After the initial exclamation of 'Allāh is the greatest', one says 'Allāh is the greatest' another six times, that is, before one utters the dictum, 'I seek refuge in Allāh from the accursed Satan'. In the second unit, one says 'Allāh is the greatest' five times before one starts to recite. One raises one's hands each time one utters 'Allāh is the greatest' and supplicates in between them using the following dictum: 'Allāh is the ever greatest; to Allāh belongs ample praise; blessed and exalted be Allāh in the mornings and evenings; may Allāh's copious blessings and peace be upon Prophet Muhammad and his household.'

After seeking refuge in Allāh from the accursed Satan, one recites aloud al-Fātiḥa followed by al-Aʿlā (Qur'ān 87); and in the second unit, al-Ghāshiyat (Qur'ān 88) after al-Fātiḥa. Once the imam has finished the festive prayer, he gives two sermons. The rules pertaining to the two sermons are similar to that of the Friday prayer; however, it is recommended to commence the first sermon by saying 'Allāh is the greatest' nine times; and the second by saying it seven times. If one performed the festive prayer in the manner of a regular voluntary prayer, it will be correct because the additional exclamations of 'Allāh is the greatest'; the dictum in between them; and the two sermons are recommended elements.

باب صلاة العيدين

وهي فرضُ كفايةٍ. وشروطُها: كالجمعةِ، ما عدا: الخطبتينِ. وتسنُّ: في الصحراءِ. ويكرهُ: النفلُ قبلَها وبعدَها، قبلَ مفارقةِ المصلَّى. ووقتُها: كصلاةِ الضحَى. فإنْ لم يعلمْ بالعيدِ إلا بعدَ الزوالِ، صلوا مِن الغدِ قضاءً.

وسنَّ: تبكيرُ المأمومِ، وتأخرُ الإمامِ إلى وقتِ الصلاةِ. وإذا مضى في طريقٍ رجعَ في أخرى، وكذا الجمعةُ.

وصلاةُ العيدِ ركعتانِ؛ يكبرُ في الأولى - بعدَ تكبيرةِ الإحرامِ وقبلَ التعوذِ - ستًّا، وفي الثانيةِ - قبلَ القراءةِ - خمسًا، يرفعُ يدَيْهِ مع كلِّ تكبيرةٍ، ويقولُ بينهُما: (اَللَّهُ أَكْبَرُ كَبِيرًا، والحَمْدُ لِلَّهِ كثيرًا، وسُبحَانَ اللَّهِ بُكرةً وأصِيلًا، وصَلَّى اللَّهُ عَلى مُحَمَّدٍ النَّبِيِّ وآلِهِ وسَلَّمَ تَسْلِيمًا).

ثمَّ يستعيذُ، ثمَّ يقرأُ جهرًا (الفاتحةَ)، ثم (سبحَ) في الأولى، و(الغاشيةَ) في الثانيةِ. فإذا سلمَ خطبَ خطبتَيْنِ وأحكامهُما: كخطبتَي الجمعةِ، لكنْ يسنُّ: أنْ يستفتحَ الأولَى بتسعِ تكبيراتٍ، والثانيةَ بسبعٍ. وإنْ صلَّى العيدَ كالنافلةِ، صحَّ؛ لأنَّ التكبيراتِ الزوائدَ، والذكرَ بينهُما والخطبتَينِ سنةٌ.

If one misses the festive prayer, it is recommended to make it up – even if it happens to be after the sun has passed its zenith.

وسنَّ: لمَن فاتتْهُ قضاؤُها، ولو بعدَ الزوالِ.

Subsection

The unrestricted[71] *takbīr* is recommended to be recited audibly on the night before each *ʿīd* until the imam completes the sermon; equally, it is recommended during the first ten days of Dhū al-Ḥijja.

The restricted *takbīr* is to be recited during the days surrounding *ʿīd al-aḍḥā,* namely from the dawn prayer on the Day of ʿArafa to the mid-afternoon prayer on the 13th day of Dhū al-Ḥijja; it is only recited after the obligatory prayers that are performed in a group (in the stated days). However, pilgrims begin from the noon prayer on the 10th of Dhū al-Ḥijja (i.e. the day of *ʿīd al-aḍḥā*). The imam recites it facing the attendees after completing the obligatory prayer.

One says, twice: 'Allāh is the greatest, Allāh is the greatest; there is no god but Allāh; and Allāh is the greatest, Allāh is the greatest; and all praise belongs to Allāh.'

There is no problem if one greeted others with the statement, 'Allāh accept it from us and from you.'

71 It is termed 'unrestricted' as the dictums are not confined to a particular circumstance unlike the case of the 'restricted' – the dictum can only be recited after one performs the obligatory prayers.

فصل

يسنُّ: التكبيرُ المطلقُ، والجهرُ بِهِ في ليلتَيْ العيدينِ إلى فراغِ الخطبةِ، وفي كلِّ عشرِ ذِي الحجةِ.

والتكبيرُ المقيدُ في الأضحَى: عقبَ كلَّ فريضةٍ صلاها في جماعةٍ، مِن صلاةِ فجرِ يومِ عرفةَ إلى عصرِ آخرِ أيامِ التشريقِ، إلا المحرمَ، فيكبرُ مِن صلاةِ ظهرِ يومِ النحرِ. ويكبِّرُ الإمامُ مستقبلَ الناسِ.

وصفتُهُ شفعًا: (اَللَّهُ أَكْبَرُ اَللَّهُ أَكْبَرِ، لَا إِلَهَ إِلَّا اِللَّهُ وَاللَّهُ أَكْبَرِ، اللَّهُ أَكْبَرِ، وَلِلَّهِ الْحَمْدُ).

ولا بأسَ بقولِهِ لغيرِهِ: (تقبَّل اللَّهُ مِنَّا وَمِنْكَ).

The Eclipse Prayer

The eclipse prayer is recommended and has no sermons. Its time is from when the eclipse occurs until it passes; one is not required to make-up the prayer if the eclipse has passed.

The eclipse prayer consists of two units. It is performed in the following manner:

One recites aloud al-Fātiḥa followed by a long chapter from the Qur'ān in the first unit and then one bows lengthily. Thereafter, one straightens up while saying the two dictums, 'Allāh hears whoever praises Him' and 'Our Lord, all praise belongs to you' (accordingly), but one does not prostrate. Instead, one recites al-Fātiḥa again followed by another long chapter from the Qur'ān. Thereafter, one bows, rises and prostrates – making the two prostrations long. The second unit of the prayer is performed in the same manner as the first unit, and upon completion one recites the Testification of Faith supplications and ends the prayer with the invocations of peace.

There is no problem if one opted to bow three, four or five bowings during each unit of the eclipse prayer. The bows after the initial one are recommended elements; therefore, a prayer unit will not be caught if a latecomer missed its first bowing. If one performed the eclipse prayer in the manner of a regular voluntary prayer, it will be valid.

باب صلاة الكسوف

وهي سنةٌ مِن غيرِ خطبةٍ، ووقتُها: مِن ابتداءِ الكسوفِ إلى ذهابِهِ، ولا تقضَى إنْ فاتتْ.

وهي ركعتانِ:

يقرأُ في الأولى جهرًا: (الفاتحة) وسورةً طويلةً، ثمَّ يركعُ طويلًا، ثمَّ يرفعُ، فيسمعُ ويحمدُ ولا يسجدُ، بلْ يقرأُ: (الفاتحةَ) وسورةً طويلةً، ثمَّ يركعُ، ثمَّ يرفعُ، ثمَّ يسجدُ سجدتينِ طويلتينِ، ثمَّ يصلِّي الثانيةَ كالأولى، ثمَّ يتشهدُ ويسلمُ.

وإنْ أتى في كلِّ ركعةٍ بثلاثِ ركوعاتٍ أو أربعٍ، أو خمسٍ فلا بأسَ. وما بعدَ الأولِ سنةٌ لا تدركُ بِهِ الركعةُ. ويصحُّ أنْ يصليَها كالنافلةِ.

The Drought Prayer

The drought prayer is recommended. Its time, its manner, and its rulings are similar to the festive prayers.

If the imam intends to perform the drought prayer, he encourages and instructs the people to repent and return anything acquired unjustly. Prior to setting forth, one purifies oneself and does not apply perfume. The imam goes forth to the prayer in a humble and lowly manner escorted by religious, pious, and elderly members of the community. It is permissible for the young, old women, and animals to be present. It is permissible to plea to Allāh through godly-people.

After performing the drought prayer, one gives a single sermon. One begins the sermon in a similar fashion to the festive sermons, exclaiming 'Allāh is the greatest' nine times. In the sermon, the imam asks Allāh's forgiveness frequently; recites verses that command people to request Allāh's forgiveness; and supplicates by raising and turning the back of his hands towards the sky. The imam supplicates using the Prophetic invocation while the attendees say, *'āmīn'* (O Allāh, accept our prayers).

Thereafter, the imam faces the direction of prayer during the sermon and quietly utters: 'Allāh! You have ordered us to call upon you and promised to answer our calls. We have called upon you as you have commanded us. Allāh! Answer our pleas as you have promised us!'

Then the imam switches his cloak around, putting the right side on his left and vice versa; the people present at the sermon do the same. The cloaks are left in this manner until one needs to change out of them along with one's clothes.

If no rain is given, the drought prayer is repeated a second time and a third time.

باب صلاة الاستسقاء

وهيَ سنةٌ ووقتُها، وصفتُها، وأحكامُها: كصلاةِ العيدِ.

وإذا أرادَ الإمامُ الخروجَ لها، وَعَظَ الناسَ وأمرَهم بالتوبةِ، والخروجِ مِن المظالمِ، ويتنظفُ لها، ولا يتطيبُ، ويخرجُ متواضعًا، متخشعًا، متذللًا، متضرعًا، ومعه أهلُ الدينِ، والصلاحِ والشيوخُ. ويباحُ: خروجُ الأطفالِ، والعجائزِ، والبهائِمِ، والتوسلِ بالصالحينَ.

فيصلِّي، ثمَّ يخطبُ خطبةً واحدةً، يفتتحُها بالتكبيرِ كخطبةِ العيدِ، ويكثرُ فيها الاستغفارَ، وقراءةَ آياتٍ فيها الأمرُ بهِ، ويرفعُ يديهِ وظهورُهما نحوَ السماءِ، فيدعو بدعاءِ النبيِّ صلى الله عليه وسلم، ويؤمنُ المأمومُ.

ثمَّ يستقبلُ القبلةَ في أثناءِ الخطبةِ، فيقولُ سرًّا: (اللَّهُمَّ إنَّكَ أَمَرْتَنَا بِدُعَائِكَ، وَوَعَدْتَنَا إجَابَتَكَ، وَقَدْ دَعَوْنَاكَ كَمَا أَمَرْتَنَا، فَاستَجِبْ لَنَا كَمَا وَعَدْتَنَا).

ثمَّ يحولُ رداءهُ، فيجعلُ الأيمنَ على الأيسرِ، والأيسرَ على الأيمنِ، وكَذَا الناسَ، ويتركونَهُ حتَّى ينزعُوهُ مع ثيابِهِم.

فإنْ سقُوا، وإلَّا عادُوا ثانيًا وثالثًا.

At first rain, it is recommended to stand in it, to perform ablution [from it,] bathe from it, and to bring out one's clothes and saddles for the rain to strike.

If it rained too much to the extent that it's feared, it is recommended to supplicate:

> Allāh! Pour it around us, and not upon us. Allāh! Upon the hills, bluffs, valley floors, and copses. Lord, do not burden us with more than we have strength to bear (Qur'ān 2: 286)

It is recommended to say, 'it rained because of Allāh's grace and mercy.' It is prohibited to say, 'it has rained due to such-and-such star' but it is permissible for one to say, 'it has rained when such-and-such star was present'.

ويسنُّ: الوقوفُ في أولِ المطرِ، والوضوءُ، والاغتسالُ مِنهُ، وإخراجُ رحلِهِ، وثيابِهِ ليصيبَها.

وإنْ كثرَ المطرُ حتَّى خيفَ مِنهُ، سنَّ: قولُ: (اللَّهمَّ حوالينا ولا علينا، اللَّهُمَّ على الآكامِ، والظرابِ، وبطونِ الأوديةِ، ومنابتِ الشجر، ﴿رَبَّنَا وَلا تُحَمِّلْنَا مَا لا طَاقَةَ لَنَا بِهِ﴾ [البقرة: ٢٨٦] الآية.

وسنَّ قولُ: (مُطِرْنا بِفَضْلِ اللَّهِ وَرَحْمَتِهِ)، ويحرمُ: (مُطِرْنَا بِنَوءِ كذَا)، ويباحُ: (في نوءِ كذَا).

Funerals

It is recommended to prepare for death and remember it often. It is reprehensible to groan; similarly it is reprehensible for one to wish for death unless one fears some tribulation in one's religion.

It is recommended to visit the sick Muslim; to instruct the dying person to say, 'There is no god but Allāh' once – one does not go beyond this unless the dying person speaks; to recite al-Fātiḥa to the dying person; and likewise to recite Yāsin (Qur'ān 36). It is also recommended to turn the dying person to face the direction of the prayer by laying him on his right side, that is, if space allows, otherwise he is laid on his back.

If the person died, it is recommended to close his eyes while one says, 'In the name of Allāh and according to the Messenger of Allāh's death.' There is no problem if one kissed or looked at the deceased – even after shrouding.

كتاب الجنائز

يسنُّ: الاستعدادُ للموتِ، والإكثارُ مِن ذكرِهِ. ويكرَهُ: الأنينُ، وتمنِّي الموتِ، إلا لخوفِ فتنةٍ.

وتسنُّ عيادةُ المريضِ المسلمِ، وتلقينُهُ عندَ موتِهِ (لا إله إلَّا اللَّهُ) مرةً، ولَم يزِد إلَّا أنْ يتكلمَ، وقراءةُ (الفاتحةِ)، و(يس)، وتوجيهُهُ إلى القبلةِ على جنبِهِ الأيمنِ مع سعةِ المكانِ، وإلا فعلى ظهرِهِ.

فإذا ماتَ، سنَّ: تغميضُ عينيهِ، وقولُ: (بسمِ اللَّهِ وعلى وفاةِ رسولِ اللَّهِ). ولا بأسَ: بتقبيلِهِ، والنظرِ إليهِ، ولو بعدَ تكفينِهِ.

Washing the Body

Washing the body is a communal obligation. The water to be used for the washing must be purifying and permissible; the person washing the body must be Muslim, sane, and be of discernment.

The best suited to wash the body is a trustworthy person who is well acquainted with the rules for washing bodies. The most entitled to wash the body is an upright person who was appointed in the will.

It is obligatory for the washer to keep the nakedness of the deceased covered once he begins. Thereafter, one wraps a small cloth over one's hand and uses it to clean the private parts; it is obligatory to use water to wash away filth. It is prohibited to touch the nakedness of a person who is over the age of seven. It is recommended for the washer not to touch the rest of the body except with a cloth.

It is permissible for a man to wash the body of his wife, his female slave, and girls under the age of seven. A woman can wash the body of her husband, her master, and boys under the age of seven.

The rulings surrounding the *ghusl* for washing a dead body are similar to the *ghusl* when one is in a state of sexual impurity, that is, in terms of the obligatory and recommended elements. However, when washing the dead, water is not inserted into the mouth or the nose; instead, a wet cloth is used to wipe the teeth and the nostrils.

It is reprehensible to limit it to a single wash, that is, even if nothing exited from the body. However, if something kept exiting the body, it is obligatory to wash the body until seven washings are reached. If anything exits the body after the seventh wash, the area is blocked off using cotton pads; and if that does not hold, then pure clay is used. The area is purified and an ablution is given to the body but another *ghusl* is not performed; the ablution here is obligatory to do. Ablution and *ghusl* are not repeated if anything leaves the body after shrouding.

فصل

وغسلُ الميتِ، فرضُ كفايةٍ. وشرطَ في الماءِ: الطهوريةُ والإباحةُ. وفى الغاسلِ: الإسلامُ، والعقلُ، والتمييزُ.

والأفضلُ: ثقةٌ عارفٌ بأحكامِ الغسلِ. والأولى بِهِ وصيُّهُ العدلُ.

وإذا شرعَ في غسلِهِ سترَ عورتَهُ وجوبًا، ثمَّ يلفُّ على يدِهِ خرقَةً فينجيهِ بها. ويجبُ: غسلُ ما بِهِ مِن نجاسةٍ، ويحرمُ: مسُّ عورةِ مَن بلغَ سبعَ سنينَ، وسنَّ: أنْ لا تمسَّ سائِرَ بدنِهِ، إلَّا بخرقةٍ.

وللرجلِ: أنْ يغسلَ زوجتَهُ، وأمتَهُ، وبنتاً دون سبعٍ. وللمرأةِ غسلُ زوجِها وسيدِها، وابنٍ دونَ سبعٍ.

وحكمُ غسلِ الميتِ فيما يجبُ ويسنُّ، كغسلِ الجنابةِ، لكنْ لا يدخِلُ الماءَ في فمِهِ وأنفِهِ، بل يأخذُ خرقةً مبلولةً، فيمسحُ بها أسنانَهُ، ومنخرَيْهِ.

ويكرهُ: الاقتصارُ في غسلِهِ على مرةٍ، إنْ لمْ يخرجْ مِنهُ شيءٌ، فإنْ خرجَ، وجبَ إعادةُ الغسلِ إلى سبعٍ، فإنْ خرجَ بعدَها، حشيَ بقطنٍ، فإنْ لم يستمسِكْ، فبطينٍ حرٍّ، ثمَّ يغسلُ المحلَّ، ويوضأ وجوبًا، ولا غسلَ. وإنْ خرجَ بعدَ تكفينِهِ، لم يعِدِ الوضوءَ، ولا الغسلَ.

The martyr killed in battle and the one killed unjustly are not washed, shrouded, or prayed over. It is obligatory to leave the blood of the martyr on his body and to bury him in his clothes. Though, if someone injured was being carried away[72] and he ate, drank, slept, spoke, sneezed, or took a long time according to custom before his passing, then such a case is treated contrarily to others (i.e. such martyrs are washed, shrouded, and prayed over). The same applies to the one who was killed and an obligatory *ghusl* was due on him, for instance, a person who was killed in a state of sexual impurity.

Miscarried foetuses, which died after four months or more are treated as though they were born alive.

It is prohibited for a Muslim to wash, shroud, pray over, or to attend the funeral of a non-Muslim or a non-Muslim subject of the Islamic state. A non-Muslim is buried if there is none to bury him (i.e. from the non-Muslims).

72 After incurring an injury by the enemy, whether one is being carried away from a battlefield or otherwise.

وشهيدُ المعركةِ، والمقتولُ ظلماً: لا يغسلُ، ولا يكفنُ، ولا يصلَّى عليهِ، ويجبُ بقاءُ دمِهِ عليهِ، ودفنُهُ في ثيابِهِ. وإنْ حملَ فأكلَ، أو شربَ، أو نامَ، أو بالَ، أو تكلمَ، أو عطسَ، أو طالَ بقاؤُهُ عرفاً، أو قتلَ وعليهِ ما يوجبُ الغسلَ مِن نحوِ جنابةٍ، فهو كغيرِهِ.

وسقطٌ لأربعةِ أشهرٍ، كالمولودِ حياً.

ولا يغسلُ مسلمٌ كافراً، ولو ذميًا ولا يكفنُهُ، ولا يصلِّي عليهِ، ولا يتبعُ جنازتَهُ، بل يوارى لعدمِ مَن يواريه.

Shrouding the Body

Shrouding the body is a communal obligation. It is obligatory to cover the entire body using clothing that renders the skin imperceptible; however, a male pilgrim's (*muḥrim*) head, and the face of a female pilgrim, are left uncovered. It is obligatory for the quality of the shrouding material to be relevant to the dead person's standard, unless one willed to be shrouded with something below standard.

It is recommended for a male to be wrapped in three white cotton sheets. The sheets are spread one on top of the other and the body is placed on the sheets on his back. The top sheet's edge is folded from the left side to the deceased's right side, then the other edge over his left side; the other two sheets are folded in the same manner.

It is recommended for a deceased female to be dressed in five white garments made of cotton: a lower body wrap, a head covering; a shirt; and two sheets. It is recommended for a child to be dressed in one garment, although three can be used. A young girl is dressed using one shirt and two sheets.

It is reprehensible to shroud the body using hair, wool, garments that were dyed with saffron and safflower, or decorative clothing. It is prohibited to wrap the body with leather, silk, or gold-infused clothing.

فصل

وتكفينُهُ، فرضُ كفايةٍ. والواجبُ: سترُ جميعِهِ، سوَى رأسِ المحرمِ ووجهِ المحرمةِ بثوبٍ لا يصفُ البشرةَ، ويجبُ أنْ يكونَ مِن ملبوسِ مثلِهِ، ما لم يوصِ بدونِهِ.

والسنةُ: تكفينُ الرجلِ في ثلاثِ لفائفَ بيض، مِن قطنٍ تبسطُ على بعضِها، ويوضعُ عليها مستلقِيا، ثمَّ يردُّ طرفُ العليَا مِن الجانبِ الأيسرِ، على شقِّهِ الأيمنِ، ثمَّ طرفُها الأيمنُ على الأيسرِ، ثمَّ الثانيةُ ثمَّ الثالثةُ كذلك.

والأنثى في: خمسةِ أثوابٍ بيضٍ مِن قطنٍ؛ إزارٌ، وخمارٌ، وقميصٌ، ولفافتينِ. والصبيُّ في ثوبٍ، ويباحُ في ثلاثةٍ. والصغيرةُ في قميصٍ، ولفافتينِ.

ويكرهُ: التكفينُ بشعرٍ، وصوفٍ، ومزعفرٍ، ومعصفرٍ، ومنقوشٍ. ويحرمُ: بجلدٍ، وحريرٍ، ومذهبٍ.

The Prayer over the Dead

It is a communal obligation and the ruling rescinds if an accountable person prayed over the dead - even a female.

There are eight pre-requisites: intention; the performer of the prayer is legally accountable; to face the direction of the prayer; to cover one's nakedness; to be free from filth; presence of the body, that is, if it was within the country; the one performing the prayer and the deceased are Muslims; and both are in a state of purity – even if purifying earth was used due to an excuse.

There are seven integrals: standing when the prayer is obligatory; to exclaim 'Allāh is the greatest' four times; to recite al-Fātiḥa; to supplicate for the Prophet to be blessed; to supplicate for the deceased; to say the invocations of peace; and the correct order. However, it is not necessary that the supplication for the deceased is made after the third exclamation of 'Allāh is the greatest'; it is permissible do so after the fourth.

Description of the prayer:

One intends to perform the prayer; thereafter, one exclaims the initial 'Allāh is the greatest' and recites al-Fātiḥa. One exclaims 'Allāh is the greatest' again and supplicates for the Prophet to be blessed in a similar manner to the [final] Testification of Faith supplication. One exclaims 'Allāh is the greatest' again and then supplicates for the deceased, for example, one can say, 'Allāh, have mercy on him'. One then exclaims 'Allāh is the greatest' again and remains standing for a moment, and thereafter one concludes with the invocations of peace. It is sufficient to do one invocation of peace – even if one did not add the phrase, 'and Allāh's mercy' to the dictum. It is permissible to pray over the dead up to a month after the burial, with a small leeway; thereafter, it is prohibited.

فصل

والصلاةُ عليهِ فرضُ كفايةٍ. وتسقطُ بمكلفٍ، ولو أنثَى.

وشروطُها ثمانيةٌ: النيةُ، والتكليفُ، واستقبالُ القبلةِ، وسترُ العورةِ، واجتنابُ النجاسةِ، وحضورُ الميتِ إنْ كان بالبلدِ، وإسلامُ المصلِّى، والمصلَّى عليهِ، وطهارتُهُما، ولو بترابٍ لعذرٍ.

وأركانُها سبعةٌ: القيامُ في فرضِها، والتكبيراتُ الأربعُ، وقراءةُ الفاتحةِ، والصلاةُ على محمدٍ، والدعاءُ للميتِ، والسلامُ، والترتيبُ، لكن لا يتعينُ كون الدعاءِ في الثالثةِ، بل يجوزُ بعدَ الرابعةِ.

وصفتُها:

أنْ ينويَ، ثم يكبرُ، ويقرأُ الفاتحةَ. ثمَّ يكبرُ، ويصلِّي على محمدٍ، كفِي التشهدِ. ثمَّ يكبرُ، ويدعوُ للميتِ بنحوِ: (اللّهُمَّ ارْحَمْهُ)، ثُمَّ يكبرُ، ويقفَ بعدَها قليلاً، ويسلمُ وتجزىءُ: واحدةٌ، ولو لم يقلْ (وَرَحْمَةُ اللّهِ). ويجوزُ: أنْ يصلىَ على الميتِ مِن دفنِهِ إلى شهرٍ وشيءٍ، ويحرمُ: بعدَ ذلك.

Burial

Carrying the deceased to the grave and burying the dead are communal obligations. The obligation to shroud, to carry, and to bury the dead rescinds from the Muslim community if non-Muslims can do so. It is reprehensible to take fees for carrying, burying, or washing the deceased.

Whilst following the bier, it is recommended for people on foot to be at the front, and for the riders to be behind; it is best that the attendees are close to the bier. It is reprehensible to stand up for the bier or raise one's voice for it, even if one was reciting the Qur'ān or dictums of remembrance aloud.

It is recommended to dig the grave wide and deep without limits; however, a grave that will prevent any foul odours from emerging and protect the body from animals will suffice. It is reprehensible to insert wood into a grave or anything that has been scorched by fire; similarly, it is reprehensible to place a mattress under the deceased or a pillow under his head.

It is recommended for the person burying the deceased to say the dictum, 'In the name of Allāh and according to the religion of the messenger of Allāh.' It is obligatory that the body be placed in the direction of prayer; and it is recommended for it to be placed on its right side.

It is prohibited to bury someone where another person has been buried or bury one body with another unless it is absolutely necessary. It is recommended for those present at the graveside to sprinkle three scoops of earth; thereafter, the grave is filled in. The majority of the scholars recommended to instruct the deceased after the burial (i.e. the answers for the questions in the grave). It is recommended to sprinkle water on the grave and raise the grave's surface by one hand span.

The following things are reprehensible to do: to adorn the grave; to plaster it; to perfume it with incense; to kiss it; to circumambulate it; to lean on it; to sleep by the graveside; to laugh by it; to speak about worldly matters; to place an inscription on the grave; to sit on it, to build over it; and for one to walk around with footwear unless one feared thorns and its likes.

فصل

وحملُهُ ودفنُهُ: فرضُ كفايةٍ، لكن يسقطُ الحملُ، والدفنُ، والتكفينُ بالكافرِ. ويكرهُ: أخذُ الأجرةِ على ذلك، وعلى الغسلِ.

وسنَّ: كونُ الماشي أمامَ الجنازةِ، والراكبِ خلفهَا. والقربُ مِنها، أفضلُ. ويكرهُ: القيامُ لها ورفعُ الصوتِ معها، ولو بالذكرِ، والقرآنِ.

وسنَّ: أنْ يعمقُ القبرُ، ويوسعَ بلا حدٍّ، ويكفِي: ما يمنعُ السباعَ، والرائحةَ. وكرهَ: إدخالُ القبرِ خشباً، وما مستهُ نارٌ، ووضعُ فراشٍ تحتَهُ، وجعلُ مخدةٍ تحتَ رأسِهِ.

وسنَّ: قولُ مدخلِهِ القبرَ: (بِسمِ اللّهِ، وَعَلى مِلَّةِ رَسُولِ اللّهِ). ويجبُ: أنْ يستقبلَ بِهِ القبلةَ، ويسنُّ على جنبِهِ الأيمنِ.

ويحرمُ: دفنُ غيرِهِ عليهِ، أو معهُ إلا لضرورةٍ. ويسنُ: حثوُ الترابِ عليهِ ثلاثاً، ثمَّ يهالُ. واستحبَّ الأكثرُ تلقينَهُ بعدَ الدفنِ. وسنَّ: رشُّ القبرِ بالماءِ، ورفعُهُ قدرَ شبرٍ.

ويكرَهُ: تزويقُهُ، وتجصيصُهُ، وتبخيرُهُ، وتقبيلُهُ، والطوافُ بِهِ، والإتكاءُ إليهِ، والمبيتُ، والضحكُ عندَهُ، والحديثُ في أمرِ الدنيا، والكتابةُ عليهِ، والجلوسُ، والبناءُ، والمشيُ بالنعلِ، إلا لخوفِ شوكٍ ونحوِهِ.

It is prohibited to place lamps over graves. It is also prohibited to bury the dead within mosques and in someone else's property – such buried corpses are unearthed and exhumed. It is best to bury the dead in an open area.

If a pregnant woman passed away, it is prohibited to open up her womb (to bring out the child). However, if the child is believed to be alive, other females can bring out the child. If it was impossible to bring out the child, the mother's burial is not carried out until the child passes away. If the child was out of the mother's womb partly and was still alive, the rest of the womb can be opened up.

ويحرمُ: إسراجُ المقابرِ، والدفنُ بالمساجدِ، وفي ملكِ الغيرِ، وينبشُ. والدفنُ بالصحراءِ، أفضلُ.

وإنْ ماتتِ الحاملُ حرمَ شقُّ بطنِها. وأخرجَ النساءُ مَن ترجَى حياتُهُ، فإنْ تعذرَ لم تدفنْ حتى يموتَ، وإنْ خرجَ بعضُهَ حيًا، شقَّ للباقي.

Consoling the Deceased's Relatives

It is recommended to console Muslims for a period of three days. The following dictum is said to the one afflicted by a death in the family: 'May Allāh greaten your reward, perfect your consolation, and forgive your deceased.' The one afflicted replies: 'May Allāh respond to your supplications, and may Allāh have mercy on you and us.'

There is no problem in weeping for someone who passed away. It is prohibited to eulogise the dead, namely, to weep and to enumerate praises for the deceased. It is prohibited to lament, that is, to raise one's voice in eulogising the dead with (high-pitched) sounds. Similarly, it is prohibited to rip off one's garments; to slap one's cheeks; to scream; to pull out, dishevel, and shave one's hair.

It is recommended for men to visit graves and reprehensible for women. However, if a woman passed by a grave on her way, and she sent her greetings and made supplications for the deceased, then it will be fine.

For the one visiting graves or passing by graves, it is recommended to say:

> Believers of this abode, peace be unto you. Allāh willing, we will be joining you. Allāh have mercy on all of you – the preceding ones and the later ones! We ask Allāh to keep you and us safe and protected. Allāh, do not deprive us of their reward nor put us into trial after them. Allāh, forgive them and us.

It is recommended to initiate the greeting of peace when encountering someone living; but replying to the greeting of peace is a communal obligation.

If one praised Allāh after sneezing, it is a communal obligation to implore Allāh to have mercy on the person; however, the response to this dictum by the one who sneezed is an individual obligation.

فصل

تسنُّ: تعزيةُ المسلمِ إلى ثلاثةِ أيامٍ، فيقالُ له: (أَعظَمَ اللّهُ أَجْرَكَ، وَأَحْسَنَ عزَاءَكَ، وَغَفَرَ لِمَيِّتِكَ). ويقولُ هوَ: (استَجَابَ اللّهُ دُعَاءَكَ، وَرَحِمَنَا وَإِيَّاكَ).

ولا بأسَ: بالبكاءِ على الميتِ. ويحرمُ: الندبُ، وهو: البكاءُ مع تعدادِ محاسنِ الميتِ، والنياحةُ وهي: رفعُ الصوتِ بذلك برنةٍ. ويحرمُ شقُّ الثوبِ، ولطمُ الخدِّ، والصراخُ، ونتفُ الشعرِ، ونشرُهُ وحلقُهُ.

وتسنُّ: زيارةُ القبورِ للرجالِ، وتكرهُ للنساءِ، وإنْ اجتازتْ المرأةُ بقبرٍ في طريقِها، فسلمتْ عليهِ، ودعتْ له فحسنٌ.

وسنَّ: لمَنْ زارَ القبورَ أو مرَّ بها أن يقولَ: (السَّلامُ عَلَيْكُم دَارَ قَومٍ مُؤْمِنِينَ، وَإِنَّا إنْ شَاءَ اللّهُ بِكُمْ لَلاحِقُونَ، وَيَرْحَمُ اللّهُ المُسْتَقْدِمِينَ مِنْكُمْ وَالمُسْتَأْخِرِينَ، نَسْأَلُ اللّهُ لَنَا وَلَكُم العَافِيَةَ. اللَّهُمَّ لا تَحْرِمْنَا أَجْرَهُمْ، وَلَا تَفْتِنَّا بَعْدَهُم، واغْفِرْ لَنَا وَلَهُمْ).

وابتداءُ السلامِ على الحيِّ: سنةٌ، وردُّهُ فرضُ كفايةٍ.

وتشميتُ العاطسِ - إذا حمدَ - فرضُ كفايةٍ. وردُّهُ: فرضُ عينٍ.

The deceased are aware of their visitors on Fridays, before sunrise. The deceased are harmed by objectionable acts in their presence, and profit and benefit from good actions.

ويعرفُ الميتُ زائرَهُ يومَ الجمعةِ، قبلَ طلوعِ الشمسِ. ويتأذَى بالمنكرِ عندَهُ، وينتفعُ بالخيرِ.

Obligatory Charity

There are five pre-requisites for *zakāt* to be obligatory:

- Islam; non-Muslims are not obliged to pay *zakāt,* even apostates from Islam
- Freedom; slaves are not obliged to pay *zakāt* nor *mukātab*s.[73] Partly owned slaves are required to pay *zakāt* according to their proportion of ownership
- Ownership of the *zakāt*-threshold; approximately for gold and silver,[74] and precisely for others
- Complete possession of the wealth;

Consequently, a master of a slave is not required to pay *zakāt* on debts owed to him when a slave decides to buy his freedom from him with deferred payments (*kitaba*). The same is the case for the share of a silent business partner's (*muḍārib*) profits; *zakāt* is not obligatory on it before it is shared out.

- Passing of a lunar year; there is no harm if the year fell short by half a day

It is obligatory to levy *zakāt* from the wealth of a child and an insane person.

The *zakāt* is levied from five things: free-grazing livestock; agricultural produce; honey; currency; and trade goods. Owed debts that decrease the wealth to levels below the *zakāt*-threshold rescind the obligation of *zakāt.* If a person passes away owing some *zakāt,* it is paid from his estate.

73 *Mukātab* is a slave who purchases himself from his master with deferred wealth that he earns.

74 This implies that if the *zakāt*-threshold falls slightly below the mark for gold and silver, it will not prevent a person from paying the *zakāt.* In other words, one is still required to pay. However, this is not the case for the *zakāt*-thresholds of other types of wealth; if they happen to fall below their marks, one is not required to pay the *zakāt.*

كتاب الزكاة

شرطُ وجوبِها خمسةُ أشياءَ:

- أحدُها: الإسلامُ، فلا تجبُ على الكافرِ، ولو مرتدًا.
- الثاني: الحريةُ، فلا تجبُ على الرقيقِ، ولو مكاتباً، لكن تجبُ على المبعضِ بقدرِ ملكِهِ.
- الثالثُ: ملكُ النصابِ تقريباً في الأثمانِ، وتحديداً في غيرِهَا.
- الرابعُ: الملكُ التامُّ، فلا زكاةَ على السيدِ في دينِ الكتابةِ، ولا في حصةِ المضاربِ، قبلَ القسمةِ.
- الخامسُ: تمامُ الحولِ، ولا يضرُّ لو نقصَ نصفَ يومٍ.

وتجبُ: في مالِ الصغيرِ، والمجنونِ.

وهي، في خمسةِ أشياءَ: في سائمةِ بهيمةِ الأنعامِ، وفي الخارجِ مِن الأرضِ، وفى العسلِ، وفي الأثمانِ، وفي عروضِ التجارةِ. ويمنعُ: وجوبَها دينٌ، ينقصُ النصابَ. ومَن ماتَ وعليهِ زكاةٌ، أخذتْ مِن تركتِهِ.

Free-Grazing Livestock

There are three pre-requisites for *zakāt* to be obligatory for free-grazing livestock:

- One acquires the free-gazing livestock for its milk, offspring, and to fatten up; but not for work purposes
- The animals graze freely; that is, on open range pasturage for most of the year
- The number of animals reaches the *zakāt*-threshold

Camel

The minimum *zakāt*-threshold for it is five camels for which a sheep is due. And thereafter for every five camels, there is a sheep payable until the number reaches twenty-five. A one-year old female camel (*bint makhāḍ*) is payable for twenty-five camels; a two-year old female camel (*bint labūn*) is payable for thirty-six camels; a three-year old female camel (*ḥiqqa*) is payable for forty-six camels; a four-year old camel (*jadhaʿ*) is payable for sixty-one camels; two *bint labūn*s are payable for seventy-six camels; two *ḥiqqa*s are payable for ninety-one camels; and three *bint labūn*s are payable for one-hundred and twenty-one camels and above until its number reaches one-hundred and thirty. Thereafter, a *bint labūn* is payable on every forty camels, and one *ḥiqqa* on every fifty camels.

Cattle

The minimum *zakāt*-threshold for cattle is thirty, whether domestic or wild. On cattle, the *zakāt* payable on every thirty head is a male yearling (*tabīʿ*). On forty head, a two-year-old female (*musinna*) is due. On sixty head, two male yearlings are due. Thereafter, a male yearling (*tabīʿ*) is payable on every thirty, and a two-year-old female (*musinna*) on every forty head.

باب زكاة السائمة

تجبُ فيها بثلاثةِ شروطٍ:

- أحدُها: أنْ تتخذَ للدرِ، والنسلِ، والتسمينِ، لا للعملِ.
- الثاني: أنْ تسومَ، أي: ترعى المباحَ أكثرَ الحولِ.
- الثالثُ: أنْ تبلغَ نصاباً.

[الإبل]

فأقلُّ نصابِ الإبلِ خمسٌ، وفيهَا شاةٌ، ثمَّ في كلِّ خمسٍ شاةٌ، إلى خمسٍ وعشرينَ: فتجبُ بنتُ مخاضٍ: وهي ما تمَّ لها سنةٌ، وفي ستٍّ وثلاثينَ: بنتُ لبونٍ، لها سنتانِ، وفي ستٍّ وأربعينَ: حقةٌ، لها ثلاثُ سنينَ، وفي إحدى وستينَ جذعهٌ، لها أربعُ سنينَ، وفي ستٍّ وسبعينَ. بنتا لبونٍ، وفي إحدَى وتسعينَ: حقتانِ، وفي مائةٍ وإحدى وعشرينَ: ثلاثُ بناتِ لبونٍ، إلى مائةٍ وثلاثينَ، فيستقرُّ في كلِّ أربعينَ: بنتُ لبونٍ وفي كلِّ خمسينَ: حقةٌ.

[البقر]

وأقلُّ نصابِ البقرِ - أهليةً كانتْ، أو وحشيةً - ثلاثونَ، وفيها: تبيعٌ، وهو ما له سنةٌ، وفي أربعينَ: مسنةٌ لها سنتانِ، وفى ستينَ: تبيعانِ، ثمَّ في كلِّ ثلاثينَ: تبيعٌ، وفي كلِّ أربعينَ: مسنةٌ.

Sheep and goats

The minimum *zakāt*-threshold for sheep and goats is forty, whether domestic or wild. On forty sheep, the *zakāt* payable is a one-year old female goat or a half-year-old lamb. Two are payable for one hundred and twenty-one sheep and goats; three are payable for two hundred and one; and four are payable for four hundred. Thereafter, one is payable on every one hundred sheep and goats.

[الغنم]

وأقلُّ نصابِ الغنمِ - أهليةً كانتْ أو وحشيةً - أربعونَ وفيها: شاةٌ، لها سنةٌ، أو جذعةُ ضأنٍ لها: ستةُ أشهرٍ، وفي مائةٍ وإحدى وعشرينَ: شاتانِ، وفي مائتينِ وواحدةٍ: ثلاثُ شياهٍ، وفي أربعمائةٍ: أربعُ شياهٍ، ثمَّ في كلِّ مائةٍ: شاةٌ.

Joint ownership of Livestock

Two or more people pay *zakāt* jointly as a single person if they jointly own a *zakāt*-threshold amount of livestock for an entire year. Secondly, if they jointly share the following: the same place to bed them down; to gather the livestock before grazing; to milk the animals; to share the same stud; and if they jointly shared the same pasture.

It is not a pre-requisite for an intention to be stipulated for joint ownership of livestock. Similarly, it is not a pre-requisite to jointly share watering holes, have the same shepherd, or the same stud if the animal type was different, for example cows with buffalos or sheep with goats.

Joint ownership in livestock can sometimes be heavier [on the parties] or lighter. Example of the former is when two people jointly own forty sheep, and individually own twenty sheep; in such a case, a one-year old female goat or a half-year-old lamb is binding to pay between the two. Example of the latter is when three people jointly own one hundred and twenty sheep, and individually own forty sheep; in such a scenario, a one-year old female goat or a half-year-old lamb is binding to pay but between the three partners.[75]

The division of wealth has no effect, as long as the wealth being divided is not livestock. If one's livestock is situated in two different locations and the distance between them is enough for prayers to be shortened, then the animals at each location are treated as separate entities.[76] Therefore, if one has

75 In the first case, without the joint partnership, *zakāt* will not be obligatory for either of them because individually they are both below the minimum *zakāt*-threshold number for sheep and goats, namely forty. In the second case, without the joint partnership, each individual is required to pay a one-year old female goat or a half-year-old lamb as the minimum *zakāt*-threshold number was met by each of them.

76 For instance, if location X has thirty-nine sheep and location Y has another thirty-nine sheep, and one person owned them all. The owner of the total seventy-eight sheep is not required to pay *zakāt* because the distance between the locations is enough for prayers to be shortened; regardless of collectively going beyond the minimum *zakāt*-threshold for sheep.

فصل

وإذا اختلطَ اثنانِ فأكثرُ مِن أهلِ الزكاةِ في نصابِ ماشيةٍ لهم جميعَ الحولِ، واشتركَا في المبيتِ، والمسرحِ، والمحلبِ والفحلِ، والمرعَى، زكيَا كالواحدِ.

ولا تشترطُ: نيةُ الخلطةِ، ولا اتحادُ المشربِ والراعِي، ولا اتحادُ الفحلِ، إن اختلفَ النوعُ: كالبقرِ، والجاموسِ، والضأنِ، والمعزِ.

وقد تفيدُ الخلطةُ تغليظاً: كاثنينِ اختلطَا بأربعينَ شاةً: لكلِّ واحدٍ عشرونَ؛ فيلزمُهُما شاةٌ وتخفيفًا، كثلاثةٍ اختلطوا بمائةٍ وعشرينَ شاةً لكلِّ واحد أربعونَ، فيلزمُهم شاةٌ.

ولا أثرَ لتفرقةِ المالِ، ما لم يكنْ سائمةً. فإنْ كان سائمةً بمحلينِ، بينهما مسافةُ قصرٍ، فلكلِّ حكمٌ بنفسِهِ، فإذا كان له [...]

sheep in a number of separate locations and each location has forty sheep, then one must pay *zakāt* according to the number of locations. If the number of sheep does not reach forty in each of the separate locations, one is not required to pay *zakāt* – that is, as long as there is no joint ownership in place.

This is a solitary opinion within the Ḥanbalī school.

شياهٌ بمحالَّ متباعدةٍ، في كلِّ محلٍّ أربعونَ، فعليهِ شياهٌ بعددِ المحالِّ. ولا شيءَ عليهِ إنْ لم يجتمعْ في كلِّ محلٍّ أربعونَ، ما لم يكنْ خلطةً.

Agricultural Produce

Zakāt is obligatory for all types of grains and fruits which can be measured by volume and stored. Examples of grains include: wheat, barley, maize, rice, chickpeas, lentils, broad beans, vetch seeds, sesame seeds, millet, caraway seeds, coriander seeds, cottonseed, flaxseed, watermelon seeds, and its likes. Examples of fruits include: dates, raisins, almonds, pistachios, hazelnuts, and sumac. There is no *zakāt* due on the following: jujubes, olives, walnuts, figs, apricots, buckthorn berries, hawthorn fruits, and pomegranates.

Zakāt is obligatory on grains and fruits if two pre-requisites are fulfilled:

- Once the grains have been winnowed (i.e. made free of straw) and fruits have been dried, the net dried weight of the products reaches its *zakāt*-threshold of 5 *awsuq*[77]
- One owns the produce at the time it's due; namely, when grains become firm and fruits appear ripe

77 The author mentioned 5 *awsuq* which is equivalent to 300 *ṣāʿ*. One *ṣāʿ* is equivalent to 2.06 kilogram (The Council of Senior Scholars, KSA), making 300 *ṣāʿ* a total of 612 kilograms. The author also provided some equivalences in Egyptian, Iraqi and Damascene measures which were in use during his era; all have been omitted in the translation as the measure in kilograms suffices the intended meaning of the author.

باب زكاة الخارج من الأرض

تجبُ: في كلِّ مكيلٍ مدخرٍ مِن الحبِّ، كالقمحِ، والشعيرِ، والذرةِ، والأرزِ، والحمصِ، والعدسِ، والباقلَّا، والكرسنةِ، والسمسمِ، والدخنِ، والكراويا، والكزبرةِ، وبزرِ القطنِ، والكتانِ، والبطيخِ، ونحوِهِ، ومِن الثمرِ: كالتمرِ، والزبيبِ، واللوزِ، والفستقِ، والبندقِ والسماقِ. ولا زكاةَ في عنابٍ، وزيتونٍ، وجوزٍ، وتينٍ، ومشمشٍ، ونبقٍ، وزعرورٍ، ورمانٍ.

وإنما تجبُ فيما تجبُ بشرطينِ:

- الأولُ: أنْ يبلغَ نصابًا وقدرُهُ - بعدَ تصفيةِ الحبِّ وجفافِ الثمرِ - خمسةُ أوسقٍ وهيَ: ثلاثمائةِ صاعٍ، وبالأرادبِّ: ستةٌ وربعٌ، وبالرطلِ العراقيِّ: ألفٌ وستمائةٍ، وبالقدسيِّ: مائتانِ وسبعةٌ وخمسونَ، وسبعُ رطلٍ.
- الثاني: أنْ يكونَ مالكاً للنصابِ وقتَ وجوبِها. فوقتُ الوجوبِ في الحبِّ إذا اشتدَّ، وفى الثمرةِ، إذا بداَ صلاحُها.

Subsection

It is obligatory to pay 10 per cent of the produce which has been watered without effort, and 5 per cent of the produce which has been watered with effort. One must set aside seeds for *zakāt* once they have been winnowed, and fruits once they have been dried. If one contradicts and does it while it's ripe, then the payment will not suffice and it will be considered as a voluntary charity.

Once date palms and orchards begin to bear fruit, it is recommended for the sultan to send out surveyors to estimate crop yields. It is sufficient to send one person as long as the surveyor is Muslim, trustworthy, and experienced. The owners pay for the surveyor's wage. Once the time nears to pay the *zakāt,* the sultan must send out couriers to collect *zakāt* from the owner's 'apparent wealth'.

On taxable lands (*al-arḍ al-kharājiyya*), one pays the 10 per cent (*ʿushr*) for agricultural produce as well the land tax (*kharāj*). Taxable lands are lands which were captured by force and were not divided between the Muslim fighters; examples of such lands include Egypt, Levant, and Iraq. It is invalid for owners to be made responsible (to pay a set amount) on the wealth of taxable lands and on wealth of the 10 per cent.

One pays 10 per cent on honey; the *zakāt*-threshold for honey is 160 Iraqi *ritl*s.[78]

One pays 20 per cent on treasures (*rikāz*), that is, buried treasures even if the discovered amount is little. Debts do not rescind the obligation of paying the 20 per cent on treasures.

78 The author mentioned 160 Iraqi *ritl*s which is equivalent to 30 *ṣāʿ*. One *ṣāʿ* is equivalent to 2.06 kilograms, making 30 *ṣāʿ* a total of 61.8 kilograms.

فصل

ويجبُ: فيما يسقى بلا كلفةٍ: العشرُ، وفيما يسقى بكلفةٍ: نصفُ العشرِ. ويجبُ: إخراجُ زكاةِ الحبِّ: مصفًّى، والثمرِ: يابساً، فلو خالفَ وأخرجَ رطباً لم يجزِهِ، ووقعَ نفلاً.

وسنَّ: للإمامِ بعثُ خارصٍ لثمرةِ النخلِ والكرمِ، إذا بدا صلاحُها، ويكفِي واحدٌ، وشرطَ: كونُهُ مسلماً، أميناً، خبيراً، وأجرتُهُ على ربِّ الثمرةِ. ويجبُ، عليهِ: بعثُ السعاةِ قربَ الوجوبِ، لقبضِ زكاةِ المالِ الظاهرِ.

ويجتمعُ العشرُ، والخراجُ في الأرضِ الخراجيةِ، وهي ما فتحتْ عنوةً، ولم تقسمْ بين الغانمينَ، كمصرَ، والشامِ والعراقِ. وتضمينُ أموالِ العشرِ، والأرضِ الخراجيةِ، باطلٌ.

وفي العسلِ: العشرُ ونصابُهُ: مائةٌ وستونَ رطلاً عراقيةً.

وفي الركازِ: وهو الكنزُ ولو قليلاً: الخمسُ، ولا يمنعُ مِن وجوبِهِ الدينُ.

Currency

It is namely gold and silver. On currency, 2.5 percent is payable upon reaching its *zakāt*-threshold. The *zakāt*-threshold for gold is 85 grams (20 *mithqāl*), on which 2.12 grams is payable (2.5 percent). For silver, the *zakāt*-threshold is 595 grams (200 *dirham*), on which 14.87 grams is payable (2.5 percent).[79] Gold and silver are added together to complete the *zakāt*-threshold for currency; one can pay the *zakāt* amount in gold or silver.

One is not required to pay *zakāt* on permissible jewellery prepared for personal use or for lending.

However, *zakāt* is obligatory on forbidden jewellery; similarly, it is obligatory on permissible jewellery which is prepared for renting or set aside for maintenance costs. Once the threshold has been met in weight, the value of the *zakāt* is paid, if it is more.[80]

---

79 Again, I have converted the author's medieval measurements and conversions to modern measurements for practicality and ease.

80 Weight is used to determine the threshold amount, and the value is used to determine the payment. Here, a person weighs the jewellery item to determine whether it has reached the threshold amount; if it exceeds the threshold amount, one pays on the value. On the contrary, if the threshold is not met in weight but its value exceeds the threshold amount, one is not obliged to pay the *zakāt*. For example, if one has a gold chain weighing 85 grams and its value is worth 200 grams of gold, one pays 2.5 percent on the value. On the other hand, if the gold chain weighs 60 grams and its value is worth 300 grams of gold, one will not be required to pay because the threshold in weight was not met, although it was reached in value.

باب زكاة الأثمان

وهى: الذهبُ والفضةُ. وفيها: ربعُ العشرِ، إذا بلغتْ نصاباً. فنصابُ الذهبِ بالمثاقيلِ: عشرونَ مثقالاً، وبالدنانيرِ: خمسةٌ وعشرونَ، وسبعًا دينارٍ وتسعُ دينارٍ. ونصابُ الفضةِ: مائتا درهمٍ، والدرهمُ: اثنتا عشرةَ حبةَ خروبٍ، والمثقالُ درهمٌ، وثلاثةُ أسباعِ درهمٍ. ويضمُّ الذهبُ إلى الفضةِ في تكميلِ النصابِ، ويخرجُ مِن أيهما شاءَ.

ولا زكاةَ في حليٍّ مباحٍ، معدٍّ لاستعمالٍ، أو إعارةٍ.

وتجبُ: في الحليِّ المحرمِ، وكذا في المباحِ المعدِّ للكراءِ، أو النفقةِ؛ إذا بلغَ نصاباً وزناً، ويخرجُ عن قيمتِهِ، إن زادتْ.

Subsection

It is prohibited to adorn mosques with gold or silver. Silver rings are permissible for men even if the silver content is more than 4.25 grams; it is best to wear it on the little finger of the left hand. Men can adorn the pommel of the sword only, even with gold. Likewise, it is permissible to adorn one's belt, chainmail, and helmet. The stirrup of a saddle, the bit of a bridle, and inkwells are impermissible to adorn with silver.

Gold and silver are permissible for women for whatever is customary for them to wear, even if the quantity happens to be over 4.25 kilograms worth. It is permissible for men and women to adorn themselves with jewels, pearls, and emeralds. It is reprehensible for them to wear rings made from iron, lead, and copper; however, rings made with carnelian gemstones are recommended to wear.

فصل

وتحرمُ: تحليةُ المسجدِ بذهبٍ، أو فضةٍ. ويباحُ: للذكرِ مِن الفضةِ الخاتم، ولو زادَ على مثقالٍ، وجعلُهُ بخنصِرِ يسارٍ، أفضلُ. وتباحُ: قبيعةُ السيفِ فقطْ، ولو مِن ذهبٍ، وحليةُ المنطقةِ، والجوشنِ، والخوذةِ، لا الركابِ، واللجامِ، والدواةِ.

ويباحُ للنساءِ: ما جرتْ عادتُهُنَّ بلبسِهِ، ولو زادَ على ألفِ مثقالٍ. وللرجلِ، والمرأةِ: التحليُّ بالجوهرِ، والياقوتِ والزبرجدِ. وكرِهَ: تختمُهما بالحديدِ، والرصاصِ، والنحاسِ ويستحبُّ بالعقيقِ.

Trade Goods

Trade goods are things prepared for buying and selling in order to make a profit. Once the *zakāt* year passes, the trade goods are assessed; the *zakāt* year begins when the trade good's market value reaches the *zakāt*-threshold of gold or silver; one selects between them according to whatever is best for the poor. A *zakāt* of 2.5 percent is obligatory to pay if the trade goods' value reaches the *zakāt*-threshold; otherwise, one is not obliged to pay. The same pertains to the wealth of money-exchangers.[81]

The value of silver and gold utensils are disregarded (when trade goods are being assessed), rather their weight is taken account of instead. The same applies to anything which has had elements of unlawful manufacturing processes applied to it; assessments for *zakāt* are made without taking such elements into account.

If one owns goods for trade or acquires it as inheritance but intends to keep it for personal use, and then decides to trade with it, such goods will not be treated as trade goods as soon as an intention is made. However, this is not the case for jewellery items.

A 2.5 percent *zakāt* is due immediately on anything extracted from mines; that is, if the value reaches the *zakāt*-threshold after the ore is refined.

---

81 The author mentioned an issue which was common during his era; the applicable currencies used to be weighed. This of course is not applicable in modern times as the money-exchanges deal with paper money.

باب زكاة العروض

وهي ما يعدُّ للبيعِ، والشراءِ، لأجلِ الربحِ، فتقومُ إذا حالَ الحولُ، وأولُهُ مِن حِينِ بلوغِ القيمةِ نصاباً بالأحظِّ للمساكينِ مِن ذهبٍ أو فضةٍ. فإنْ بلغتْ القيمةُ نصاباً، وجبَ ربعُ العشرِ، وإلَّا فلا، وكذَا أموالُ الصيارفِ.

ولا عبرةَ بقيمةِ آنيةِ الذهبِ، والفضةِ، بل بوزنِها، ولا بِما فيهِ صناعةٌ محرمةٌ، فيقومُ عارياً عنها.

ومَن عندَهُ عرضٌ للتجارةِ، أو ورثَهُ، فنواهُ للقنيةِ، ثمَّ نواهُ للتجارةِ، لم يصرْ عرضاً بمجردِ النيةِ، غير حليِّ اللبسِ.

وما استخرجَ مِن المعادنِ، ففِيهِ بمجردِ إحرازِهِ: ربعُ العشرِ، إنْ بلغتِ القيمةُ نصاباً بعدَ السبكِ، والتصفيةِ.

Zakāt al-fiṭr

Zakāt al-fiṭr becomes obligatory on the night before *ʿīd.* If one passes away before sunset or it becomes too difficult for one to pay before sunset, then one is not required to pay, otherwise the obligation remains.

Zakāt al-fiṭr is obligatory for every Muslim, provided that one has an excess amount of what one needs to feed oneself and one's family on the night before *ʿīd* and on *ʿīd* itself; and after meeting one's basic needs, for example, to sustain one's house, servant, vehicle, the clothes one requires (i.e. for work purposes), and one's books of knowledge.

The payment is binding for oneself and for any Muslim one supports. If one does not have enough to pay for them all, then one begins by paying one's own, then that of one's wife, slave, mother, father, children, and then the closest according to the rules of inheritance.

If one undertakes the responsibility of supporting another person during Ramadan, then it is obligatory to pay *zakāt al-fiṭr* for the person. But, this is not the case for a person that one hires as a labourer in return for food. It is recommended to pay *zakāt al-fiṭr* for a fetus.

باب زكاة الفطر

تجبُ: بأولِ ليلةِ العيدِ، فمَن ماتَ أو أعسرَ قبلَ الغروبِ، فلا زكاةَ عليهِ، وبعدَهُ تستقرُّ في ذمتِهِ.

وهي واجبةٌ على كلِّ مسلمٍ، يجدُ ما يفضلُ عن قوتِهِ، وقوتِ عيالِهِ يومَ العيدِ وليلتَهُ، بعدَ ما يحتاجُهُ مِن مسكنٍ وخادمٍ، ودابةٍ، وثيابِ بذلةٍ، وكتبِ علمٍ.

وتلزمُهُ: عن نفسِهِ، وعن مَن يمونُهُ مِن المسلمِينَ. فإنْ لم يجِد لجميعِهم بدأَ بنفسِهِ، فزوجتِهِ، فرقيقِهِ، فأمِّهِ، فأبيهِ، فولدِهِ، فأقرَبَ في الميراثِ.

وتجبُ على مَن تبرعَ بمؤنةِ شخصٍ شهرَ رمضانَ، لا على مَن استأجرَ أجيراً بطعامِهِ. وتسنُّ: عن الجنينِ.

Subsection

It is best to pay *zakāt al-fiṭr* on the day of *ʿīd* before the prayer, whereas paying it after the prayer is reprehensible. It is prohibited to delay the payment beyond the day of *ʿīd,* that is, if one was capable of doing it earlier, and for which one must make it up. It is permissible to pay *zakāt al-fiṭr* two days in advance.

One must either pay one *ṣāʾ* (2.06 kilograms) of dried dates, raisins, wheat, barley or cheese made from sour milk. The flour from wheat and barley is acceptable providing the flour weighs the same as its grains. If the aforementioned foodstuff is unavailable, then one substitutes them with other staple grains, for example the likes of maize, millet, and broad beans.

A group of people can give their *zakāt al-fiṭr* to one person; similarly, one person may give to a group of people.

Paying the value of *zakāt al-fiṭr* does not suffice under any circumstance.

It is prohibited for one to purchase one's *zakāt* or voluntary charity – even if one purchases from someone other than the person it was donated to.

فصل

والأفضلُ: إخراجُها يومَ العيدِ قبلَ الصلاةِ، وتكرهُ بعدَها، ويحرمُ: تأخيرُها عن يومِ العيدِ مع القدرةِ، ويقضيها. وتجزىء: قبلَ العيدِ، بيومينِ.

والواجبُ: عن كلِّ شخصٍ صاعُ تمرٍ، أو زبيبٍ، أو برٍّ أو شعيرٍ، أو أقطٍ. ويجزىءُ: دقيقُ البرِّ، والشعيرِ، إذا كانَ وزنَ الحبِّ. ويخرجُ مع عدمِ ذلك ما يقومُ مقامَهُ مِن حبٍّ يقتاتُ، كذرةٍ، ودخنٍ، وباقلَّا.

ويجوزُ: أنْ يعطيَ الجماعةُ فطرتَهم لواحدٍ، وأنْ يعطيَ الواحدُ فطرتَهُ لجماعةٍ.

ولا يجزىءُ: إخراجُ القيمةِ في الزكاةِ مطلقاً.

ويحرمُ: على الشخصِ شراءُ زكاتِهِ وصدقتِهِ، ولو اشتراها مِن غيرِ مَن أخذَها مِنهُ.

Paying *Zakāt*

It is obligatory to pay the *zakāt* straightaway just like the payments for vows and expiations. It is permissible for one to delay the payment for a time of need or if one anticipates paying the *zakāt* to a relative or a neighbour. One can delay payment because of difficulties in arranging the due amount from one's *zakāt*-threshold capital, even if one has other means to pay.

One becomes a non-Muslim if one knowingly denies the obligation of paying *zakāt*, even with payment; but if one refuses to pay out of stinginess or carelessness, it is taken by force and the person is chastised. If one claims to have paid the *zakāt* or that one's *zakāt*-year is incomplete or that one is below the *zakāt*-threshold amount or that one no longer owns the wealth, then in such scenarios the person's claims are accepted without an oath. For children and insane individuals, it is binding for the guardian to pay *zakāt* on their behalf.

It is recommended for the owner to pay *zakāt* openly and distribute it, and while it is being handed out, one supplicates, 'Allāh, make it fruitful, and not futile.' The recipient responds, 'Allāh reward you for what you have given, bless you in what you have retained, and make it a means of purification.'

باب إخراج الزكاة

يجبُ: إخراجُها فوراً كالنذرِ والكفارةِ، ولهُ تأخيرُها لزمنِ حاجةٍ، ولقريبٍ وجارٍ، ولتعذرِ إخراجِها مِن النصابِ ولو قدرَ أنْ يخرِجَها مِن غيرِه.

ومَن جحدَ وجوبَها عالماً: كفرَ، ولو أخرجَها. ومَن منعَها بخلاً وتهاوُنا؛ أخذتْ مِنهُ، وعزِّرَ. ومِن ادعى إخراجَها، أو بقاءَ الحولِ، أو نقصَ النصابِ، أو زوالَ الملكِ؛ صدقَ بلا يمينٍ. ويلزمُ: أنْ يخرجَ عنِ الصغيرِ، والمجنونِ وليهُما.

ويسنُّ: إظهارُها وأنْ يفرقَها ربُّها بنفسِهِ، ويقولُ عندَ دفعها: (اللَّهُمَّ اجْعَلهَا مَغْنَماً، ولا تَجْعَلْهَا مَغْرَماً)، ويقولُ الآخذُ: (آجَرَكَ اللهُ فِيمَا أَعْطَيْتَ، وَبَارَكَ لَكَ فِيمَا أَبْقَيْتَ، وَجَعَلَهُ لَكَ طَهُوراً).

Subsection

The intention from a legally accountable person is a pre-requisite to pay the *zakāt.* It is permissible to make the intention shortly before the payment, although it is best to make it when the *zakāt* is being paid. A person makes the intention to give the payment as the *zakāt* or as the obligatory alms. Therefore, if he made an intention to give it as a general donation, it will not suffice – even if all of his wealth is donated in this manner. A person is not required to specify in one's intention that the *zakāt* is obligatory or specify which wealth his payment is for. If a person assigns a Muslim to make the payment, his intention will suffice as long as the payment follows shortly; otherwise, the deputy will also need to make the intention.

It is best to give all of the payments of *zakāt* to the poor of one's locality. Transferring the payment to another place beyond the distance for shortening one's prayers is prohibited, but nevertheless it will suffice.

Paying the *zakāt* in advance of a maximum of two years is permissible, that is, if someone reaches the *zakāt*-threshold; otherwise, it will not be acceptable to pay for the two years. If the *zakāt*-threshold amount gets destroyed or it diminishes, the advance payment becomes a voluntary donation.

فصل

ويشترطُ لإخراجِها نيةٌ مِن مكلفٍ، ولهُ تقديمُها بيسيرٍ، والأفضلُ: قرنُها بالدفعِ، فينوِي الزكاةَ أو الصدقةَ الواجبةَ، ولا يجزيءُ: إنْ نوى صدقةً مطلقةً ولو تصدقَ بجميعِ مالِهِ. ولا تجبُ: نيةُ الفرضيةِ، ولا تعيينُ المالِ المزكَّى عنهُ. وإنْ وكلَ في إخراجِها مسلمًا، أجزأتْ نيةُ الموكلِ مع قربِ الإخراجِ، وإلا نوى الوكيلُ أيضاً.

والأفضلُ: جعلُ زكاةِ كلِّ مالٍ في فقراءِ بلدِهِ، ويحرمُ نقلُها إلى مسافةِ قصرٍ، وتجزئُ.

ويصحُّ: تعجيلُ الزكاةِ لحولينِ فقطْ، إذا كمل النصابُ، لا منه للحولين، فإنْ تلف النصابُ أو نقصَ وقعَ نفلاً.

The Recipients of *Zakāt*

The recipients of *zakāt* are of eight categories:

- the poor; people who have less than half of what one needs
- the needy; people who have half or more than half of what one needs
- the administrators of *zakāt*; for example, its collectors, treasurers, clerks, and its distributors
- those whose hearts need winning over;

Namely, for the chief personage of tribes: who is hoped to enter Islam; or whose evil is feared; or whose Islam may be strengthened if already Muslim; or those who have the ability to recover it from those who would not normally pay.

- slaves purchasing their freedom;
- those in debt; debtors who borrowed money to reconcile between people or borrowed for themselves and are in financial straits
- the fighters in Allāh's cause;
- the travellers who are stranded in a foreign place

The *zakāt* is given to every category according to their needs, except for the administrators of *zakāt,* who receive according to their wages – whether one is rich or a slave. If the payment is given to Khawārij or rebels of the state, it will suffice; similarly, if given to sultans who take payments by force or otherwise, whether the sultan is just or unjust in dealing with the payments.

باب أهل الزكاة

وهم ثمانيةٌ:

- الأولُ: الفقيرُ، وهو مَن لم يجدْ نصفَ كفايتِهِ.
- الثاني: المسكينُ، وهو مَن يجدُ نصفَها أوْ أكثرَها.
- الثالثُ: العاملُ عليها، كجابٍ وحافظٍ وكاتبٍ وقاسمٍ.
- الرابعُ: المؤلفُ:

وهو السيدُ المطاعُ في عشيرتِهِ مِمَّن يرجَى إسلامُهُ، أو يخشى شرُّهُ، أو يرجى بعطيتِهِ قوةُ إيمانِهِ، أو جبايتُها مِمَّنْ لا يعطيها.

- الخامسُ: المكاتبُ.
- السادسُ: الغارمُ، وهو مَن تدينَ للإصلاحِ بين الناسِ، أو تدينَ لنفسِهِ وأعسرَ.
- السابعُ: الغازِي في سبيلِ اللهِ.
- الثامنُ: ابنُ السبيلِ، وهو الغريبُ المنقطعُ بغيرِ بلدِهِ.

فيعطى الجميعُ مِن الزكاةِ بقدرِ الحاجةِ، إلاَّ العاملُ فيعطَى بقَدرِ أجرتِهِ، ولو غنياً أو قنًّا. ويجزئُ دفعُها إلى الخوارجِ والبغاةِ، وكذلك من أخذها مِن السلاطينِ قهراً، أو اختياراً، عدلَ فيها أو جارَ.

Subsection

It does not suffice to give *zakāt* to a non-Muslim, or to a slave, or a rich person who has wealth or earnings, or to someone whom one is obliged to support, or to one's husband, or to descendants of (*banī*) Hāshim.

If one gives the *zakāt* to other than those who qualify unknowingly but then realises later, it will not suffice; one must demand back the *zakāt* along with any surplus made from the payment. The payment suffices if one gives it to a poor person believing that the person is poor but then it turns out the person is rich.

It is recommended to distribute one's *zakāt* to relatives other than those one is obliged to support in proportion to their needs; likewise, to one's close family members such as one's paternal aunt and one's niece. It is acceptable to give *zakāt* to a relative whom one supports voluntarily.

فصل

ولا يجزئُ: دفعُ الزكاةِ للكافرِ، ولا للرقيقِ، ولا للغنيِّ بمالٍ أو كسبٍ، ولا لمَن تلزمُه نفقتُهُ، ولا للزوجِ، ولا لبنِي هاشمٍ.

فإنْ دفعَها لغيرِ مستحقِّها وهو يجهلُ، ثمَّ علمَ، لم يجزِهِ، ويستردُّها مِنه بنمائِها. وإنْ دفعَها لمَن يظنُّهُ فقيراً فبانَ غنيًّا: أجزأَ.

وسنَّ: أنْ يفرقَ الزكاةَ على أقاربِهِ الذينَ لا تلزمُهُ نفقتهُم على قدرِ حاجتِهِم، وعلى ذوي أرحامِهِ كعمتِهِ، وبنتِ أخيهِ. وتجزئُ: إن دفعَها لمَن تبرعَ بنفقتِهِ بضمِّه إلى عيالِهِ.

Subsection

Giving voluntary charity at all times is recommended, especially in secret and at all noble times and places; similarly, giving to one's neighbour, and to one's blood relatives – giving to the latter will be counted as charity as well as keeping ties with kinship.

One is sinful for giving charity if it cuts one's obligatory financial support, or leads to harming oneself or one's creditor. It is reprehensible for one to give one's entire livelihood if the person cannot be patient or if the person is unable to come out from such a shortage. Reminding a recipient of one's charity is a major sin and consequently, nullifies the reward.

فصل

وتسنُّ: صدقةُ التطوعِ في كلِّ وقتٍ لا سيمَا سرًا، وفي الزمانِ والمكانِ الفاضلِ، وعلى جارِهِ وذوِي رحمِهِ، فهيَ صدقةٌ وصلةٌ.

ومن تصدقَ بما ينقصُ مؤنةً: تلزمُهُ، أو أضرَّ بنفسِهِ أو غريمِهِ، أثم بذلك. وكرِهَ: لمَن لا صبرَ لهُ، أو لا عادةَ لهُ على الضيقِ أنْ ينقصَ نفسَهُ عن الكفايةِ التامةِ. والمنُّ بالصدقةِ كبيرةٌ، ويبطلُ بِهِ: الثوابُ.

Fasting

It is obligatory for everyone to fast the month of Ramadan upon sighting the crescent moon. Similarly it is obligatory for those who are prevented from sighting the moon owing to it being too overcast with clouds or with the presence of dust during the thirtieth night of Shaʿbān. This fast is done with the intention of fasting for Ramadan as a safety measure. Commencing the month this way is acceptable even if the crescent moon appeared in another location. Similarly, the Ramadan night-prayers can be performed. However, the remaining Islamic legislations cannot come into effect (which are related to the start of the month) such as the occurrence of divorces, manumission of slaves, and the deadline of deferred payments.

The statement of a single trustworthy accountable Muslim is accepted for the moon sighting of Ramadan – even if the person happens to be a slave or a female, the statement is accepted.

Subsequently, the remaining Islamic legislations come into effect.

The statement of a single person is not accepted for any of the other months besides Ramadan; two trustworthy persons' affirmations are required.

كتاب الصيام

يجبُ: صومُ رمضانَ برؤيةِ هلالِهِ على جميعِ الناسِ، وعلى مَن حالَ دونَهُم ودونَ مطلعِهِ غيمٌ، أو قترٌ، ليلةَ الثلاثينَ مِن شعبانَ، احتياطاً بنيةِ رمضانَ، ويجزئُ: إنْ ظهرَ منهُ، وتصلَّى التراويحُ، ولا تثبتُ بقيةُ الأحكامِ: كوقوعِ الطلاقِ، والعتقِ، وحلولِ الأجلِ.

وتثبُتُ رؤيةُ هلالِهِ بخبرِ مسلمٍ مكلفٍ عدلٍ، ولو عبداً، أو أنثى.

وتثبتُ بقيةُ الأحكامِ تبعاً.

ولا يقبلُ في بقيةِ الشهورِ إلَّا رجلانِ عدلانِ.

Subsection

There are four pre-requisites for the fast to be obligatory:

- Islam
- Maturity
- Sanity
- Capability

Whoever is incapable of fasting owing to old age or an incurable medical condition, such a person can break the fast and feed a poor person one *mudd* (0.65 kilogram) of wheat or half a *ṣāʿ* (1.03 kilograms) of other foodstuff, for each day.

There are six pre-requisites for the fast to be correct:

- Islam
- Cessation of a woman's menstrual bleeding
- Cessation of a woman's postnatal lochia
- Discernment

It is obligatory for the guardian of the discerning child who is able to endure fasting to command the child to fast and it's imposed upon the child so that he or she gets accustomed to fasting.

- Intellect

If a person makes the intention to fast at night but then lost his sanity or became unconscious for the whole day only regaining consciousness for a small portion of it, such fasts will be considered to be correct.

- Intention

فصل

وشرطُ وجوبِ الصومِ أربعةُ أشياءَ:

- الإسلامُ
- والبلوغُ
- والعقلُ
- والقدرةُ عليهِ.

فمَن عجزَ عنهُ لكبرٍ، أو مرضٍ لا يرجى زوالُهُ أفطرَ، وأطعمَ عن كلِّ يومٍ مسكيناً مدَّ برٍّ، أو نصفَ صاعٍ مِن غيرِهِ.

وشروطُ صحتِهِ ستةٌ:

- الإسلامُ
- وانقطاعُ دمِ الحيضِ
- والنفاسِ.
- الرابعُ: التمييزُ، فيجبُ على ولي المميزِ المطيقِ للصومِ أمرُهُ بِهِ، وضربُهُ عليهِ ليعتادَهُ.
- الخامسُ: العقلُ، لكن لو نوَى ليلاً ثمَّ جنَّ، أو أغميَ عليهِ جميعَ النهارِ، وأفاقَ مِنهُ قليلاً: صحَّ.
- السادسُ: النيةُ مِن اللَّيلِ لكلِّ يومٍ واجبٍ.

It is obligatory to make the intention at night to fast each day. Whoever brought to his mind at night that he will be fasting, then he has made his intention. Similarly, if a person eats or drinks with the objective of fasting, then he has made his intention.

After having made the intention at night, there is no harm in doing actions that would oppose a fast [i.e. such as eating, drinking, sexual intercourse]. Similarly there is no harm if a person says, 'God willing I will fast' without being hesitant about fasting the following day. The same is the case for a person who says during the thirtieth night of Ramadan, 'If tomorrow is Ramadan, it's obligatory upon me otherwise it's not.' However, if a person says something to this effect at the start of Ramadan, it will be problematic.

Its obligation is to refrain from its invalidators from the emergence of 'true dawn' until sunset.

There are six recommended acts for fasting. It is recommended to hasten in breaking the fast and delay the pre-dawn meal. A person should also increase in good actions. If a person is verbally abused, it is recommended to say: 'I am fasting'. When breaking the fast, a person should say: 'Allāh! For you I have fasted and with your provisions I have broken my fast. Glorified and praised be you. Allāh! Accept it from me, certainly you are hearing and knowing.' Finally, it is recommended to break the fast with ripe dates and if ripe dates are unavailable, then with dried ones. If dried dates are not available, then with water.

فمَن خطرَ بقلبِهِ ليلاً أنَّهُ صائمٌ، فقد نوى، وكذا الأكلُ والشربُ بنيةِ الصومِ.

ولا يضرُّ إن أتى بعدَ النيةِ بمنافٍ للصومِ، أو قال: (إنْ شاءَ اللهُ)، غيرَ مترددٍ، وكذا لو قالَ ليلةَ الثلاثينَ مِن رمضانَ: (إن كان غداً مِن رمضانَ ففرضِي، وإلا فمفطرٌ ويضرُّ إنْ قالهُ في أولِهِ.

وفرضُهُ، الإمساكُ عن المفطراتِ مِن طلوعِ الفجرِ الثاني إلى غروبِ الشمسِ.

وسننُهُ ستةٌ: تعجيلُ الفطرِ، وتأخيرُ السحورِ، والزيادةُ في أعمالِ الخيرِ وقولُهُ جهراً إذا شتمَ: (إني صائِمٌ) وقولُهُ عندَ فطرِهِ: (اللَّهُمَّ لَكَ صَمْتُ وعَلى رِزْقِكَ أفطرتُ، سُبحانَكَ وبِحَمْدِكَ، اللَّهُمَّ تَقَبَّلْ مِنِّي إنَّكَ أَنْتَ السَّمِيعُ العَليمُ). وفطرُهُ على رطبٍ، فإنْ عدمَ فتمرٌ فإنْ عدمَ فماءٌ.

Subsection

It is prohibited for those who do not have a legitimate excuse to break their fast during Ramadan.

It is obligatory for the menstruating woman and the woman experiencing postpartum bleeding to break their fast. It is also obligatory for those who need to save someone's life that's inviolable.

It is recommended for a traveller who can shorten his prayers, and the sick person who apprehends harm by fasting to break their fast.

It is permissible for the resident to break his fast if he travels during the daytime in Ramadan. It is also permissible for a pregnant woman and a breast-feeding woman who apprehend harm for themselves or apprehend harm for the child to break their fasts. However, if they broke their fasts apprehending harm for the child only, it becomes binding upon the guardian of the child to feed a poor person for each day missed.

It is binding to refrain from the nullifiers of fasting and make up fasts at a later date for the following scenarios which occur during the daytime: if a disbeliever becomes a Muslim; if a menstruating woman becomes pure; if a sick person recovers from his illness; if a traveller returns from his journey; if a child reaches puberty; and if an insane person regains his consciousness.

The one who is allowed to break his fast during Ramadan is not allowed to fast other than it in its place.

فصل

ويحرمُ: على مَن لا عذرَ له الفطرُ برمضانَ.

ويجبُ الفطرُ على الحائضِ والنفساءِ، وعلى مَن يحتاجُهُ لإنقاذِ معصومٍ مِن مهلكةٍ.

ويسنُّ: لمسافرٍ يباحُ لهُ القصرُ، ولمريضٍ يخافُ الضررَ.

ويباحُ: لحاضرٍ سافرَ في أثناءِ النهارِ، ولحاملٍ، ومرضعٍ خافتَا على أنفسِهما، أو على الولدِ، لكنْ لو أفطرتَا للخوفِ على الولدِ فقطْ، لزمَ وليهُ إطعامُ مسكينٍ لكلِّ يومٍ.

وإنْ أسلمَ الكافرُ، وطهرتِ الحائضُ، وبرئَ المريضُ، وقدم المسافرُ، وبلغَ الصغيرُ أو عقلَ المجنونُ في أثناءِ النهارِ، وهم مفطرونَ، لزمَهُم الإمساكُ، والقضاءُ.

وليس لمَن جازَ لهُ الفطرُ برمضانَ، أنْ يصومَ غيرَهُ فيهِ.

Nullifiers of Fasting

There are twelve things that nullify the fast, they include:

- the start of menstruation and postpartum bleeding
- death
- apostasy
- one's resolving to break the fast
- one's hesitation in breaking the fast
- one inducing vomit
- one inserting something into the anus
- one swallowing mucus after it reaches the mouth
- one undertaking 'wet' cupping (*ḥijāma*) specifically, whether it relates to the person performing the 'wet' cupping or having it performed upon oneself
- one ejaculating because of looking repetitively; single gazes, thoughts, nocturnal emissions, and emission of pre-ejaculatory fluid (*madhī*) do not nullify the fast
- ejaculation or emission of pre-ejaculatory fluid or semen as a result of kissing, touching, masturbation or foreplay without involving the genitals
- liquid substances or solids reaching the body cavity (core), or the throat or the upper skull

فصل في المفطرات

وهي اثنَا عشرَ:

- خروجُ دمِ الحيضِ والنفاسِ
- الموتُ
- الردةُ
- العزمُ على الفطرِ
- الترددُ فيهِ
- القيءُ عمداً
- الإحتقانُ مِن الدبرِ
- بلعُ النخامةِ إذا وصلتْ إلى الفمِ.
- التاسعُ: الحجامةُ خاصةً، حاجماً كانَ، أو محجوماً.
- العاشرُ: إنزالُ المنيِّ بتكرارِ النظرِ، لا بنظرةٍ، ولا بالتفكرِ الاحتلامِ، ولا بالمذي.
- الحاديَ عشرَ: خروجُ المنيِّ، أو المذيِ بتقبيلٍ، أو لمسٍ، أو استمناءٍ أو مباشرةٍ دونَ الفرجِ.
- الثانيَ عشرَ: كلُّ ما وصلَ إلى الجوفِ، أو الحلقِ، أو الدماغِ مِن مائعٍ وغيرِهِ.

Consequently, the following will nullify one's fast: anything reaching the brain owing to the application of eardrops; anything reaching the body cavity as result of treating deep-wounds; applying kohl[82] to the eyelids and it is known to have travelled to the throat; chewing or sucking on Frankincense gum (mastics); tasting food that reaches the throat; and swallowing saliva which reached between the lips.

If one did any of the aforementioned nullifiers absent-mindedly or through compulsion, the fast will not be nullified. One's fast does not nullify if dust particles or a fly enters one's throat involuntarily. Similarly, if one gathers spit in one's mouth and then swallows it, the fast will remain intact.

82 A preparation of pulverised antimony used for darkening the edges of the eyelids.

فيفطرُ إنْ قطرَ في أذنِهِ ما وصلَ إلى دماغِهِ، أو داوَى الجائفةَ فوصلَ إلى جوفِهِ، أو اكتحلَ بما علمَ وصولَهُ إلى حلقِهِ، أو مضغَ علكاً، أو ذاق طعاماً ووجدَ الطعمَ بحلقِهِ، أو بلعَ ريقهُ بعدَ أنْ وصلَ إلى بينَ شفتيهِ.

ولا يفطرُ إنْ فعلَ شيئاً مِن جميعِ المفطراتِ ناسياً، أو مكرهاً، ولا إنْ دخلَ الغبارُ حلقَهُ، أو الذبابُ بغيرِ قصدِهِ، ولا إنْ جمعَ ريقَهُ، فابتلعَهُ.

Subsection

If one has sexual intercourse in Ramadan during the daytime, whether it be vaginal or anal, or whether it is with a corpse or an animal, at a time when it is binding for him to refrain [from the nullifiers of fasting,] then it becomes obligatory for the person to make up for that day and expiate – whether it was done out of compulsion or because of absent-mindedness. It also applies to the person (i.e. the female) who complies and consents to the sexual intercourse, unless she was ignorant or absent-minded.

The expiation is to emancipate a believing slave. If one is incapable of doing that, one has to fast two lunar months consecutively; and if one is unable to do that, one needs to feed sixty poor people. If one cannot find anything to feed the sixty people, the expiation rescinds – unlike the other expiations.

There is no expiation for breaking the fast in Ramadan except in the case of sexual intercourse and orgasms owing to lesbianism.

فصل

ومنْ جامعَ نهارَ رمضانَ في قبلٍ، أو دبرٍ ولو لميتٍ، أو بهيمةٍ في حالةٍ يلزمُهُ فيها الإمساكُ، مكرهًا كانَ، أو ناسياً، لزمَهُ القضاءُ، والكفارةُ. وكذا مَن جومعَ إنْ طاوعَ، غيرَ جاهلٍ، وناسٍ.

والكفارةُ: عتقُ رقبةٍ مؤمنةٍ، فإنْ لم يجِد فصيامُ شهرَينِ متتابعَين، فإنْ لم يستطعْ فإطعامُ ستينَ مسكيناً، فإنْ لم يجدْ: سقطتْ، بخلافِ غيرِها مِن الكفاراتِ.

ولا كفارةَ فِي رمضانَ بغيرِ الجماعِ، والإنزالِ بالمساحقةِ.

Subsection

If one misses the fasts of Ramadan, one must make-up the unperformed days. It is recommended to make-up the unperformed days immediately; however, it becomes obligatory if there is a set number of days left of Shaʿbān to make-up the unperformed fasts.

It is incorrect to start a voluntary fast whilst one has unperformed fasts to make-up for Ramadan. If one intends to fast an obligatory or an unperformed fast and then decides to change it to a voluntary fast, it will be considered correct.

It is recommended to perform the voluntary fasts. The best voluntary fast is to fast every other day.

It is recommended to fast:

- The full-moon days of every lunar month, namely, the 13th, 14th, and 15th
- Mondays and Thursdays
- Six days of Shawwāl
- The month of Muḥarram, and the most emphasised day therein is ʿĀshūrā, which expiates the sins for a year
- The initial nine days of the month of Dhū al-Ḥijja, and the most emphasised day therein is ʿArafa, which expiates the sins for two years

It is reprehensible to single out fasting in the following times:

- The month of Rajab
- Fridays
- Saturdays

فصل

ومَن فاتَهُ رمضانُ قضَى عددَ أيامِهِ. ويسنُّ: القضاءُ على الفورِ، إلا إذا بقيَ مِن شعبانَ بقدرِ ما عليهِ فيجبُ.

ولا يصحُّ: ابتداءُ تطوعٍ مَن عليهِ قضاءُ رمضانَ، فإنْ نوى صوماً واجباً، أو قضاءً، ثمَّ قلبَهُ نفلاً صحَّ.

ويسنُّ: صومُ التطوعِ، وأفضلُهُ: يومٌ ويومٌ.

وسنَّ:

- صومُ أيامِ البيضِ: وهي ثلاثُ عشرةَ، وأربعُ عشرةَ، وخمسُ عشرةَ
- وصومُ الخميسِ والإثنينِ
- وستةٍ مِن شوالٍ.
- وسنَّ: صومُ المحرمِ، وآكدُهُ عاشوراءُ وهو كفارةُ سنةٍ
- وصومُ عشرِ ذي الحجةِ، وآكدُهُ: يومُ عرفةَ، وهو كفارةُ سنتينِ.

وكرِهَ:

إفرادُ رجبٍ والجمعةِ والسبتِ بالصومِ.

It is reprehensible to fast on the Day of Uncertainty; this refers to the 30th day of Shaʿbān, without the presence of cloud or dust.

It is prohibited to fast during the two days of *ʿīd* and the three days following *ʿīd al-adḥā*.

If one starts a voluntary act of worship, it is not obligatory for one to complete it; and if one starts a mandatory act of worship, it becomes obligatory to complete it as long as one did not change it into a voluntary act of worship.

وكرِهَ: صومُ يومِ الشكِّ، وهو: الثلاثونَ مِن شعبانَ إذا لَمْ يكن غيمٌ، أو قترٌ.

ويحرمُ: صومُ العيدينِ، وأيامِ التشريقِ.

ومَن دخلَ في تطوعٍ لم يجبْ إتمامُهُ، وفي فرضٍ يجبْ ما لَمْ يقلبْهُ نفلاً.

Devotional Seclusion

Devotional seclusion is recommended; but if one vows to perform it then it becomes obligatory.

There are six pre-requisites for the devotional seclusion to be correct:

- Intention
- Islam
- Sanity
- Discernment
- To be free from things that obligate the mandatory bath (*ghusl*)
- To be performed in a mosque

Additionally, for those who it is obligatory to pray in congregation, the mosque (selected for the devotion seclusion) must be one which establishes the congregational prayers.

The annexes from the mosque are considered to be part of the mosque. This includes the mosque's roof, its wall-bordered courtyard, its minaret therein, or doors of the minaret within the mosque's vicinity.

If one specifies to perform the devotional seclusion in a certain mosque other than the three holy mosques, then one may perform it in any mosque.

The devotional seclusion is nullified by the following:

- To leave the mosque without a valid reason
- To make the intention to leave the mosque, even if the person did not exit
- Sexual intercourse through the private parts

كتاب الاعتكاف

وهو سنةٌ، ويجبُ بالنذرِ.

وشرطُ صحتِهِ ستةُ أشياءَ:

- النيةُ
- والإسلامُ
- والعقلُ
- والتمييزُ وعدمُ ما يوجبُ الغسلَ
- وكونُهُ بمسجدٍ

ويزادُ في حقِّ مَن تلزمُهُ الجماعةُ: أنْ يكونَ المسجدُ ممَّا تقامُ فيهِ.

ومِن المسجدِ ما زيدَ فيهِ، ومِنهُ: سطحُهُ، ورحبتُهُ المحوطةُ، ومنارتُهُ التي هي، أو بابُها فِيهِ.

ومَن عينَ الاعتكافَ بمسجدٍ غيرَ الثلاثةِ: لم يتعينْ.

ويبطلُ الاعتكافُ:

- بالخروجِ مِن المسجدِ لغيرِ عذرٍ
- وبنيةِ الخروجِ ولو لم يخرجْ
- وبالوطءِ في الفرجِ

- Orgasms resulting from fondling with other than the private parts
- Apostasy
- Intoxication

If the devotional seclusion happens to be nullified, it becomes obligatory for one to re-start the devotional seclusion, that is, one who vowed to perform it consecutively but did not specify a time. There is no expiation for this scenario. However, if one stipulated for the vowed devotional seclusion to be done at a fixed time, then one must restart it and the expiation of violating an oath is due for missing its timing.

Leaving the mosque for the following reasons does not nullify the devotional seclusion:

- Urination
- Defecation
- Obligatory purifications
- For cleaning and removing physical impurities
- Friday prayers for whom it's binding
- To get food and drink if there is no one to do so

It is permissible for one to walk at one's normal pace.

It is befitting for those who come to the mosques (i.e. for prayers etc.) to intend devotional seclusion for the period of their stay, especially those people who will be in a state of fasting.

- وبالإنزالِ بالمباشرةِ دون الفرجِ
- وبالردةِ
- وبالسكرِ.

وحيثُ بطلَ الاعتكافُ، وجبَ استئنافُ النذرِ المتتابعِ غيرِ المقيدِ بزمنٍ ولا كفارةَ، وإنْ كان مقيداً بزمنٍ معينٍ، استأنفَهُ، وعليهِ كفارةُ يمينٍ؛ لفواتِ المحلِّ.

ولا يبطلُ الاعتكافُ إنْ خرجَ مِن المسجدِ:

- لبولٍ
- أو غائطٍ
- أو طهارةٍ واجبةٍ
- أو لإزالةِ نجاسةٍ
- أو لجمعةٍ تلزمُهُ
- ولا إنْ خرجَ للإتيانِ بمأكلٍ ومشربٍ؛ لعدمِ خادمٍ.

ولهُ المشيُ على عادتِهِ.

وينبغِي لِمَن قصدَ المسجدَ: أنْ ينويَ الاعتكافَ مُدَّةَ لُبْثِهِ فِيهِ، لا سيمَا إنْ كانَ صائماً.

Pilgrimage

It is obligatory once in a person's lifetime along with *'umra*; it becomes an obligation when five pre-requisites are met:

- Islam
- Sanity
- Maturity
- Complete freedom

Pilgrimage and *'umra* performed by minors or slaves are valid, but they will not suffice one's lifetime pilgrimage and *'umra*. However, if a child reaches puberty or a slave gains freedom before the standing at 'Arafa or even after it, providing one returns to the planes of 'Arafa and presents oneself within its timing, then in such scenarios the pilgrimage will suffice as one's lifetime pilgrimage. However, if an *ifrād* or a *qirān* pilgrimage was initially intended, and one already walked between the points of Ṣafā and Marwa (*sa'ī*) after the arrival circumambulation (*ṭawāf al-qudūm*), the pilgrimage will not be counted as a person's lifetime pilgrimage. The same relates to *'umra*; namely, if a child reaches puberty or a slave gains freedom before its circumambulation, it will suffice as one's lifetime *'umra*.

- Capability

Capability is to have provisions for the trip and transportation suitable to someone like oneself, or to have assets that will permit one to attain the provisions and transportation for the trip. It is a requirement to pay with money one has that is in excess of the amount required for one's personal needs, for example books, accommodation, and servants. And similarly, in excess of one's on-going sustenance to support oneself and one's family.

كتاب الحج

وهو: واجبٌ مع العمرةِ في العمرِ مرةً. وشرطُ الوجوبِ خمسةُ أشياءَ:

- الإسلامُ
- والعقلُ
- والبلوغُ
- وكمالُ الحريةِ.

لكنْ يصحانِ مِن الصغيرِ والرقيقِ، ولا يجزئانِ عن حجةِ الإسلامِ وعمرتِهِ، فإنْ بلغ الصغيرُ، أو عتقَ الرقيقُ قبلَ الوقوفِ، أو بعدَهُ إنْ عادَ، فوقفَ في وقتِهِ، أجزَأَهُ عن حجةِ الإسلامِ، ما لمْ يكنْ أحرَمَ مفرداً، أو قارناً، وسعَى بعدَ طوافِ القدومِ، وكذا تجزئُ العمرةُ إنْ بلغَ، أو عتقَ قبلَ طوافِها.

- الخامسُ: الاستطاعةُ:

وهي ملكُ زادٍ، وراحلةٍ تصلحُ لمثلِهِ، أو ملكَ ما يقدرُ بِهِ على تحصيلِ ذلك، بشرطِ كونِهِ فاضلاً عمَّا يحتاجُهُ مِن كتبٍ ومسكنٍ، وخادمٍ، وأنْ يكونَ فاضلاً عَن مؤنتِهِ، ومؤنةِ عيالِهِ على الدوامِ.

If the aforementioned pre-requisites are fulfilled for an individual, it becomes binding to perform the pilgrimage straightaway, that is, if one's safety is not compromised en route.

If one is incapable owing to an excuse such as old age or an incurable illness, it is binding to support a free representative to perform pilgrimage and *'umra* on one's behalf from one's home country – even if the representative happens to be a woman. A representative's pilgrimage will suffice the sender, that is, if the excuse has not ceased before the representative's entry into the state of sanctification (*iḥrām*). If he dies beforehand, it is obligatory to use money from the person's estate to pay for the representative's expenses towards the pilgrimage and *'umra*. A representative's pilgrimage for others will be considered incorrect if the representative has not performed his own pilgrimage.

A sixth pre-requisite is added for females; namely to have a husband or a legally accountable unmarriageable male relative (to accompany her). She must be capable of covering the unmarriageable male relative's costs; she must also have the provisions and transportation for herself and her unmarriageable male relative. If a woman performed the pilgrimage without an unmarriageable male relative, (her travel) is prohibited; nevertheless, the pilgrimage will stand and suffice.

فمَن كملتْ لهُ هذهِ الشروطُ، لزِمَهُ السعيُ فوراً إنْ كانَ في الطريقِ أمنٌ.

فإنْ عجزَ عن السعي لعذرٍ ككبرٍ، أو مرضٍ لا يرجَى برؤُهُ: لزِمَهُ أنْ يقيمَ نائباً حرًّا، ولو امرأةً يحجُّ، ويعتمرُ عنهُ مِن بلدِهِ، ويجزئُهُ ذلك ما لم يزلِ العذرُ قبل إحرامِ نائبِهِ فلو ماتَ قبلَ أنْ يستنيبَ؛ وجبَ أنْ يدفعَ مِن تركتِهِ لمَن يحجُّ، ويعتمرُ عنهُ. ولا يصحُّ ممَّن لم يحجَّ عن نفسِهِ حجٌّ، عنْ غيرِهِ.

وتزيدُ الأُنثى شرطاً سادساً، وهو: أنْ تجدَ لهَا زوجاً، أو محرماً مكلفاً، وتقدرُ على أجرتِهِ، وعلى الزادِ، والراحلةِ لها ولهُ. فإنْ حجتْ بلا محرمٍ؛ حرمَ، وأجزأَها.

State of Sanctification

It is obligatory to enter the state of sanctification (*iḥrām*)[83] from the designated sites of entry. If one's residence is located within the sites of entry, one can enter the state of sanctification at one's residence.

It will not be considered to have begun validly in the cases of insanity, unconsciousness, and intoxication. Once the state of sanctification has begun validly, nothing will nullify it except for apostasy. It is spoiled and not nullified by having sexual intercourse before the partial release from the state of sanctification (*al-taḥallul al-awwal*). In such a circumstance, it is obligatory to still complete the spoiled pilgrimage and then make it up.

If one wants to enter the state of sanctification, one chooses and intends between one of the ways of performing the pilgrimage, namely *tamattuʿ*, *ifrād*, or *qirān*. The best is *tamattuʿ*.

- *Tamattuʿ* is to enter the state of sanctification for *ʿumra* in the months of pilgrimage; after finishing one's *ʿumra,* one enters the state of sanctification again to perform one's pilgrimage.
- *Ifrād* is to enter the state of sanctification for pilgrimage; upon its completion, one enters it for performing *ʿumra*.
- *Qirān* is to enter the state of sanctification to perform pilgrimage and *ʿumra* simultaneously. Or one may enter the state of sanctification for *ʿumra* and before doing the circumambulation of *ʿumra,* one adds (the intention of performing) pilgrimage.

If one enters the state of sanctification for pilgrimage and then incorporates *ʿumra,* the *ʿumra* will be incorrect.

---

83 *Iḥrām* in the technical sense refers to one's intention for entering into a state for doing the rites of pilgrimage, *ʿumra* or both. It is an integral element of pilgrimage and *ʿumra.* The word, *iḥrām,* is also used to refer to the garments worn by pilgrims. Namely the two white unhemmed sheets; one for the lower body (*izār*), and another for the upper body (*ridāʾ*).

باب الإحرام

وهو واجبٌ مِن الميقاتِ. ومَن منزلُهُ دونَ الميقاتِ، فميقاتُهُ منزلُهُ.

ولا ينعقدُ الإحرامُ مع وجودِ الجنونِ، أو الإغماءِ، أو السكرِ. وإذا انعقدَ لم يبطلْ إلا بالردةِ، لكن يفسدُ بالوطءِ في الفرجِ قبلَ التحللِ الأولِ، ولا يبطلُ، بل يلزمُهُ إتمامُهُ، والقضاءُ.

ويخيرُ مَن يريدُ الإحرامَ بينَ أن ينويَ التمتعَ، وهو أفضلُ، أو ينويَ الإفرادَ، أو القرانَ.

- فالتمتعُ: هو أنْ يحرمَ بالعمرةِ في أشهرِ الحجِّ، ثمَّ بعدَ فراغِهِ مِنها يحرمُ بالحجِّ.
- والإفرادُ: هو أنْ يحرمَ بالحجِّ، ثمَّ بعدَ فراغِهِ مِنه يحرمُ بالعمرةِ.
- والقرانُ: هو أنْ يحرمَ بالحجِّ العمرةِ معاً، أو يحرمَ بالعمرةِ، ثمَّ يدخلَ الحجَّ عليها قبلَ الشروعِ في طوافِها.

فإنْ أحرمَ بِهِ، ثُمَّ بِها لم يصِحَّ.

A person's state of sanctification will be correct if one enters it unconditionally.[84] In such a case, one may use the unconditional state of sanctification as one wishes; the actions carried out before (specification) are therefore ignored. However, it is recommended to specify what one intends to do of the rites. Similarly, it is recommended to stipulate, and it's done so by uttering: 'O Allāh! I intend to do such-and-such rite, so make it easy for me and accept it from me. If something obstructs me (from completing it), then the point of terminating my state of sanctification is from where you made me incapable of proceeding further.'

84 This is when one does not specify what one will do, one merely intends entering into the performance of rites.

وَمَن أحرَمَ وأطلقَ: صحَّ، وصرفَهُ لِما شاءَ. وما عملَ قبلُ، فلغوٌ.

لكنَّ السنةَ لمَن أرادَ نسكاً أنْ يعينَهُ، وأنْ يشترطَ، فيقولَ:

(اللَّهُمَّ إنيِّ أُرِيدُ النُّسُكَ الفُلَانِيَّ، فَيَسِّرْهُ لِي وَتَقَبَّلْهُ مِنِّي، وإنْ حَبَسَنِي حَابِسٌ، فَمَحِلِّي حيثُ حَبَسْتَني).

Things Forbidden in *Iḥrām*

Seven things are forbidden in the state of sanctification:

- To wear fitted-sewn garments intentionally for men – even leather socks
- To cover the head intentionally for men

It even includes covering one's head with soil or even being under the shade of a *maḥmal*.[85] It is forbidden for a woman to veil her face but she may drape something in front of her face if there is a need.

- To intentionally smell perfume, to touch fragranced things that attaches on, and using anything of a perfume base in food and drink in such a manner that the taste and scent manifests

If one wears something sewn, applies perfume, or covers one's head absent-mindedly, ignorantly, or forcefully, then there is nothing upon him. But whenever one's excuse ceases, one is required to stop doing the prohibited action straightaway or otherwise, one will be required to pay the expiation.

- To remove hair from one's body – even from the nostrils; and to clip one's nails
- To kill wild game animals that are permissible to eat

It includes guiding another to the game animal, assisting with its killing, and destroying its eggs. It is forbidden to kill locusts and lice but not fleas. In fact, it is recommended to kill all that harms under any circumstance.

85 The *maḥmal* is an embroidered palanquin (a form of travelling tent). In its general meaning, it denotes a covered construction perched on the back of an animal, usually a camel, and used to carry people. Since the late thirteenth century, ceremonial *maḥmal*s were used for the annual pilgrimage caravans to Mecca. These *maḥmal*s, however, were empty and no longer used as a method of transport. Instead, they were a symbol of the authority and the protective role played by the ruler of the Holy Places; it often represented the sultan's presence. See: Jacques Jomier, "Mahmal," and Jane Hathaway, "Amīr al-ḥajj," in *Encyclopedia of Islam, Three* (Leiden: Brill, 2015)

باب محظورات الإحرام

وهي سبعةُ أشياءَ:

- أحدُها: تعمدُ لبسِ المخيطِ على الرجالِ حتَّى الخفينِ.
- الثاني: تعمدُ تغطيةِ الرأسِ مِن الرجلِ ولو بطينٍ، أو استظلالٍ

بمحملٍ وتغطيةُ الوجهِ مِن الأنثَى، لكِن تسدلُ على وجهِها لحاجةٍ.

- الثالثُ: قصدُ شمِّ الطيبِ، ومسِّ ما يعلقُ، واستعمالُهُ في أكلٍ، أو شربٍ بحيثُ يظهرُ طعمُهُ، أو ريحُهُ.

فمَن لبسَ، أو تطيبَ، أو غطَّى رأسَهُ ناسياً، أو جاهلاً، أو مكرهاً، فلا شيءَ عليهِ، ومتَى زالَ عذرُهُ، أزالَهُ في الحالِ، وإلَّا فدَى.

- الرابعُ: إزالةُ الشعرِ مِن البدنِ، ولو مِن الأنفِ، وتقليمُ الأظفارِ.
- الخامسُ: قتلُ صيدِ البرِّ الوحشيِّ المأكولِ

والدلالةُ عليهِ، والإعانةُ على قتلِهِ، وإفسادُ بيضِهِ، وقتلُ الجرادِ، والقملِ، لا البراغيثِ، بل يسنُّ قتلُ كلِّ مؤذٍ مطلقاً.

- To marry; such a marriage contract is invalid
- To have sexual intercourse through the private parts including its foreplay; to touch non-genital areas intimately; and to masturbate

Expiation is due for all the forbidden things except in the case of contracting a marriage and killing lice. If one killed locusts or destroyed eggs (of a game animal), one is to pay its estimated value. If one removes a hair or nail, one poor person is fed; two poor people are fed for removing two hair strands or nails; thereafter, the expiation is due for anything higher. Dire necessities render the forbidden as permissible, but one is required to expiate thereafter.

- السادسُ: عقدُ النكاحِ، ولا يصحُّ.
- السابعُ: الوطءُ في الفرجِ ودواعِيهِ، والمباشرةُ دونَ الفرجِ، والاستمناءُ.

وفي جميعِ المحظوراتِ الفديةُ، إلَّا قتلَ القملِ، وعقدَ النكاحِ، وفي البيضِ، والجرادِ: قيمتُهُ مكانهُ، وفي الشعرةِ، أو الظفرِ: إطعامُ مسكينٍ، وفي اثنينِ: إطعامُ اثنينِ، والضروراتُ تبيحُ للمحرمِ المحظوراتِ، ويفدِي.

Expiation

The expiation becomes obligatory as a result of infringements in the state of sanctification or in the sacred precinct of Mecca. Expiation is of two categories; in the first category one can choose a given method to expiate, whereas in the second category, a sequential method must be observed.

The first category includes expiating when one wears fitted-sewn garments; applies perfume; covers one's head; removes more than two hair strands or nails; ejaculates sperm as a result of one look; and when one touches another in non-genital areas but did not ejaculate. One can expiate by choosing any of the following ways:

- by slaughtering a sheep
- by fasting three days
- or by feeding six poor people; each person is given one *mudd* (0.65 kilogram) of wheat or half of a *ṣāʿ* (1.03 kilograms) of other foodstuff

As for hunting a game animal, one can expiate by choosing either:

- by slaughtering an animal from domestic livestock that is like the killed wild game
- or by assessing its value based on an equivalent animal from the site where the game was killed

One purchases food with its value; it will suffice to purchase the foodstuff fitting for *zakāt al-fiṭr*. One gives to each poor person one *mudd* (0.65 kilogram) of wheat or half of a *ṣāʿ* (1.03 kilograms) of other foodstuff or alternatively, fasts one day for feeding each poor person.

The second category includes offering a sacrificial animal whilst performing *tamattuʿ* or *qirān*; when omitting an obligatory element; when obstructed (from completing the rites); and as a result of sexual intercourse and its likes.

باب الفدية

وهي ما يجبُ بسببِ الإحرامِ، أو الحرمِ. وهي قسمانِ: قسمٌ على التخييرِ، وقسمٌ على الترتيبِ.

فقسمُ التخييرِ: كفديةِ اللبسِ، والطيبِ، وتغطيةِ الرأسِ، وإزالةِ أكثرَ مِن شعرَتَين أو ظفرَينِ، والإمناءِ بنظرةٍ، والمباشرةِ بغيرِ إنزالِ منيٍّ؛ يخيرُ بينَ:

- ذبحِ شاةٍ
- أو صيامِ ثلاثةِ أيامٍ
- أو إطعامِ ستةِ مساكينَ، لكلِّ مسكينٍ مدُّ برٍّ، أو نصفُ صاعٍ مِن غيرِهِ.

ومِن التخييرِ جزاءُ الصيدِ يخيرُ فِيهِ بينَ:

- المثلِ مِن النعمِ
- أو تقويمِ المثلِ بمحلِّ التلفِ

ويشترِي بقيمتِهِ طعاماً: ما يجزئُ في الفطرةِ، فيطعمُ كلَّ مسكينٍ مدَّ برٍّ، أو نصفَ صاعٍ مِن غيرِهِ، أو يصومُ عَن إطعامِ كلِّ مسكينٍ يوماً.

وقسمُ الترتيبِ: كدمِ المتعةِ، والقرانِ وتركِ الواجبِ، والإحصارِ، والوطءِ ونحوِهِ.

It is obligatory to offer a sacrifice whilst performing *tamattu'* or *qirān*; similarly, for the one who omitted an obligatory element. If one is unable to find an animal to sacrifice or did not have the funds, one must fast three days during the pilgrimage and the remaining seven when one returns to one's family. It is best to observe the final fast (i.e. of the three fasts) on the Day of 'Arafa; if the fasts were observed on the 11th, 12th and 13th, it will be correct.

A pilgrim obstructed (from completing the rites) must offer a sacrifice. If one is unable to find an animal to sacrifice, one must fast for ten days and thereafter one can exit the state of sanctification.

It is obligatory to sacrifice a camel if one had sexual intercourse before the partial release from the state of sanctification; the same applies if one ejaculated semen because of foreplay, masturbation, kissing, touching with desire, and looking repetitively. If one is unable to find a camel to sacrifice, one must fast three days during the pilgrimage and the remaining seven upon one's return. A sheep must be sacrificed when one spoils one's *'umra* (by having sexual intercourse) before going between Ṣafā and Marwa.

The partial or first release from the state of sanctification occurs when two of the following three rites are performed: stoning, cutting the hair, and the going-forth circumambulation. Once done, it will be permissible for one to do all things except matters relating to women. The full or second release occurs when one completes all three rites including the walks between Ṣafā and Marwa; that is, if one has not done so already before the partial release.

فيجبُ: على متمتعٍ، وقارنٍ، وتاركِ واجبٍ: دمٌ، فإنْ عدمَهُ، أو ثمنَهُ، صامَ ثلاثَةَ أيامٍ في الحجِّ، والأفضلُ: كونُ آخرِها يومَ عرفَةَ، ويصحُّ: أيامَ التشريقِ، وسبعةً إذا رجعَ إلى أهلِهِ.

ويجبُ: على محصرٍ دمٌ، فانْ لم يجدْ صامَ عشرةَ أيامٍ، ثمَّ حلَّ.

ويجبُ على مَن وطءَ في الحجِّ قبلَ التحللِ الأولِ، أو أنزلَ منيًّا بمباشرةٍ، أو استمناءٍ، أو تقبيلٍ، أو لمسٍ بشهوةٍ، أو تكرارِ نظرٍ: بدنةٌ.

فإنْ لم يجدْها صامَ عشرةَ أيامٍ: ثلاثةَ أيامِ في الحجِّ، وسبعةً إذا رجعَ. وفي العمرةِ إذا أفسدَها قبلَ تمامِ السعيِ شاةٌ.

والتحللُ الأولُ: يحصلُ باثنينِ مِن رميٍ، وحلقٍ، وطوافٍ، ويحلُّ له كلُّ شيءٍ إلا النساءَ والثاني: يحصلُ بما بقيَ مع السعيِ، إنْ لم يكنْ سعَى قبلُ.

Expiation for Hunting in *Iḥrām*

Animals killed which have a domestic counterpart include:

- ostriches; in its place, a camel is sacrificed as expiation
- zebras and addaxes; in each of its place, a cow is sacrificed
- hyenas; a ram is sacrificed in its place
- gazelles; a sheep is sacrificed in its place
- hyraxes and lizards; in each of its place, a male goat of six months is sacrificed
- jerboas; a female goat of four months is sacrificed in its place
- rabbits; a female goat less than four months is sacrificed in its place
- pigeon-like birds; that is, all birds which are able to immerse their beaks and drink continuously[86] such as sandgrouses, wood pigeons, and Barbary doves. For such pigeon-like birds, a sheep is sacrificed in their place.

Other birds which do not have a domestic counterpart, for example the likes of geese, bustards, partridges, and cranes, then for such cases one must distribute its value.

---

86 The way pigeons and doves drink water is different to most birds. A lot of birds drink by dipping their beaks in water and throwing their head back to send the water down the gullet. This is not the case for pigeons and doves; they are able to immerse their beaks and drink continually without tipping their head back.

فصل

والصيدُ الذي له مثلٌ مِن النعمِ:

- كالنعامةِ ففيها بدنةٌ
- وفي حمارِ الوحشِ وبقرهِ بقرةٌ
- وفي الضبعِ كبشٌ
- وفي الغزالِ شاةٌ
- وفي الوبرِ والضبِّ جديٌ، له نصفُ سنةٍ
- وفي اليربوعِ جفرةٌ، لها أربعةُ أشهرٍ
- وفي الأرنبِ: عناقٌ، دونَ الجفرةِ
- وفي الحمامِ - وهو كلُّ ما عبَّ الماءَ كالقطَا، والورشينِ، والفواختِ شاةٌ

وما لا مثل له كالأوزِّ، والحبارَى، والحجلِ، والكركيِّ، ففيهِ قيمتُهُ مكانَهُ.

Hunting in the Sacred Precinct of Mecca

It is prohibited to hunt in the sacred precinct of Mecca; the rules of hunting therein are akin to the rules of hunting whilst in a state of sanctification.

Cutting down its trees and grass is prohibited. The prohibition applies equally to non-pilgrims and pilgrims; one must compensate, therefore:

- for cutting down a small tree; that is, small according to custom, a sheep is sacrificed
- for cutting down larger trees, a cow is sacrificed
- for cutting leaves and grasses, its value is distributed

It will suffice to offer a cow as a sacrifice instead of a camel and vice versa; a single cow or camel fulfils and suffices for seven sheep.

Sacrificial animal specification for an obligatory expiation; it is namely what suits a general sacrifice:

- a six month old male sheep
- a one year old goat
- a seventh of a camel or a cow; however, it is best to slaughter a whole camel or cow (as expiation)

فصل

ويحرمُ: صيدُ حرمِ مكةَ، وحكمُهُ حكمُ صيدِ الإحرامِ.

ويحرُمُ: قطعُ شجرِهِ وحشيشِهِ، والمحلُّ والمحرمُ في ذلكَ سواءٌ، فتضمنُ

- الشجرةُ الصغيرةُ عرفاً بشاةٍ
- وما فوقَها ببقرةٍ
- ويضمنُ الحشيشُ والورقُ بقيمتِهِ.

ويجزئُ عنِ البدنةِ بقرةٌ كعكسِهِ، ويجزئُ عن سبعِ شياهٍ: بدنةٌ أو بقرةٌ.

والمرادُ بالدمِ الواجبِ: ما يجزئُ في الأضحيةِ:

- جذع ضأنٍ
- أو ثنيُّ معزٍ
- أو سبعُ بدنةٍ أو بقرةٍ، فإنْ ذبحَ أحدهُما، فأفضلُ وتجبُ كلهَا.

Integral and Obligatory elements of Pilgrimage

The integral components of pilgrimage are four things:

- The state of sanctification

It is namely one's intention; if the state of sanctification is left out, the pilgrimage will not be considered to have begun validly.

- Standing at ʿArafa

Its timing is (at some point) between the dawn of the Day of ʿArafa and the dawn of the Day of Sacrifice. Anyone who is present at ʿArafa within the stated time, even for a few moments, and is considered amongst 'the people of pilgrimage',[87] his pilgrimage is valid. It even includes if one merely passes through ʿArafa, if one was asleep therein, if one is in one's menstrual period or if one was simply ignorant of one's presence at ʿArafa. But if someone spends time at ʿArafa intoxicated, in a state of insanity, or whilst unconscious, then one's presence at ʿArafa is invalid. If the people as a whole, or all of them except a small number, stand at ʿArafa on the 8th or 10th day by mistake, their pilgrimage is valid.

- The going-forth circumambulation (*ṭawāf al-ifāḍa*)

Its timing begins from midnight of the Day of Sacrifice, that is, for those who completed standing at ʿArafa; if one did not stand, the timing begins when one completes the standing. There is no time limit for the going-forth circumambulation's end time.

- Going between Ṣafā and Marwa

The obligatory elements of pilgrimage are seven things:

---

87 For a person to be considered from 'the people of pilgrimage' one must be Muslim, sane, and be in the state of sanctification.

باب أركان الحج وواجباته

أركانُ الحجِّ أربعةٌ:

- الأولُ: الإحرامُ

وهو مجردُ النيةِ. فمَن تركَهُ لمْ ينعقِدْ حجُّهُ.

- الثاني: الوقوفُ بعرفَةَ:

ووقتُهُ مِن طلوعِ فجرِ يومِ عرفَةَ إلى طلوعِ فجرِ يومِ النحرِ. فمَن حَصَلَ في هذا الوقتِ بعرفةَ لحظةً واحدةً، وهو أهلٌ، ولو مارًّا أو نائماً، أو حائضاً، أوْ جاهلاً أنَّها عرفةُ؛ صحَّ: حجُّهُ، لا إنْ كانَ سكراناً، أو مجنوناً أو مغمًى عليهِ. ولو وقفَ الناسُ كلُّهُم، أو كلُّهُم إلا قليلاً في اليومِ الثامنِ، أو العاشرِ خطأً أجزأَهُم.

- الثالثُ: طوافُ الإفاضةِ

وأولُ وقتِهِ: مِن نصفِ ليلةِ النحرِ لمَن وقفَ، وإلا فبعدَ الوقوفِ، ولا حدَّ لآخِرِهِ.

- الرابعُ: السعيُ بينَ الصَّفَا والمروَةِ.

واجباتُهُ سبعةٌ:

- to enter the state of sanctification at the designated sites of entry
- to stay at ʿArafa until sunset for an individual who stood during the day
- to stay at Muzdalifa until midnight during the night of *ʿīd*
- to stay the nights at Minā after *ʿīd*
- to stone the stoning sites in the correct order
- to shave or shorten one's hair
- the farewell circumambulation (*ṭawāf al-wadāʿ*)

The integral components of *ʿumra* are three things: the state of sanctification, circumambulation, and going between Ṣafā and Marwa. The obligatory elements are two matters: to enter the state of sanctification from outside the sacred precinct of Mecca, and to shave or shorten one's hair.

The recommended acts of pilgrimage include:

- staying overnight at Minā before ʿArafa
- the arrival circumambulation (*ṭawāf al-qudūm*)
- trotting for the first three rounds during the arrival circumambulation
- baring the right shoulder during it
- for the male to rid himself of fitted-sewn garments upon intending to enter the state of sanctification
- to wear a white and clean lower body sheet and upper body sheet
- to chant the dictum, 'O Allāh! Here I am...' starting from the time one enters the state of sanctification until one begins to stone the stoning sites

If one misses out an integral component of pilgrimage, the pilgrimage will be considered incomplete; it must be done to complete the pilgrimage. If one misses an obligatory element, it is obligatory for the person to sacrifice an animal; and the pilgrimage will be considered correct. There is nothing owed for leaving out recommended acts.

- الإحرامُ مِنَ الميقَاتِ
- الوقوفُ إلى الغروبِ لِمَن وقفَ نهاراً
- المبيتُ ليلةَ النحرِ بمزدَلِفَةَ، إلى بعدَ نصفِ الليلِ
- المبيتُ بمِنى في ليالِي التشريقِ
- رميُ الجمارِ مرتَّباً
- الحلقُ أو التقصيرُ
- طوافُ الوداعِ.

وأركانُ العمرةِ ثلاثةٌ: الإحرامُ والطوافُ والسعيُ. وواجباتُها شيئان: الإحرامُ بها مِنَ الحلِّ، والحلقُ أو التقصيرُ.

والمسنونُ:

- كالمبيتِ بمنى ليلةَ عرفَةَ
- وطوافِ القدومِ
- والرملِ في الثلاثةِ أشواطِ الأولِ مِنهُ
- والاضطباعِ فيهِ
- وتجرُّدِ الرجلِ مِنَ المخيطِ عندَ الإحرامِ
- ولبسِ إزارٍ ورداءٍ أبيضينِ نظيفينِ
- والتلبيةِ مِن حينِ الإحرامِ إلى أولِ الرمي.

فمَن تركَ ركناً؛ لم يتمَّ حجهُ إلا بِهِ، ومَن تركَ واجباً؛ فعليهِ دمٌ، وحجهُ صحيحٌ، ومَن تركَ مسنوناً؛ فلا شيءَ عليهِ.

Circumambulation

Eleven pre-requisites are required for the circumambulation to be valid: intention; Islam; sanity; to perform it (i.e. *ṭawāf al-ifāḍa*) in the correct time; one's *ʿawra* is clothed; one is free from filth; pure from ritual impurity; completes seven rounds; the Kaʿba is on one's left side; if able, on foot; and without long intervals between the rounds.

If one becomes ritually impure during the circumambulation, one starts again; likewise if there is a prolonged interval between the rounds. If the interval is short between the rounds, one continues (from where one left off) at the Black stone. The same applies when the call for a prayer's imminent beginning is made or when a funeral prayer is to be performed.

The recommended acts include: touching the Yamani corner with one's right hand; similarly, touching the Black stone and kissing it; supplicating during the rounds; reciting dictums of remembrance; staying close to the Kaʿba; and performing the two units of prayer after the circumambulation.

فصل

وشروطِ صحةِ الطوافِ أحدَ عشرَ: النيةُ، والإسلامُ، والعقلُ، ودخولُ وقتِهِ، وسترُ العورةِ، واجتنابُ النجاسةِ، والطهارةُ مِنَ الحدثِ، وتكميلُ السبعِ، وجعلُ البيتِ عَن يسارِهِ، وكونُهُ ماشياً مَعَ القدرةِ، والموالاةُ.

فيستأنفُهُ لحدثٍ فيهِ، وكذا لقطعٍ طويلٍ. وإنْ كان يسيراً، أو أقيمتِ الصلاةُ، أو حضرتْ جنازةٌ، صلى وبنى مِن الحجرِ الأسودِ.

وسننُهُ: استلامُ الركنِ اليمانيِّ بيدِهِ اليمنَى، وكذا الحجرِ الأسودِ، وتقبيلُهُ، والدعاءُ، والذكرُ، والدنوُّ مِنَ البيتِ، والركعتانِ بعدَهُ.

Going between Ṣafā and Marwa (*sa'ī*)

Eight pre-requisites are required to be fulfilled for the going between Ṣafā and Marwa to be valid: intention; Islam; sanity; one completes the seven lengths without long intervals between them; one performs it on foot if capable; it takes place after circumambulation – even if the circumambulation happens to be a recommended one, such as the arrival circumambulation; one completes the seven lengths; and one covers the entire distance between Ṣafā and Marwa. If one begins at Marwa, it does not count. The recommended acts include: purification; one's nakedness is clothed; and to not have a long interval between it and the circumambulation.

It is recommended to drink Zamzam water for whatever one wishes; one sprinkles Zamzam water over one's body and clothes and utters the supplication:

> In the name of Allāh. O Allāh, grant us through it knowledge that is beneficial, a livelihood that is ample, moistening and fulfilling, and let it be a cure for all maladies. O Allāh, wash my heart with Zamzam and fill it with your reverence.

It is recommended for one to visit the grave of the Prophet and those of his two companions. It is recommended to pray at the Prophet's Mosque; a prayer therein is 1000 fold. In the Holy Mosque of Mecca, a prayer therein is 100,000 fold, and in Al-Aqsa Mosque, it is 500 fold.

فصل

وشروطُ صحةِ السعيِ ثمانيةٌ: النيةُ، والإسلامُ، والعقلُ، والموالاةُ، والمشيُ مع القدرةِ، وكونُهُ بعدَ طوافٍ ولو مسنونًا كطوافِ القدومِ، وتكميلُ السبعِ، واستيعابُ ما بينَ الصفَا والمروةِ. وإنْ بدأَ بالمروةِ، لم يعتدَّ بذلك الشوطِ. وسننُهُ: الطهارةُ، وسترُ العورةِ، والموالاةُ بينَهُ وبينَ الطوافِ.

وسنَّ أنْ يشربَ مِن ماءِ زمزمَ لما أحبَّ، ويرشَّ على بدنِهِ، وثوبِهِ، ويقولُ: (بِسْمِ اللهِ، اللَّهُمَّ اجْعَلْهُ لَنَا عِلْمًا نافِعاً، وَرِزْقاً وَاسِعاً، وَرِياً وَشَبَعاً، وَشِفَاءً مِنْ كُلِّ داءٍ، وَاغْسِلْ بِهِ قَلبِي، وَامْلَأْهُ مِنْ خَشْيَتِكَ).

وسنَّ: زيارةُ قبرِ النبيِّ صلى الله عليه وسلم، وقبرِ صاحبيهِ رضوانُ اللهِ عليهِما. وتستحبُّ: الصلاةُ بمسجدِهِ صلى الله عليه وسلم وهي بألفِ صلاةٍ. وفي المسجدِ الحرامِ بمائةِ ألفٍ. وفي المسجدِ الأقصَى بخمسمائةٍ.

Missing Out and Being Prevented

If one could not stand at ʿArafa before dawn of the Day of Sacrifice owing to the excuse of being prevented or for any other reason, then the person has missed his pilgrimage. In such a scenario, the person changes his intention to perform *ʿumra* and releases from one's pilgrimage rites by performing the *ʿumra*; the person must sacrifice an animal and make up the pilgrimage the following year. The *ʿumra* performed here will not suffice as one's lifetime *ʿumra*. If a person is prevented from standing at ʿArafa but manages to release from his pilgrimage rites before the end timing of ʿArafa, then he is not required to make up the pilgrimage.

If someone is prevented from entering the Sacred Precinct, even if it happens to be after standing at ʿArafa, the person sacrifices his sacrificial animal with the intention of releasing from one's pilgrimage rites. If the person did not have a sacrificial animal, one observes ten fasts with the intention of release, and thereafter one becomes released.

If someone is only prevented from performing the going-forth circumambulation and he has already stoned and cut his hair, then he cannot be released until he performs the circumambulation.

If a person stipulated at the beginning of his intention, 'the point of release is from where you made me incapable of proceeding further' or if he said, 'if I become unwell, incapable, or when my sustenance ends, then that will be the point of my release' – in such cases, a person may release from his pilgrimage rites when he wishes. The person is not required to do anything else nor make up his pilgrimage.

باب الفوات والإحصار

مَن طلعَ عليهِ فجرُ يومِ النحرِ، ولم يقفْ بعرفةَ لعذرِ حصرٍ أو غيرِهِ؛ فاتَهُ الحجُّ، وانقلبَ إحرامُهُ عمرةً، ولا تجزئُ عَن عمرةِ الإسلامِ، فيتحللُ بِها، وعليهِ دمٌ، والقضاءُ في العامِ القابلِ. لكن لو صدَّ عن الوقوفِ، فتحللَ قبلَ فواتِهِ، فلا قضَاءَ.

ومَن حُصر عنِ البيتِ، ولو بعدَ الوقوفِ، ذبحَ هدياً بنيةِ التحللِ، فإنْ لم يجدْ؛ صامَ عشرةَ أيامٍ بنيةِ تحللٍ، وقد حلَّ.

ومَن حُصرَ عن طوافِ الإفاضةِ فقطْ، وقدْ رمَى وحلقَ لمْ يتحلَّلْ حتَّى يطوفَ.

ومنْ شرطَ فِي ابتداءِ إحرامِهِ: أنَّ (مَحِلِّي حَيْثُ حَبَسْتَنِي)، أو قالَ: (إنْ مَرِضْتُ، أوْ عَجَزْتُ، أو ذَهَبَتْ نَفَقَتِي، فَلِي أَنْ أَحِلَّ)؛ كان له أنْ يتحللَ متَى شاءَ مِن غَيْرِ شيءٍ، ولا قضاءَ عليهِ.

Sacrifice on *ʿīd al-aḍḥā*

Sacrifice on *ʿīd al-aḍḥā* is strongly recommended; it is obligatory if one vows and when one says, 'this is a sacrifice' or 'this is for Allāh'. The best sacrifice is a camel, followed by a cow, then a sheep; other animals besides these three are not acceptable.[88] A single sheep fulfils and suffices for one person, his family, and his dependants whereas a single camel or cow suffices for seven (people and their households).

At the youngest, a sheep must be over six months, goats over one full year, cows and buffalos over two full years, and camels over five full years – for them to be sufficient and acceptable.

The following animals will be sufficient and acceptable for a sacrifice: an animal that is naturally hornless; an animal that is naturally tailless or its tail was severed; a castrated animal; a pregnant animal; an animal that is earless naturally or lost half of its fat tail (namely, sheep) or half of its ear.

The following animals will not suffice:

- a sick animal whose infirmity is clear
- an obviously one-eyed animal; namely, when the pupils completely disappear
- a blind animal that has lost sight in both eyes
- an emaciated animal that has no marrow or fat
- a lame animal that cannot keep up with a healthy one
- an animal which has lost its front teeth from the root
- an animal that has the covering of its horn broken (i.e. core bone)

88 In *An Epitome of Ḥanbalī Substantive Law,* Yūsuf b. ʿAbd al-Hādī al-Ḥanbalī (d. 909/1503) stated, 'in my opinion, it is acceptable to sacrifice animals besides the livestock animals'. So, according to him, as long as the animal or bird was lawful to eat, then it will be sufficient and acceptable to offer it as a sacrifice; the opinion was unique to him and something which he singled out from the mainstream Ḥanbalī opinion.

باب الأضحية

وهيَ سنةٌ مؤكدةٌ. وتجبُ بالنذرِ، وبقولِهِ: (هَذِهِ أُضْحِيَّةٌ) أو: (لِله). والأفضلُ: الإبلُ فالبقرُ فالغنمُ. ولا تجزئُ: مِن غيرِ هذِهِ الثلاثةِ. وتجزئُ: الشاةُ عنِ الواحدِ، وعن أهلِ بيتِهِ وعيالِهِ. وتجزئُ: البدنةُ والبقرةُ عن سبعٍ.

وأقلُّ ما يجزئُ مِن الضأنِ: ما لَهُ نصفُ سنةٍ، ومِن المعزِ: ما له سنةٌ، ومِن البقرِ، والجاموسِ: ما لهُ سنتانِ، ومِن الإبلِ: ما له خمسُ سنينَ.

وتجزئُ: الجماءُ، والبتراءُ والخصيُّ والحاملُ وما خلقَ بلَا أذنٍ، أو ذهبَ نصفُ أَليتِهِ، أو أذنِهِ.

- لا بينةُ المرضِ
- ولا بينةُ العورِ، بأنِ انخسفتْ عينُها
- ولا قائمةُ العينينِ مع ذهابِ أبصارِهِما
- ولا عجفاءُ: وهي الهزيلةُ التي لا مخَّ فِيها.
- ولا عرجاءُ: لا تطيقُ مشياً مع صحيحةٍ
- ولا هتماءُ: وهي التي ذهبتْ ثنايَاها مِن أصلِها
- ولا عصمَاءُ: وهي ما انكسرَ غلافُ قرنِها.

- a castrated animal with a severed penis
- an animal that has lost most of its ear or horn

- ولا خصيٌّ مجبوبٌ.
- ولا عضباءُ: وهيَ ما ذهبَ أكثرُ أذنِها، أو قرنِها.

Subsection

It is recommended to slaughter a camel from the bottom of its neck while it is standing (with its left leg tied), whereas a cow and a sheep are slaughtered while on their left side and facing the direction of prayer. One mentions the name of Allāh when one moves his hand to slaughter, one then utters, 'Allāh is the greatest' and says, 'O Allāh, this is from you and for you'.

The earliest time for slaughtering is from the first *ʿīd* prayer of one's locality or long enough after the time to have completed the *ʿīd* prayer for one who does not pray; a sacrifice done prior to this will not suffice. The time to sacrifice continues throughout the day and night until the end of the second day of *tashrīq*. If the time is missed, a mandatory sacrifice is made up, whereas a recommended sacrifice is rescinded.

It is recommended for one to eat the meat from his voluntary sacrificial animals (i.e. for the purpose of sacrificing in pilgrimage); equally, it is recommended to eat the meat from one's animal sacrificed for *ʿīd* – even if it happens to be a mandatory *ʿīd* sacrifice. It is permissible for one to eat the meat from animals sacrificed for *tamattuʿ* and *qirān*.

It is obligatory to give some away as charity, that is, at the very least what can be considered as 'meat'. It should be given to the poor (for ownership) and not to feed them. It is recommended that a third of one's *ʿīd* sacrifice be eaten, a third be given away, and a third be donated as charity. It is prohibited to sell anything from the *ʿīd* sacrifice – even its fur and hide. The butcher is not given anything from the sacrifice as a payment; however, one can donate or gift something to the butcher from the sacrifice.

When the ten days of Dhu l-Ḥijja begin, it is prohibited for one who intends to sacrifice or someone who is assigned to sacrifice on another's behalf to cut any hair or trim nails until the animal is sacrificed. It is recommended to shave one's head after the sacrifice.

فصل

ويسنُّ: نحرُ الإبلِ قائمةً، وذبحُ البقرِ، والغنمِ على جنبِها الأيسرِ، موجهةً إلى القبلةِ. ويسمِّي حينَ يحركُ يدهُ بالفعلِ، ويكبرُ، ويقولُ: (اللَّهُمَّ هَذَا مِنْكَ وَلَكَ).

وأولُ وقتِ الذبحِ مِن بعدِ أسبقِ صلاةِ العيدِ بالبلدِ، أو قدرِها لِمَن لَم يصلِّ، فلا يجزئُ: قبلَ ذلكَ. ويستمرُّ وقتُ الذبحِ نهاراً وليلاً، إلى آخرِ ثاني أيامِ التشريقِ. فإنْ فاتَ الوقتُ، قضى الواجبَ، وسقطَ التطوعُ.

وسنَّ لهُ: الأكلُ مِن هدي التطوعِ ومِن أضحيتِهِ، ولو واجبةً. ويجوزُ: مِن المتعةِ، والقِرانِ.

ويجبُ: أنْ يتصدقَ بأقلِّ ما يقعُ عليهِ اسمُ اللحمِ. ويعتبرُ تمليكُ الفقيرِ فلا يكفي إطعامُهُ. والسنةُ: أنْ يأكلَ مِن أضحيتِهِ ثلثَها ويهديَ ثلثَهَا ويتصدقَ بثلثِها ويحرمُ: بيعُ شيءٍ مِنها حتَّى مِن شعرِها وجلدِها. ولا يعطِي الجازرَ أجرتَهُ مِنها شيئاً ولَهُ إعطاؤُهُ صدقةً وهديةً.

وإذا دخلَ العشرُ: حرمَ على مَن يضحِّي أو يضحَّى عنه أخذُ شيءٍ مِن شعرِهِ أو ظفرِهِ إلى الذبحِ. ويسنُّ الحلقُ بعدَهُ.

Sacrifice for a Newborn

Sacrifice for a newborn is recommended for the father to do even if he happens to be under financial difficulty. For a baby boy, one slaughters two sheep; and for a baby girl, one slaughters one sheep. A camel or a cow will not suffice as a sacrifice unless one offers the whole camel or the whole cow.

It is recommended to sacrifice for a newborn on the seventh day;[89] if missed, then on the fourteenth day; and if that is missed, then on the twenty-first day. Thereafter, the weekly increments from birth are disregarded.[90]

It is reprehensible to smear the newborn's head with blood from the animal.

It is recommended to give the call to prayer in the right ear of the newborn and the call to the prayer's immediate commencement in the left ear.

On the seventh day, it is recommended to shave a newborn boy's hair and thereafter donate the hair's weight in silver; the child is given a name on the seventh day. The most beloved names are ʿAbdullāh and ʿAbd al-Raḥman. It is prohibited to name a child with the name "ʿAbd' (slave) when it's annexed to others beside Allāh; for instance, ʿAbd al-Nabī (i.e. slave of the Prophet) or ʿAbd al-Masīḥ (i.e. slave of Messiah). It is reprehensible to name a child with the following names: Ḥarb, Yasār, Mubārak, Mufliḥ, Khayr, and Surūr. And it is not reprehensible to name with the names of angels and prophets.

If the time of the sacrifice for a newborn coincides with the sacrifice for *ʿīd,* one suffices the other and vice versa.

---

89 The author in his extended epitome, *Ghāyat al-muntahā,* mentioned that if one offers the sacrifice before the seventh day, it would suffice. But if the sacrifice is made before the child's birth, it would not suffice.

90 The author added in *Ghāyat* that one may sacrifice any day one wishes after the third week.

فصل في العقيقة

وهي سنةٌ فِي حقِّ الأبِ، ولو معسراً. فعنِ الغلامِ شاتانِ، وعنِ الجاريةِ شاةٌ ولا تجزئُ: بدنةٌ، ولا بقرةٌ، إلا كاملةً.

والسنةُ: ذبحُها في سابعِ يومِ ولادتِهِ، فإن فاتَ، ففِي أربعةَ عشرَ، فإنْ فاتَ، ففي أحدٍ وعِشرينَ، ولا تعتبرُ الأسابيعُ بعدَ ذلكَ.

وكرِهَ لطخُهُ مِن دمِها.

ويسنُّ: الأذانُ في أذنِ المولودِ اليمنَى حِينَ يولدُ، والإقامةُ في اليسرى.

ويسنُّ: أنْ يحلقَ رأسُ الغلامِ فِي اليومِ السابعِ، ويتصدقَ بوزنِهِ فضةً، ويسمَّى فِيهِ. وأحبُّ الأسماءِ: عبدُ اللهِ، وعبدُ الرحمنِ. وتحرمُ: التسميةُ بعبدِ غيرِ اللهِ، كعبدِ النبيِّ، وعبدِ المسيحِ. وتكرَهُ: بحربٍ، ويسارٍ، ومباركٍ، ومفلحٍ، وخيرٍ، وسرورٍ. ولا بأسماءِ الملائكةِ والأنبياءِ.

وإنِ اتفقَ وقتُ عقيقةٍ وأضحيةٍ، أجزأتْ إحداهُما عن الأخرى.

Warfare

Jihad is a communal obligation; and if sufficient numbers participate in it to accomplish it successfully, then jihad is recommended (for others).

Jihad is obligatory for free Muslim men, who are accountable and in good health. One must possess enough wealth to meet one's expenses and one's family's needs while one is away; furthermore, for journeys in which prayers can be shortened, one must have a mode of transport.

It is recommended to see off the one who will carry out a military expedition but it is not recommended to receive him. The best form of voluntary acts of worship is jihad; military sea expeditions are superior. Martyrdom expiates all sins except for debts.

It is not permissible for the one in debt and incapable of clearing it to participate in voluntary jihads; however, one can participate with the creditor's permission. The same rule applies to someone with at least one free Muslim parent, that is, it is impermissible to participate unless permission is granted.

It is recommended to participate in manning borders (*ribāṭ*), which is namely to be stationed at the frontiers. The shortest duration for manning borders is any small moment of time whereas its optimum duration is forty days. Manning borders is superior to a sojourn in Mecca; and manning borders at the frontiers with extreme perils and fears is more virtuous.

It is impermissible for Muslims to flee (from non-Muslims) that are twice the size of the Muslim force; this applies even if one Muslim was up against two combatants. However, if the enemies are more than twice the size of the Muslim force, it is permissible to retreat.

Emigration is obligatory for Muslims incapable of observing their religion openly in places where the rule of non-Muslims and misguided innovations predominate. However, emigration is recommended from such places if one was able to observe one's religion openly.

كتاب الجهاد

وهو فرضُ كفايةٍ. ويسنُّ: مع قيامٍ من يكفِي بِهِ.

ولا يجبُ إلا على ذكرٍ، حرٍّ، مسلمٍ، مكلفٍ، صحيحٍ، واجدٍ مِن المالِ ما يكفِيهِ، ويكفِي أهلَهُ فِي غيبتِهِ، ويجدُ مع مسافةِ قصرٍ ما يحملُهُ.

وسنَّ: تشييعُ الغازي، لا تلقِّيهِ. وأفضلُ متطوعٍ بِهِ: الجهادُ، وغزوُ البحرِ: أفضلُ. وتكفرُ الشهادةُ جميعَ الذنوبِ، سوى الدينِ.

ولا يتطوَّعُ بِهِ: مدينٌ لا وفاءَ لَهُ، إلا بإذنِ غريمِهِ، ولا مَن أحدُ أبويهِ حرٌّ مسلمٌ إلا بإذنِهِ.

ويسنُّ الرباطُ: وهو لزومُ الثغرِ للجهادِ، وأقلُّهُ ساعةٌ، وتمامُهُ أربعونَ يوماً وهو أفضلُ مِن المقامِ بمكةَ، وأفضلُهُ: ما كانَ أشدَّ خوفاً.

ولا يجوزُ للمسلمينَ الفرارُ مِن مثليهِم، ولو واحداً مِن اثنينِ، فإنْ زادُوا على مثليهِم، جازَ.

والهجرةُ واجبةٌ على كلِّ مَن عجزَ عَن إظهارِ دينِهِ، بمحلٍّ يغلبُ فِيهِ حكمُ الكفرِ، والبدعِ المضلةِ، فإنْ قدرَ على إظهارِ دينِهِ فمسنونةٌ.

Non-Muslim Prisoners

Non-Muslim prisoners are of two categories:

- Women and children: the individuals in this category become slaves by the fact of mere capture
- Adult male combatants: the individuals in this category do not become slaves automatically. The imam decides the prisoner's fate between death, slavery, release, or ransoming him in exchange for money or for a Muslim prisoner. It is obligatory for the caliph to opt for what is most beneficial (i.e. in the interests of Muslims).

It is incorrect to sell an enslaved person to non-Muslims.

The children of non-Muslims who have not reached puberty are regarded as Muslims providing one of three things occurred:

- One of the child's parents specifically accepted Islam and became Muslim
- One of the child's parents went missing within the Islamic state
- If a child was captured by himself alone by a Muslim

If a non-Muslim subject (*dhimmī*) captured a child, the child will be regarded to be on the religion of the non-Muslim subject. And if a child was captured along with both parents, the child will be considered to be on the religion of the parents.

فصل

والأسارَى مِن الكفارِ على قسمينِ:

- قسمٌ يكونُ رقيقاً بمجردِ السبيِ، وهم النساءُ والصبيانُ.
- وقسمٌ لا، وهمُ الرجالُ البالغونَ المقاتلونَ، والإمامُ فيهِم مخيرٌ بينَ: قتلٍ، ورقٍّ، ومنٍّ، وفداءٍ بمالٍ، أو بأسيرٍ مسلمٍ ويجبُ عليهِ فعلُ الأصلحِ.

ولا يصحُّ: بيعُ مسترقٍّ مِنهم لكافرٍ.

ويحكمُ بإسلامِ مَن لم يبلغْ مِن أولادِ الكفارِ عندَ وجودِ أحدِ ثلاثةِ أسبابٍ:

- أحدُها: أنْ يسلمَ أحدُ أبويهِ خاصةً.
- الثانِي: أنْ يعدمَ أحدُهُما بدارنَا.
- الثالثُ: أنْ يسبيهُ مسلمٌ، منفرداً عنْ أحدِ أبويهِ.

فإنْ سباهُ ذميٌّ فعلى دينِهِ، أو سبيَ مع أبويهِ، فعلى دينهِما.

The Spoils of Battle

If a Muslim fighter kills one of the enemies during battle, then he is entitled to the personal booty (*salab*). The personal booty includes the enemy soldier's clothes, jewellery, weaponry, and the mount (the enemy used for combat) along with the gear on the mount. The enemy soldier's money, baggage, tent, and his alternate-mount are part of the collective spoils of battle.

The collective spoils of battle (*ghanīma*) are distributed between the fighters who witnessed the battle.[91] Four fifths of the spoils of war are apportioned to the fighters: one share to each infantryman; two shares to each cavalryman mounted on a half-breed (Arabian) horse; and three shares to each cavalryman mounted on an Arabian horse.[92] Shares from the spoils of war are not appointed for other mounts besides horses. Equally, the shares are not appointed to individuals unless four pre-requisites are fulfilled: namely, the person being a free male who has reached puberty and is sane. If a participant does not meet one of the pre-requisites, a token payment is given instead of allocating a share from the spoils of battle.

The remaining fifth is further divided into five shares:

- A share for Allāh and his Messenger; it is used for the public welfare of Muslims
- A share for the relatives of the Prophet; namely, Banū Hāshim and Banū al-Muṭṭalib wherever they be. Each male relative receives twice the amount of each female relative.

---

91 It is not a condition for the fighters who witnessed the battle to have participated in combat. The spoils of war are allocated to the fighters as long as they intended to participate in the battle – whether they fought or otherwise.

92 A cavalryman receives one share of the spoils of war and the remaining is allocated for the horses. Therefore, a cavalryman with a half-breed horse will get one share for himself and one share for his horse. Whereas a cavalryman with an Arabian horse will get a share for himself and two shares for his horse.

فصل

ومَن قتلَ قتيلاً، في حالةِ الحربِ، فلَهُ سلبُهُ، وهو: ما عليهِ مِن ثيابٍ، وحليٍّ، وسلاحٍ، وكذا دابتُهُ التِي قاتلَ عليهَا، وما عليهَا، وأمَّا نفقتُهُ، ورحلُهُ، وخيمتُهُ، وجنيبُهُ فغنيمَةٌ.

وتقسمُ الغنيمةُ بينَ الغانمينَ، فيعطَى لهم أربعةُ أخماسِها. للراجل: سهمٌ، وللفارسِ على فرسٍ هجينٍ: سهمانِ، وعلى فرسٍ عربيٍّ: ثلاثةٌ. لا يسهمُ لغيرِ الخيلِ، ولا يسهمُ إلا لمَن فِيهِ أربعةُ شروطٍ: البلوغُ، والعقلُ، والحريةُ، والذكورةُ. فإنَ اختلَّ شرطٌ، رضخَ لهُ، ولم يسهمْ.

ويقسمُ الخمسُ الباقِي خمسةَ أسهمٍ:

- سهمٌ للهِ ولرسولِهِ، يصرفُ مصرفَ الفيءِ
- وسهمٌ لذوِي القربَى، وهم: بنو هاشمٍ، وبنو المطلبِ حيثُ كانوا، للذكرِ مثلُ حظِّ الأنثيينِ

- A share for the orphans who are poor; an orphan is a child who is under the age of puberty and does not have a father
- A share for the poor
- And a share for the wayfarers

- وسهمٌ لفقراءِ اليتامَى وهم مَن لا أبَ له ولم يبلغْ
- وسهمٌ للمساكينِ
- وسهمٌ لأبناءِ السبيلِ.

Subsection

Wealth acquired lawfully from non-Muslims, without combat, is considered to be *fay'*. The non-Muslim poll tax, the land tax, the 10% business tax imposed on non-Muslims without a covenant, and the 5% business tax imposed on non-Muslim subjects are part of this category. Wealth left behind by non-Muslims fearing Muslims is also considered to be *fay'*; similarly, wealth left behind by deceased non-Muslims who had no inheritors is treated as *fay'*.

Such wealth is used for the public welfare of Muslims, starting with the most important affairs. It begins with fortifying defences on the frontiers and empowering the people manning the borders; then meeting the needs of those who protect the Muslims; then moving to building infrastructure; and thereafter the wealth is used towards the salaries of Islamic judges, jurists, and etc. If there was surplus wealth (after the core expenditure), the wealth is divided between free Muslims, whether they are rich or poor.

The Muslim common fund is owned by the Muslims. One is liable if wealth from the Muslim common fund was tampered with and damaged. It is prohibited to use wealth from the Muslim common fund without the Sultan's permission.

فصل

والفيءُ: هو ما أخذَ مِن مالِ الكفارِ بحقٍّ مِن غيرِ قتالٍ، كالجزيةِ، والخراجِ، وعشرِ التجارةِ مِن الحربيِّ، ونصفِ العشرِ مِن الذميِّ وما تركوهُ فزعاً، أو عن ميتٍ، ولا وراثَ لَهُ.

ومصرفُهُ فِي مصالحِ المسلمينَ. ويبدأُ بالأهمِّ فالأهمِّ مِن سدِّ ثغرٍ، وكفايةِ أهلِهِ، وحاجةِ مَن يدفعُ عن المسلمينَ، وعمارةِ القناطرِ، ورزقِ القضاةِ، والفقهاءِ وغيرِ ذلك، فإنْ فضلَ شيءٌ، قسمَ بينَ أحرارِ المسلمينَ غنيِّهِم وفقيرِهِم.

وبيتُ المالِ ملكٌ للمسلمينَ، ويضمنُهُ متلفُهُ، ويحرُمُ الأخذُ مِنهُ، بلا إذنِ الإمامِ.

Agreement of Protection for Non-Muslim Subjects

The formal agreement of protection will not be effective unless it is made with people with a Sacred Book or with people who possess something similar to the Sacred Books, such as the Zoroastrians. It is obligatory for the caliph to make the formal agreement of protection providing that the caliph feels safe from any deception and trickery. It is binding for the subjected people to fulfil four conditions:

- To pay the non-Muslim poll tax willingly in a humbled state
- To only speak well of Islam
- To not do things which are harmful to Muslims
- To conform to the Islamic laws pertaining to one's safety and indemnity of life, property, and reputation. Equally, to conform to the Islamic legal punishments for things which the non-Muslim subjects consider to be unlawful (in their religion), such as fornication; but not for matters they consider to be lawful, such as consuming wine.

The non-Muslim poll tax is not levied on the following: women; hermaphrodites; children; people who are insane; slaves; the chronically ill; the blind; decrepit old men; and monks residing in monasteries.

If anyone from the non-Muslim subjects of the Islamic State accepts Islam after the passing of a year, the non-Muslim poll tax rescinds.

باب عقد الذمة

لا تعقدُ إلا لأهلِ الكتابِ، أو لِمَنْ لَهُ شبهةُ كتابٍ، كالمجوسِ. ويجبُ على الإمامِ عقدُها حيثُ أمنَ مكرَهُم. والتزمُوا لنا بأربعةِ أحكامٍ:

- أحدُها: أن يعطُوا الجزيةَ عن يدٍ، وهم صاغرُون.
- الثاني: أن لا يذكرُوا دينَ الإسلامِ، إلا بالخيرِ.
- الثالثُ: أنْ لا يفعلُوا ما فِيهِ ضررٌ على المسلمينَ.
- الرابعُ: أنْ تجرِي عليهِم أحكامُ الإسلامِ في نفسٍ، ومالٍ، وعرضٍ وإقامةِ حدٍّ، فيما يحرمونَهُ كالزِّنا، لا فِيمَا يحلونَهُ، كالخمرِ.

ولا تؤخذُ الجزيةُ مِن امرأةٍ، وخنثَى، وصبيٍّ، ومجنونٍ، وقنٍّ، وزمنٍ، وأعمى، وشيخٍ فانٍ، وراهبٍ بصومعَةٍ.

ومَن أسلمَ مِنهم بعدَ الحولِ، سقطتْ عنهُ الجزيةُ.

Subsection

It is prohibited to kill non-Muslim subjects of the Islamic State or seize their properties. It is obligatory for the caliph to protect them and stop those who harm non-Muslim subjects.

The non-Muslim subjects are forbidden from the following:

- To ride horses
- To carry weapons
- To build new churches
- To rebuild demolished structures (of churches etc.)
- To openly exhibit abominable acts
- To make public displays of their festive celebrations; to display crosses; to ring church bells; and to recite their Sacred Books aloud
- To openly eat and drink during the daylight hours of Ramadan
- To openly consume wine and pork

The non-Muslim subjects are forbidden:

- To recite the Qur'ān
- To purchase copies of the Qur'ān
- To purchase books of Islamic law and Prophetic narrations
- To build buildings higher than the Muslims'

فصل

ويحرمُ: قتلُ أهلِ الذمةِ، وأخذُ مالِهم. ويجبُ على الإمامِ حفظُهُم ومنعُ مَن يؤذِيهم.

ويمنعونَ مِن:

- ركوبِ الخيلِ
- وحملِ السلاحِ
- ومِن إحداثِ الكنائسِ
- ومِن بناءِ ما انهدمَ مِنها
- ومِن إظهارِ المنكرِ
- والعيدِ، والصليبِ، وضربِ الناقوسِ، ومِن الجهرِ بكتابِهم
- ومِن الأكلِ والشربِ نهارَ رمضانَ
- ومِن شربِ الخمرِ، وأكلِ الخنزيرِ

ويمنعونَ مِن:

- قراءةِ القرآنِ
- وشراءِ المصحفِ
- وكتبِ الفقهِ والحديثِ
- ومِن تعليةِ البناءِ على المسلمينَ.

It is binding for them to be distinguished from Muslims in dress, and it is reprehensible for Muslims to resemble the non-Muslim subjects.

It is prohibited:

- To stand for non-Muslim subjects
- To place them in honorary seats in gatherings
- To initiate the greeting of peace
- To start asking how was their morning or evening or how they are

It is also prohibited to congratulate the non-Muslim subjects; to console them; and to visit the ill.

If one greeted a non-Muslim subject with the greeting of peace but then realised that he was a non-Muslim subject, it is recommended to say, 'Return my greeting of peace upon me.'

If a non-Muslim subject greeted with the greeting of peace, one must reply to the greeting and say, 'And upon you.'

If a Muslim praised Allāh after sneezing and a non-Muslim implored Allāh to have mercy on him, one responds to the dictum.[93] It is reprehensible to shake hands with them.

93 The Muslim replies to the dictum by saying, 'May Allāh guide you and rectify your affairs.' The same is the case when a non-Muslim subject sneezes and praises Allāh; one invokes Allah for his guidance and betterment rather than implore Allāh to have mercy on him.

ويلزمُهُم التميزُ عنَّا بلبسِهِمْ. ويكرهُ لنا التشبُّهُ بِهِم.

ويحرمُ:

- القيامُ لهم
- وتصديرُهُم في المجالسِ
- وبداءتُهُم بالسلامِ
- وبكيفَ أصبحتَ أو أمسيتَ؟ وكيفَ أنتَ أو حالُك؟

وتحرُمُ: تهنئتُهم، وتعزيتُهم، وعيادتُهم.

ومَن سلمَ على ذميٍ ثمَّ علمَهُ سنَّ قولُهُ: (رَدَّ عَلَيَّ سَلَامِي).

وإنْ سلمَ الذميُّ لزمَ ردهُ، فيقالُ: (وَعَلَيْكُمْ).

وإنْ شمتَ كافرٌ مسلماً؛ أجابَه. وتكرهُ مصافحتُهُ.

Subsection

The following violates the agreement of protection for non-Muslim subjects in the Islamic State: one refuses to pay the non-Muslim poll tax or to pay it willingly in a humbled state; one rejects adhering to Islamic laws; one commits adultery with a Muslim woman or marries her; one commits highway robberies; one mentions Allāh or the Prophet in an evil manner; and if one kills a Muslim or leads a Muslim away from Islam.

In such scenarios, the caliph chooses between the opinions in connection with prisoners of war. The individual's property and wealth are treated as *fay'*. The person's womenfolks' and children's agreement of protection is not annulled consequently. If such a person accepts Islam, it is prohibited to kill him – even if one insulted the Prophet.

فصل

ومَن أبى مِن أهلِ الذمةِ بذلَ الجزيةِ، أو أبى الصغارَ، أو أبى التزامَ حكمِنا، أو زنى بمسلمةٍ، أو أصابَها بنكاحٍ، أو قطعَ الطريقَ، أو ذكرَ اللهَ تعالى، أو رسولَهُ بسوءٍ، أو تعدَّى على مسلمٍ بقتلٍ، أو فتنةٍ عن دينِهِ، انتقضَ عهدُهُ.

ويخيرُ الإمامُ فِيهِ كالأسيرِ، ومالُهُ: فيءٌ، ولا ينتقضُ عهدُ نسائِهِ وأولادِهِ. فإنْ أسلمَ، حرمَ: قتلُهُ ولو كانَ سبَّ النبيَّ صلى الله عليه وسلم.

Addendum

Substantive law, Legal Theory, and Schools of Law

Substantive law (*fiqh*)

Fiqh (substantive law) has several linguistic meanings, including comprehension, understanding, and knowledge. The term *fiqh* has been used in this manner in the Qur'ān and the Prophetic sunna; such as in the passage, 'They said, 'Shu'ayb, we do not understand (*lā nafqahu*) much of what you say.'[1] Technically, the term is used to denote understanding of the rules of Islamic law through analysis; some legal theorists defined *fiqh* as 'the knowledge concerning the rules of Islamic law (*aḥkam al-sharī'a*) through investigation and deduction.'[2] Others have expanded on the classical definition and added that *fiqh* is 'the knowledge of divinely legislated rulings from its detailed evidences, pertaining to bodily actions.'

This last definition mentions some important points: firstly, the emphasis of 'divinely legislated' to suggest that *fiqh* is concerned with the matters of prohibitions, permissibilities, and etc.; secondly, the legislated rulings are deduced from 'detailed evidences' such as texts of the Qur'ān and the Prophetic sunna; and thirdly, *fiqh* pertains to 'bodily actions', acts which include prayer, pilgrimage, warfare, social dealings, capital punishment and etc. So the knowledge of *fiqh* is not concerned with creedal nor dogmatic issues. In sum, *fiqh* is the law itself, which deals with the detailed rules of Islamic law that regulate the conduct of a legally competent person (*mukallaf*).

---

1 M.A.S Abdelhaleem, *The Qur'an* (Oxford: Oxford University Press, 2005), 142.
2 Abū al-Wafā' 'Alī b. 'Aqīl, *Al-Wāḍiḥ fī uṣūl al-fiqh* (Beirut: Orient-Institut, 1996), vol.1 p.1-2.

Legal theory (*uṣūl al-fiqh*)

Uṣūl al-Fiqh (legal theory), on the other hand is concerned with methods which are applied to infer the law from its sources, such as the Qur'ān and the Prophetic sunna. Some classical legists define legal theory as 'the principles of law, on which substantive laws are built and inferred from its different source evidences and its varying grades.' This suggests that *fiqh* and *uṣūl al-fiqh* are closely affiliated; the substantive law is the end product of legal theory; the latter acts as a deduction mechanism for the production of the former. According to the Islamic legists, legal theory provides a sort of standard criteria for the correct deduction of substantive law from the sources[3] – this appears to be one of the main objectives for the appearance of this genre of literature.

Legal theory is primarily concerned with the general principles for substantive law, how to deduce its rulings, and qualities of the diligent enquirer (*mujtahid*). The general principles include brief expressions such as 'an imperative form (in language) is indicative for an obligation' (*al-amr li-l-wujūb*); 'a prohibitive form (in language) signposts a prohibition' (*al-nahy li-l-taḥrīm*); and so forth. These general principles are applied to the 'detailed evidences' by a diligent enquirer to infer substantive laws to regulate the conduct of the legally competent person. To illustrate this, for example if the principle, 'an imperative form is indicative for an obligation' is applied to the Qur'ānic passage, 'You who believe, fulfil (*awfū*) contracts.'[4] – this would imply that the ruling for fulfilling contracts is an obligation upon a legally competent person as the verb (*awfū*) in the passage is in the imperative form.[5]

Concise substantive law manuals were generally authored for people aspiring to be jurists and judges. They do not normally include passages of the Qur'ān or Prophetic traditions as supportive material for the legal opinions

3 Mohammad Kamali, *Principles of Islamic Jurisprudence* (Cambridge: ITS, 2003), 2-3.

4 Qur'ān 5:1

5 'Abd al-Wahhāb Khallāf, *'Ilm uṣūl al-fiqh* (Beirut: Beirut: Mu'assasat al-Risāla, 2008), 12.

in the manuals.[6] A typical substantive law manual generally divides into two main sections; the first part deals with acts of worship (*ʿibādāt*), which includes prayer, charity, fasting, pilgrimage, and warfare; the latter section pertains to social dealings (*muʿāmalāt*), this includes trades and sales, family law, criminal law, and judgeship. The works of legal theory are structured differently. The manuals begin by exploring the sources for the substantive law; normally commencing with the sources that are agreed upon by the Islamic legists such as the Qurʾān, the Prophetic sunna, and consensus. Thereafter, the different types of Islamic rulings are discussed, normally starting with defining law (*al-ḥukm al-taklīfī*) followed by declaratory law (*al-ḥukm al-waḍʿī*). The authors usually conclude with a discussion about the diligent enquirer and the legally competent person. The style and layout of substantive law manuals and legal theory manuals differ from one law school to another but generally follow the aforementioned pattern.

Schools of Law (*madhāhib*, sing. *madhhab*)

Madhāhib, sing. *madhhab* (schools of law or thought), the lexical meaning of the word *madhhab* denotes a path or a way that's followed. In the legal sense, the term 'school of law' generally refers to a body of rulings, which an imam has opted for; it specifically refers to the juristic opinions of a diligent enquirer. It can also refer to the opinions of his followers, that is, legal opinions that were derived from the imam's methodology and law principles.[7] The concept of law schools was not acknowledged during the Prophetic era or in the succeeding generation, the era of the Successors (*tābiʿūn*). However, during this period a number of Companions of the Prophet (*ṣaḥāba*), prominent in law, had some enthusiastic followers from the succeeding generation; these Successors settled in different parts of the Islamic State (Madīna, Mecca, Baṣra, Kūfa, Shām, and Yemen).

The concentration of Successors in these centres varied depending on the number of Companions that originally settled in the centres. This is probably why Hijāz and Iraq became two main epicentres for learning Islamic

6 Jewel Jalil, *An epitome of Ḥanbalī substantive law* (Birmingham: Dar al-Arqam, 2018), 17.
7 Abdullāh bin ʿAbd al-Muḥsin al-Turkī, *Al-Madhhab al-ḥanbalī* (Beirut: Muʾassasat al-Risāla, 2002), vol.1 p.14.

law. Medina was the first capital for the Islamic State; a great number of Companions resided and settled therein. Thereafter the capital was relocated to Kūfa before it was eventually moved to Shām. The relocations of the capital caused a number of Companions to also relocate, including some of the prominent law experts.

There were two major trends for interpreting Islam: personal interpretation based on legal reasoning (*qiyās*) and transmission-based interpretation. Personal interpretations were predominant in Kūfa; whereas in Hijāz, with the widespread circulation of Prophetic narrations and reports of the Companions, transmission-based interpretation became more prevailing. After the death of the Companions and the Successors, the early scholars generally divided into two camps: the rationalists (*ahl-rảy*) and the traditionalists (*ahl al-ḥadīth*). The epicentre for the rationalists was based in Kūfa, whereas the epicentre for the traditionalists was in Ḥijāz.[8] Since a lot of the Islamic knowledge and education was confined to these epicentres, arguments and discourses occurred between the two parties; there seemed to be a strong sense of competition between the two.

With the growing Islamic civilization followed the spread of aspiring jurists, exchange of dialogues, frequent debates, legal verdicts, and the documentation of law commenced. During this era, numerous Successors and their followers became leading figures in the fields of Islamic law; substantive law (*fiqh*) began to flourish across the empire. Medina eventually became to be headed by Mālik b. Anas (d. 179/796); Mecca by Muḥammad b. Idrīs al-Shāfiʿī (d. 204/820); Egypt by al-Layth b. Saʿad (d. 175/791); Kūfa by Abū Ḥanīfa (d. 150/767); and Baṣra by ʿUthmān al-Battī (d. 143/760-761). By the third century of the Islamic era, legal opinions of these scholars began to be attributed explicitly to distinct authorities rather than to a particular epicentre of knowledge. This shift occurred owing to geographical, social, and political factors; not merely a reaction to the 'traditionalist challenge' as suggested by some academics.[9]

8 ʿAbd al-Raḥmān b. Khaldūn, *Muqaddimat Ibn Khaldūn* (Damascus: Dār Yaʿrib, 2004), 185.

9 Christopher Melchert, *The formation of the Sunni Schools of Law, 9th-10th Centuries C.E.* (Leiden: Brill, 1999), 32.

Although Islamic legal history produced numerous established diligent enquirers, only four of the Sunnī schools had adherents in numbers sufficient to guarantee them institutional roles in the governance of Islamic societies – the Mālikī, Ḥanafī, Shāfiʿī, and Ḥanbalī law schools. The Malikī law school is affiliated with the teachings of Mālik b. Anas, who lived in Medina and was thought to represent the legal opinions of the people of Medina. The Ḥanafī law school is associated with the teaching of Abū Ḥanīfa, who for most of his life lived in Kūfa, Iraq. The Shāfiʿī law school is affiliated with the teaching of Muḥammad b. Idrīs al-Shāfiʿī. Al-Shāfiʿī studied with many authorities including Mālik b. Anas in Medina, and Muḥammad b. al-Ḥasan al-Shaybānī (d. 189/805) and Abū Yūsuf (d. 182/798) in Baghdad, before he settled permanently in Egypt, where he died at the beginning of the third Islamic century. The Ḥanbalī law school is connected with the teaching of Aḥmad b. Ḥanbal. Aḥmad attended the study circles of the famous Ḥanafī jurist, Abū Yūsuf for three years, and studied with al-Shāfiʿī for a short period. Aḥmad did not encounter Mālik, but it is believed that Mālik influenced Aḥmad through al-Shāfiʿī. The study of ḥadīth was more beloved to Aḥmad, for which he became a celebrated scholar. The exposure to learning law through its dual approach enabled Aḥmad to develop his own jurisprudence.[10] However, the law school of Aḥmad crystallised properly almost a century after his death.

Unlike the Mālikī and Ḥanafī law schools, which succeeded to the geographically based schools of the Hijāz and Iraq, respectively, the Shāfiʿī and the Ḥanbalī law schools were to a much greater degree defined by their self-conscious adherence to an explicit method of systematic legal reasoning. In particular, al-Shāfiʿī is credited with developing an explicit methodology for legal argumentation set forth in his legal theory treatise, *al-Risāla*. Ibn Khaldūn (d. 806/1408) discussed about the law schools of al-Shāfiʿī and Aḥmad. To him, the former was merely a unification of the methodologies of the rationalists and the traditionalists; whereas the latter's dependence on abundant narrations, singled it out to be another school of law.

Ibn Khaldūn considered Aḥmad to be an elite from amongst the tradition-

10 Abdul Hakim al-Matroudi, *The Ḥanbalī School of Law and Ibn Taymiyyah* (New York: Routledge, 1999), 7.

alists;[11] a point, which is much debated among the earlier scholars and academics. He explained that Aḥmad's law school was not received well by the masses because of the Ḥanbalī law school's remoteness in diligent enquiry (*ijtihād*) and Aḥmad's excessive use of sacred texts to foster one another, and this prevented the school from growing substantially.[12] Abū Zahra (d. 1974), mentioned three notable points regarding the Ḥanbalī school's formation: substantive law was communicated through Aḥmad's students; al-Khallāl, (d. 311/923) a second generation Ḥanbalī, was responsible for collecting and transmitting it; and his companionship with al-Marrūdhī (d. 275/889), a senior student of Aḥmad, greatly influenced this process.[13]

In response to the centrality that the Shāfiʿīs afforded methodology, the Mālikīs and the Ḥanafīs reconstructed the 'methodology' that lay behind the *ijtihād* of their founders. In doing so, the Mālikīs and the Ḥanafīs developed legal principles that justified the doctrines of their predecessors while at the same time acknowledging the basic proposition of al-Shāfiʿī—*ijtihād* was not applicable in the face of conclusive textual evidence. For example, the Ḥanafīs introduced the interpretive concept of *ʿumūm al-balwā*, which was used to justify ignoring the apparent rule communicated by a *ḥadīth* in circumstances where the alleged rule would be one of general applicability, but the practice of the community as documented in the opinion of a Prophetic Companion or prominent scholars was not in conformity with the teaching of that *ḥadīth*.

The Mālikī concept of 'the practice of the people of Madīna' (*ʿamal ahl al-madīna*) preserved normative practices that appeared to conflict with formally authentic traditions (*aḥādīth*). In each case, the Ḥanafī and the Mālikī doctrines appear to reinforce the authority of Prophetic traditions, while at the same time challenging Shāfiʿī's theory that *aḥādīth* with formal transmission chains were the most reliable historical source for discovering normative Prophetic practice, especially when solitary transmissions (*khabar al-wāḥid*) conflicted with well-known and widespread religious

11 Ibn Khaldūn, *Muqaddima*, 188.
12 Ibn Khaldūn, *Muqaddima*, 189.
13 Muhammad Abu Zahra, *The Four Imams,* trans. Aisha Bewley (London: Dar al-Taqwa, 2001), 462-470.

practices.

It seems, the Mālikīs and the Ḥanafīs developed such theories that distinguished their approach to the Prophet's Sunna from that of the Shāfiʿīs and the Ḥanbalīs without challenging the supremacy of the Prophet's practice. The Mālikīs and the Ḥanafīs were also more willing to give practical reasoning a greater role in the derivation of legal rules than the Shāfiʿīs and the Ḥanbalīs. Thus, whereas the Shāfiʿīs deprecated techniques such as *istiḥsān* (equity in law), *maṣlaḥa mursala* (considerations of public interest), and *sadd al-dharāʾiʿ* (blocking the means) as little more than arbitrary personal opinions; the Mālikīs and the Ḥanafīs deemed them to be central to the development of Islamic substantive law.

Historically, the Ḥanafī law school has had the greatest institutional impact of all the law schools, as a result of its close relationship first with the ʿAbbāsids and then with the Ottomans. To the extent that when Islamic law is still applied in modern jurisdictions, it is often Ḥanafī law, subject to legislative reforms in particular areas. Geographically, Ḥanafism spread from Iraq to Iran, Central Asia, the Indian subcontinent, and Eastern Europe. Mālikīs dominated the political and social life of Islamic Spain, North Africa, and Islamic sub-Saharan Africa, and in earlier periods of Islamic history, were influential in Egypt.

Shafiʿīs historically have been predominant in Cairo and Lower Egypt, Syria, and Palestine and, prior to the Mongol invasion, Iran. Shafiʿīs dominated the judicial administration during the Ayyūbid and Mamlūk periods and continued to predominate in Egypt, Syria, Palestine, and Yemen. They have also become the dominant school of law followed by the Muslims living on the East African coast and Southeast Asia. The Ḥanbalīs, prior to the modern period, were politically the least significant of the law schools, both in terms of their impact on the administration of the law and in numbers of adherents. Nevertheless, in the fourth century the Ḥanbalī school established itself in Levant and then in the sixth century, it spread to Egypt. The Ḥanbalī school acquired a prominent position in the Arabian Peninsula under Muḥammad b. ʿAbd al-Wahhāb's propagation (d. 1206/1791); it is currently the official school of law in Saudi Arabia and Qatar.[14]

14 Al-Matroudi, *The Ḥanbalī School of Law and Ibn Taymiyyah*, 13.

Bibliography

[Arabic]

Abū Zayd, Bakr b. ʿAbdallāh. *Al-Madkhal al-mufaṣṣal ilā fiqh al-Imām Aḥmad bin Ḥanbal.* Riyadh: Dār al-ʿĀṣima, 1997.

ʿAfāna, Ḥusām al-Dīn Mūsā. "Al-Shaykh al-ʿAllāma Marʿī bin Yūsuf al-Karmī al-Maqdisī al-Ḥanbalī wa kitābuhu dalīl al-ṭālib li-nayl al-maṭālib." Research thesis., Al-Quds University, 2000.

Ḍuwayyān, Ibrāhīm. *Manār al-sabīl fī sharḥ al-dalīl*, 3 vols., edited by Muḥammad al-ʿAbbāsī. Riyadh: Maktabat al-Maʿārif, 1997.

Al-Asqalānī, Aḥmad. *Fatḥ al-bārī bi-sharḥ ṣaḥīḥ al-Bukhārī*. Riyadh: Dār al-Ṭayyiba, 2010.

Al-Bughā, Muṣṭafā. *Nuzhat al-muttaqīn.* Damascus: Dār al-Muṣṭafā, 2006.

Al-Fawzān, ʿAbdullāh. *Al-Fawāʾid al-majmūʿa fī sharḥ fuṣūl al-ādāb wa makārim al-akhlāq al-mashrūʿa.* Riyadh: Dār Ibn al-Jawzī, 2012.

Al-Dūmānī, Muṣṭafā, *Ḥāshiyat dalīl al-ṭālib*, 2 vols., edited by Nūr al-Dīn Ṭālib. Damascus: Dār al-Nawādir, 2010.

Al-Futūḥī, Muḥammad. *Muntahā al-irādāt,* edited by Mubārak al-Ḥathlān. Kuwait: Ghirās, 2013.

Al-Ḥajjāwī, Mūsā. *Zād al-Mustaqniʿ fī ikhtiṣār al-muqniʿ*, edited by ʿAbd al-Raḥmān al-ʿAskar. Riyadh: Madār al-Waṭn, 2004.

Al-Jibrīn, ʿAbdullāh b. ʿAbd al-Raḥmān. *Shifāʾ al-ʿalīl sharḥ manār al-sabīl*, Riyadh: Dār al-Qāsim, 1999.

Al-Jurjānī, ʿAdī. *Al-Kāmil fī ḍuʿafāʾ al-rijāl,* Beirut: Dār al-Kutub al-ʿIlmiyya, 1997.

Al-Karmī, Marʿī b. Yūsuf. *Dalīl al-ṭālib li-nayl al-maṭālib*, edited by Naẓr M. al-Fāriyābī. Riyadh: Dār al-Ṭayyiba, 2004.

Al-Khathlān, S'ad. *Al-Salsabīl fī sharḥ al-dalīl,* 4 vols., Riyadh: Dār Aṭlās, 2019.

Al-Khiraqī, 'Umar. *Al-Mukhtaṣar fī al-fiqh,* Damascus: Dār al-Nawādhir, 2009.

Al-Maqdisī, 'Abdullāh b. Aḥmad. *Sharḥ dalīl al-ṭālib li-nayl al-maṭālib,* 3 vols., edited by Aḥmad al-Jammāz. Riyadh: Dar al-Aṭlas, 2015.

Al-Maqdisī, Shams al-Dīn. *Al-Sharḥ al-kabīr,* edited by 'Abdullāh bin 'Abd al-Muḥsin al-Turkī. Riyadh: Dār 'Ālam al-Kutub, 2011.

Al-Mardāwī, 'Alā'. *Al-Inṣāf fī ma'rifat al-rājiḥ min al-khilāf,* edited by 'Abdullāh bin 'Abd al-Muḥsin al-Turkī. Riyadh: Dār 'Ālam al-Kutub, 2011.

Al-Mubārakfūrī, Muḥammad. *Tuḥfat al-aḥwadhī,* Beirut: Dār al-Kutub al-'Ilmiyya, 2010.

Al-Nawawī, Muḥī al-Dīn. *Al-Minhāj,* Beirut: Dār al-Ma'rifa, 2009

Al-Rabbāṭ, Khālid. *Al-Jāmi' li-ulūm al-Imām Aḥmad,* 22 vols., Riyadh: Dār al-Fallāḥ, 2009.

Al-Taghlibī, 'Abd al-Qādir. *Nayl al-ma'ārib,* 2 vols., edited by Muhammad Sulaymān al-Ashqar, Amman: Dar al-Nafā'is, 2013.

Al-Ṭūfī, Najm al-Dīn. *Sharḥ mukhtaṣar al-rawḍat,* 3 vols., Damascus: Mu'assasat al-Risāla, 2011.

Al-Ṭurīqī, 'Abdullāh. *Al-Ḥanābila khilāl thalātha 'ashar qarnā,* 14 vols., Beirut: 2012.

Al-Turkī, 'Abdullāh bin 'Abd al-Muḥsin, *Al-Madhhab al-Ḥanbalī,* Beirut: Mu'assasat al-Risāla, 2002.

Al-Zūmān, Aḥmad. *Ghāyāt al-muqtaṣidīn sharḥ manhaj al-sālikīn,* Riyadh: Dār Ibn al-Jawzī, 2014.

Ibn 'Abd al-Hādī, Yūsuf. *Kitāb furū' al-fiqh,* edited by 'Abd al-Salām b. al-Shuwai'ir. Riyadh: Maktabat al-Rushd, 2007.

Ibn 'Awad, Aḥmad b. Aḥmad. *Ḥāshiyat ibn 'Awad (Fatḥ wahhāb al-maʾārib),* 3 vol., edited by Fayṣal Yūsuf Aḥmad al-'Alī. Kuwait: Ghirās, 2013.

Ibn Badrān, 'Abd al-Qādir. *Al-Madkhal ilā madhhab al-Imām Aḥmad b. Ḥanbal,* edited by 'Abdullāh bin 'Abd al-Muḥsin al-Turkī. Damascus: Mu'assasat al-Risāla, 2011.

Ibn Ḥumayd, Muḥammad b. 'Abdullāh, *Al-Suḥub al-wābila,* edited by 'Abd al-Raḥman al-'Uthaymīn. Beirut: Mu'assasat al-Risāla, 2017.

Ibn Qudāma, 'Abdullāh. *Al-Muqni',* edited by Maḥmūd al- al-Arnā'ūṭ. Jeddah: Maktabat al-Sawādī, 2000.

_____. *'Umdat al-fiqh,* edited by Sa'īd Muḥammad. Riyadh: Maktabat al-Rushd, 2007.

Ibn al-'Uthaymīn, Muḥammad. *Al-Sharḥ al-mumti'.* 'Unayza: Dār Ibn al-Jawzī, 2001.

_____. *Al-Uṣūl min 'ilm al-uṣūl,* Cairo: Dār 'Umar b. Khaṭṭāb, 2006.

_____. *Sharḥ riyāḍ al-ṣāliḥīn,* Riyadh: Madār al-Waṭn, 2006.

[English]

Abdul-Raof, Hussein. *Cultural Aspects in Qur'an Translation.* Clevedon: Multilingual Matters Ltd, 2005.

Alwazna, Rafat. *Translating Ḥanbalī Sharī'a code from Arabic to English.* Saarbrucken: Lambert Academic Publishing, 2013.

Al-Fawzān, Ṣālīḥ. *A Summary of Islamic Jurisprudence.* Riyadh: Al-Maiman Publishing House, 2005.

Al-Haj, Hatim. *Fiqh of Worship,* Riyadh: International Islamic Publishing House, 2011.

Al-Ḥanbalī, Yūsuf b. 'Abd al-Hādī. *An Epitome of Ḥanbalī Substantive Law.* Translated by Jewel Jalil. Dar al-Arqam: Birmingham, 2018.

Al-Matroudi, Abdul Hakim. *The Hanbalī School of Law and Ibn Taymiyyah,* New York: Routledge, 2006.

Hatim, Basil. *Discourse and the Translator,* New York: Longman, 1990.

Ibn Balbān, Muḥammad. *Hanbali acts of Worship.* Translated by Musa Furber. Great Britain: Islamosaic, 2016.

Khalid, Anas. "The Mukhtaṣar of Al-Khiraqī: A Tenth Century work on Islamic Jurisprudence." PhD diss., New York University, 1992.

Keller, Nuh Ha Mim. *Reliance of the Traveller.* Maryland: Amana Publication, 1994.

Makdisi, George. *Ibn 'Aqil: Religion and culture in Classical Islam.* Edinburgh: Edinburgh University Press, 1997.

Newmark, Paul. *A Textbook of Translation.* Hertfordshire: Prentice Hall International Ltd, 1998.

Nyazee, Imran. *The Distinguished Jurist's Primer.* Reading: Garnet Publishing Limited, 2000.

Sarcevic, Susan. *New Approach to Legal Translation.* The Hague: Kluwer Law International, 1997.

Spectorsky, Susan. *Chapters on Marriage and Divorce: Responses of Ibn Ḥanbal and Ibn Rāhwayh.* Austin: University of Texas Press, 1993.

Index